Praise for The S

'Those interested in le Carré will discover much fascinating detail ... intelligent and perceptive.'

Adam Sisman, *Spectator*

'A posthumous love-letter to David Cornwell ... le Carré's private life seems to be perfectly aligned to his work.'

Celia Walden, *Daily Telegraph*

'Dawson is always aware of the complex duplicities le Carré is indulging in (she's no fool) ... A sly and clever book.'

William Boyd, *New Statesman*

'A profound character study of a great writer.'

The Times

'A fascinating insight into how the betrayal, infidelity and lies that are at the heart of le Carré's spy novels were duplicated with exhausting precision in his private life.'

Daily Mail

'This is – like le Carré's novels – a memoir with many layers ... the nuanced elegance of the prose would have made le Carré proud of "Our Sue", as he lovingly called the author.'

The Wire

'Very sharp and funny.'

Jake Kerridge, *Daily Telegraph*

'Dawson's memoir reveals a man guarded even in his most unguarded moments.'

Financial Times

'Never once claims victimhood, yet hints at the cost.'

Guardian

'I started reading Suleika Dawson's *The Secret Heart* at a London bar, intending simply to skim through as I finished my beer. Six hours and many more beers later I was still at the bar, and still reading. The book, an erotically charged, no-punches-pulled account of her affairs with the author John le Carré, is also a fascinating and important portrait of the man himself.'

Brice Stratford, *Spectator*

'…riveting stuff if you like detailed accounts of passion, adultery, jewels, flowers, chocolates, caviar and champagne. And I must say I do. I also like the way she refuses to play the poor-little-me card which is now the done thing when women speak out.'

Jennifer Selway, *Express*

The
Secret
Heart

The Secret Heart

Le Carré and Me:
Tales from a Secret Love Affair

Suleika Dawson

MUDLARK

Mudlark
HarperCollins*Publishers*
1 London Bridge Street
London SE1 9GF

www.harpercollins.co.uk

HarperCollins*Publishers*
Macken House, 39/40 Mayor Street Upper
Dublin 1, D01 C9W8, Ireland

First published by Mudlark 2022
This paperback edition published 2023

1 3 5 7 9 10 8 6 4 2

© Suleika Dawson 2022

Suleika Dawson asserts the moral right to be identified as the author of this work

For reasons of copyright, all letter extracts contained herewith are reproduced in close paraphrase

A catalogue record of this book is available from the British Library

ISBN 978-0-00-853305-2

Printed and bound in the UK using 100% renewable electricity at CPI Group (UK) Ltd

All rights reserved. No part of this publication may be reproduced, stored in a retrieval system, or transmitted, in any form or by any means, electronic, mechanical, photocopying, recording or otherwise, without the prior written permission of the publishers.

This book is produced from independently certified FSC™ paper
to ensure responsible forest management.

For more information visit: www.harpercollins.co.uk/green

Contents

For Graham Goodwin again, and this time
for Jeremy Lloyd as well.
Remembering George Greenfield, too.
And for David, of course.

And the human heart is a very mysterious thing.

Ford Madox Ford, *The Good Soldier*

By Way of an Introduction . . .

I've never let anyone this far in, David told me once, quite early in our relationship. His voice was earnest, his expression suddenly concerned. We might have been in bed, or perhaps just sitting together, I forget. We were certainly post-coital, I remember that. We almost always were. *You are safe to love, aren't you, Sue?* he urged. *I need you to be safe.*

'Safe'. A loaded word. This, after all, was the man who educated the world about safe houses. We were in one of his at the time. So – safe that I loved him as much as he loved me? That I would continue to be a safe haven for him, whenever he wanted respite from his world? Or safe, meaning I'd never call his wife? There could have been another dozen interpretations. There almost always were.

Before I could answer, he laid the underside of his forearm along my thigh.

Look, he said. *We have the same skin. The same grain. Cut from the same bale. We'll go away again soon. I think we need some more time together under our belts.*

David always pressed the 'we' of things, sparing no word or gesture to conjure up an enveloping us-ness around our times together. He was good at it, too; *really* good. I have yet to discover a word for the mistress-attending equivalent of 'uxorious', but there ought to be one, just for him. It was wholly beguiling to be an audience of one for the powerful up-close magic he could

1

summon. Nor was it entirely illusory. Real rabbits do emerge from top hats, however they get there to begin with, and large parts of our relationship, whole stretches, were as real as anything has ever been in my life. In his too, I am certain. But I have since come to wonder whether, for David, it was the illusion itself – and his own power to invoke it – that was most real of all.

There is one further interpretation of what he meant by 'safe' that may have accounted for his worry at the time. David did take me very deep into his world, into his thoughts and hopes, his memories, his besetting concerns and fears, into his carefully guarded private reality. So he might have meant safe that I wouldn't write about him. As indeed I didn't, not for the longest time, until it *was* safe – even if this book may yet constitute a breach of the Unofficial Secrets Act I never actually signed.

So – what follows is how it went. With us. This is the story of my time with le Carré the writer and with David the man; with Ronnie the father, too, whom David sent me on a secret mission to find, and in finding the father I discovered still more about the son.

My story, then, just the way I remember it happening, my memory fortified by the many dozens of letters David sent me and by my diaries and notebooks from those years. I've withheld a few details to spare some blushes – most of them my own – but otherwise this is a pretty full account of what has unquestionably been one of the most significant relationships of my life. Of his too, I like to think. And right at the beginning of it, as perhaps ought always to be the case in any last moment before things change forever, I remember I yawned …

First Approach

September 1982

Soho

It was an early start at the sound studios and I wasn't good with mornings in those days. But Graham had said, *Make sure to get your lovely arse round to Woodsie's for eight o'clock sharp, honey, all right?,* so there I was. Prior to that day we'd never begun a session before ten. Actors usually aren't so good with mornings, either, but that day we weren't going to be recording with an actor.

I yawned again as we sat amicably together, mostly in silence, on one of the well-worn blue banquettes in the seventh-floor reception of John Wood Studios at Broadwick Street, Soho. It was just the two of us there, with the senior engineer Derek French – Frenchie – setting up in his studio.

'Why the dawn run anyway?' I asked, since I hadn't been told.

'The Great Man requested it,' Graham replied.

Good to know. We'd been waiting for twenty minutes and the Great Man had yet to appear.

'Yes, but why?'

'Dunno. Maybe he gets going in the morning – unlike some. Maybe he wants to finish early so he can go home and give his wife one. Dunno.'

Graham Goodwin – a tall, silver-haired and habitually laid-back Gent-about-Town; the man who single-handedly started the whole audiobook business; my friend, mentor and employer for the last two years – was sounding less bothered than he looked. He'd been getting up periodically, smoothing his jacket collar, shooting his cuffs, checking his tie. That he was wearing a jacket in the studio at all was indicative of his state of mind. The only other session he ever smartened up for was when the reader was Prince Philip.

'Anyway,' he added, standing up again, 'he asked me nicely so I said yes.'

'*Starfucker*' Frenchie called out genially through the open door of the studio.

We heard the lift draw up just then, always heralding its own arrival with such a resounding thud that the rates for the studio nearest to the lift-shaft were significantly lower than for the other two studios on the same floor.

'Here we go,' Graham said, nudging me to get up too.

But when the lift door slid back it was the receptionist who stepped out, looking less than pleased with the early start. I sat down again and Graham went back to shooting his cuffs.

Audiobooks were known as talking books or books-on-cassette in those days, the pre-digital age, and Graham had started the whole trade. He devised the two-cassette, three-hour abridged reading as a product that was marketable at the price of a paperback and would suit factory requirements in production – C90 cassettes being the longest that were reliable for copying from the master tapes – then pitched the first six titles to EMI in the late seventies. The new product took off at speed, especially once Walkmans and car cassette players arrived, and has continued its acceleration from analogue to digital to today's download. What is currently the vast catalogue at Audible was originally just Graham Goodwin and a great idea.

With more and more clients wanting in on the business, Graham had taken me on as his abridger and assistant producer, and I had never been happier than working with him. Actors liked the work too, with the great and the good from stage and screen all keen to be signed up to read. But it wasn't every professional actor who could sight-read effectively – we'd already had a few surprising big-name duds – and a completely non-professional reader, even reading his own work, was a real wild-card. This was why Graham was so twitchy that morning.

'Has he really not read anything?' I asked, trying to get a picture of what the day might hold.

'Not a dickie bird that I know of. Apparently he's done a couple of bits of radio for the Beeb.'

Though this meant that our new reader had at least read in front of a microphone before today, Graham didn't take it as a great recommendation. He relayed the information with the same degree of disdain he normally reserved for men who wore pocket squares that matched their neckties. The BBC had their own studios, edit suites and staff engineers, with the licence-fee revenue on tap to pay for everything. Our productions had the pressure of real-world commercial budgets and deadlines, yet we were still expected to match the BBC radio standard. Ours was the tougher gig by a long way.

'But Uncle George assures me he can deliver the goods,' he added, 'so we'll have to take a punt on his judgement.'

George Greenfield was the doyen of London literary agents, handling a long list of major authors at the John Farquharson Agency. I didn't know him then – we would meet later – but he was already a staunch ally of our work, hence the fond moniker. George had fully embraced the potential of the new medium, releasing the recording rights to a lot of top titles. One of them – *The Moon's a Balloon*, David Niven's memoir, read by Niven himself – had been Graham's greatest success to date. But Niven was an actor; the Great Man was not. I could sense Graham's mood was slipping.

'Maybe he'll be all right,' I offered.

'Maybe. But he'll have to give it a helluva lot of wellie to match the pros. And he can't *possibly* do Guinness better than Jayston.'

7

The first and only other le Carré title we'd put on tape was *Tinker Tailor Soldier Spy*, the meticulously plotted tale of the unmasking of a long-term Soviet double agent – a mole – by the ageing spymaster George Smiley. This was le Carré's reworking of the Kim Philby story, the real-life double agent whose treachery, in the writer's own phrase, had turned the nation's secret services inside-out. There had been a massively successful BBC dramatisation, with Alec Guinness giving an iconic portrayal of the hitherto faceless Smiley. Michael Jayston played Smiley's younger right-hand man, Peter Guillam, and did a sterling job reading the book for us, particularly nailing the sepulchral voice of Guinness. It had been another big success for Graham and today's booking had the potential to be bigger still – John le Carré himself reading *Smiley's People*, the conclusion to his trilogy, in which the elusive figure behind the original double-agent operation, Soviet spymaster Karla, is finally brought down. A new BBC dramatisation was on the TV schedules, with Guinness revisiting his role as the lugubrious Smiley. So everything was set for another Goodwin spoken-word bestseller – as long as the Great Man could actually *read*. Graham was anticipating the fix he'd be in if it turned out he couldn't. Diplomatic forbearance was never his strong suit. He once told a renowned knight of the theatre who was unexpectedly fluffing an easy read that he could supply him with a copy of the script in Braille if it would help …

'He's bloody late too,' Graham announced, making it official by checking the reception clock against his watch. A perky whistling of the theme from *The Great Escape* drifted towards us from the studio.

'Have you met him?' I asked.

'Nope. Talked to him on the jelly-bone a couple of times, that's all.'

'Nice voice?'

'Yeah, s'pose. A bit Oxford. Touch of the Bridesheads, maybe – bit prissy on the esses. But nothing that Frenchie here can't EQ.'

'*And the rest*,' our disembodied engineer chimed in softly again.

'So's you know,' Graham said finally, forgetting he'd told me when he assigned me the abridgement a few weeks earlier, 'his real name's David Cornwell.'

'Right.'

'Like the place, but with an "e".'

'Right.'

'Right. So don't call him John.'

With that, he let the silence settle in again.

There's a sort of protective, padded-cell hush peculiar to recording studios that comes from being cocooned in an unnatural amount of sound insulation. Over the years I've made audiobooks in London, Paris, New York, Miami and LA, and the ambience is universal. I find it the most welcoming atmosphere in the world and feel instantly at home whenever I walk into a sound studio. But that morning, with the business day not yet underway, there was a distinct edge to the empty quiet. We might have been keeping watch on the deck of the *Mary Celeste*, staying frosty for whatever it was that was going to happen …

And yet somehow – although the reception area wasn't much more than six yards by five and despite our entire focus having been at all times on his arrival – the former spy managed to take us by surprise. With no sound at all, a figure appeared in the doorway; a sandy-haired individual about six feet tall, wearing a neat dull suit and offering a slight all-purpose smile. He was carrying an old-fashioned tan leather briefcase that he seemed to be holding a little ahead of himself, as if what had really arrived was not his unassuming person but what he brought with him – my abridgement of his book, our script for the day. It was only then that I realised neither of us had really known what he looked like. The world-famous name belonged to a largely incognito face. If we hadn't known better he might have been a Fuller Brush salesman with a case of samples, calling on spec.

We did know better, of course. John le Carré, our reader of the day, had joined us at last. We couldn't possibly have missed hearing the lift, so for some reason he must have taken the stairs up to the studios. All seven flights of them, soundlessly, and he wasn't even out of breath. Graham shot me a lightning-quick look, to mark that this was an altogether sneaky way to make an entrance. Thankfully, I saw that the Great Man's pocket square didn't match his tie.

'Hello, sir!' Graham said, offering his hand and his best *mea casa, sua casa* grin. 'Welcome—'

'Ah—' came the quiet-spoken reply. There was a momentary pause. Then the one-size-fits-all smile broadened out. 'Hullo!'

They moved to clasp hands as they met for the first time and before my eyes were instantaneously transformed into old chums, David and Graham, who've known each other for years, haven't we, old man? Graham could always do that. It was astounding how quickly he could determine the pitch of the hall with a reader, especially one who seemed anxious on arrival, as le Carré had just then. He had a keen sense of the exact tuning required each time, a knack which, in his cups and waxing lyrical, he was happy to call his 'whore's finesse'. More than once, after seeming to be great pals with a reader all day, he had waited until the lift doors closed on the unsuspecting actor then turned to me and muttered, 'Prick'. What he'd immediately sensed with this particular reader was that he needed to establish his credentials to handle the material – the 'deathless prose', as we less than reverently referred to it between ourselves – and had done just that in a matter of moments. He'd simply slapped all his considerable bona fides into that burly handshake – the 'sir' didn't hurt – and was now officially licensed to record le Carré on tape.

Sadly, my own credentials were established just as fast. Graham introduced me as his abridger and co-producer, but there was no handshake for me. What I received instead was what another writer – James Kennaway, whom I'd yet to read – had previously received from him and dubbed 'the wrist-watch brush-off'. It was clearly a practised manoeuvre, the hand that had readily grasped Graham's being smoothly withdrawn to adjust the watch-strap, making it conveniently unavailable to take mine. A deflected glance completed the gesture and told me more plainly than any words that I was to have no status in the day's proceedings. As a signal of the Great Man's acknowledgement of my existence, it was so distant that radio location would have been required to pick it up.

I can't say this especially troubled me. I wasn't a spurned fan; the only le Carré books I'd read at that time were the two Smiley titles Graham had paid me to abridge. Some guys could be like that about working with women, though Graham wasn't one of them and our own working relationship had been happy and equitable from the start. But now, as I watched the pair of them file into the studio ahead of me, the ho-ho-ho of new-forged male camaraderie ringing in their voices, it suddenly felt as if I'd become the *girl* of the outfit. The transformation had happened within seconds of the arrival of the Great Man, Mr David Cornwell (with an e), the so far rather uncharming international bestselling author I had a suspicion I might yet decide to call John.

Derek French was a tall chap about Graham's age, with dark brown twinkling eyes and a high forehead racing to meet his fast-receding hairline. No matter what was presented to him in the studio, his face had a permanently pleasant expression and his eyes had a look of *I'm ahead of you* in them, which, like all first-rate audio engineers, he invariably was. He and Bob Baker – until Bob moved to Magmasters – were the two engineers at John Wood whom

Graham and I most often worked with, and every session with either of them was a masterclass in How Things Should Be Done.

While Frenchie was busy in the sound booth, adjusting the microphone and making sure the new reader was comfortable at his table and chair, Graham and I lined up our scripts in the control room next door. If I wasn't directing in another studio myself, Graham always liked me in with him as an extra pair of ears (his own stereo not being so good since his wife bought him a brace of Purdeys for Christmas) and to straighten out any hitches that might crop up in the script. Not that we knew it right then, but this session was going to give all three of us a run for our money.

Once he was happy with the set-up in the sound booth, Frenchie closed the connecting door and took his seat with us in the control room. He checked all the settings on the desk in front of him, flicked a couple of dials with his fingernail for good measure and gave the thumbs-up. Graham engaged the talkback mic that fed into the reader's headphones, cleared his throat authoritatively and undertook the exposition of our recording procedures – *la méthode Goodwin* – for the benefit of his new pal.

'George tells me you're not entirely *virgo intacta* when it comes to reading your own stuff, David,' he began. 'Apparently you've done a spot of radio for the Beeb, so you'll be used to their way of recording – take one, take two, and so forth – then they edit out all the fluffs after you've gone. Well, just to let you know, we don't work that way. We use continuous editing, which means we make finished product as we go along. We call it rock and roll, it's really very simple—'

The author sat motionless at the table in the booth, staring with an expression of gravest concentration at the copy of my abridgement propped up in front of him, as Graham launched into his standard spiel for new readers. This was Gooders where he was most at home, captain of the ship of his own making, sitting comfortably at the helm in the control room, about to steer another audiobook steadily out of port. The spiel amounted to about a minute and a half of expansive and only mildly condescending instruction, ending with, '—and there you have it, my dear. Continuous editing – rock and roll. Got it?'

He sat back and waited for any of the usual first-time queries.

But there was no response from the other side of the soundproof glass. The writer still sat motionless at his table. It seemed quite as if Graham hadn't spoken. Something must have gone wrong.

'He hasn't heard a word I just said,' Graham said crossly to Frenchie. 'The bleeding talkback must've cut out.'

But Frenchie wasn't having it. He pointed to the channel light, glowing red for *ON*. The talkback, like everything else in his studio, was working perfectly, thank you very much. If anything had cut out, it was the bleeding reader.

This was what Graham had been worried about; the perils of using a non-professional. It was looking as if the Great Man had lost his bottle before we'd started.

'Er, do you copy that, David?' he asked hesitantly.

Still no response. The silence stretched out for further ragged moments.

Then David said simply, 'Yes.'

Graham exhaled.

'You sure? It's a lot to take in first time—'

'Quite sure, thanks. Stop recording at a mistake, rock the tape back, then roll forward and drop in at the agreed point. I think that's clear. Shall I read some for level?'

The silence was now on our side of the glass. We had just witnessed what could rightfully be called 'the microphone brush-off' – as masterful a way of saying *So fuck you, Sunshine* to Graham's hegemony in the studio as any yet devised. The captain of the ship couldn't have spoken with the barrel of one of his own Purdeys to his head.

Frenchie stepped discreetly into the breach. 'Any time, David,' he said into talkback and didn't need to hear more than a half paragraph before stopping him and offering another thumbs-up through the glass. The microphone level was bang on. He started up the Studer, and as the big reels turned, threading the quarter-inch magnetic tape silently over the recording heads, said quietly, 'Recording now.' After a few more moments of silence, a voice began to descend from the control-room speakers.

We listened spellbound – to the oh-so-persuasive tone and the just-so-effortless delivery, each phrase so beautifully modulated – as John le Carré began to tell us of the seemingly unconnected events that had brought the elderly British Cold Warrior out of retirement to finally bring down his Soviet nemesis. Graham grabbed my arm, clutched his heart and pulled a face of strangulated, ejaculatory bliss.

'Fuck me,' he groaned. 'Fuck *me* – the bloke can't half read!'

To which Frenchie, adding his own technical imprimatur, remarked quietly, 'And the rest.'

It was an anxious start, but now we were off and running and the going was just fine. As the narrative took flight from the page, like the descant from a hymn sheet, it was clear that our hitherto untested reader was as good as any card-carrying actor Graham had ever put a client's money on, bar none. As well as having such a beautiful voice, he was technically faultless, never moving off mic and barely misreading a word. We never once heard him turn a page or swallow or even breathe. His pace was perhaps a little studied, but seemed exactly right for the material. He read his own words with such absolute authority that the listener was bound to want him to take his time. The quality of the voice and the skill in the delivery was what our business of storytelling was all about. This particular voice had a sort of do-me-gently quality to it and the delivery was like a fabulous seduction in the back of a luxuriously upholstered high-end motor, taking us just exactly where we needed to go (or perhaps that was just me).

Soon all the familiar characters from the book were with us in the studio, the whole Circus and more,[1] each player emerging from the speakers in true form. As for Smiley himself, Graham needn't have worried. The extraordinary truth was that the Great Man didn't just do Guinness better than Jayston – he did Guinness better than *Guinness*.

Two hours into the session, after the second reel change, Graham began to do his usual calculation. X pages read, divided into Y minutes of finished tape, equalled how long it was taking the reader to deliver an average page of script. Multiplied by the total number of pages, it gave a reliable estimate of how long the finished reading would be. On a standard two-cassette pack anything between two and a half and three hours was acceptable to the client, anything under or over was not. Graham's brow contracted when he had the final figure.

'It's running long,' he said to me. 'What did you cut it to?'

'Thirty thousand words, same as always.'

'Then he's reading it long. I thought he might be.'

'Can't you get him to crank it up a bit now the plot's going?'

'Don't want to try. He's brilliant but he's still not a pro. The bloke's got no training. I don't want to lean on him in case it puts him off his stride.' He scratched his head. 'No. I think what we have to do is you take the rest of the script out into reception and make some more cuts.'

What *we* have to do? I gave Graham an *are-you-kidding-me?* stare. It was trial enough to render the convolutions of the near-four-hundred-page original down to thirty thousand words in the

---

[1] For a glossary of le Carré terminology used throughout, see page 337.

first place. This wasn't a Dick Francis or a Jeffrey Archer we were working with; it was clever stuff for grown-ups. The script was tight as a drum already; there was nothing left to cut.

'What else am I supposed to take out?' I asked. 'Main verbs?'

'You're the abridger – you figure it out.'

'Gooders—' I started to protest, immediately seeing what it would entail.

But Graham held up his hand.

'Sorry, honey, that's how it is. At the rate he's going, I reckon we need to lose forty minutes. That's twenty-four pages, twenty-five for comfort. Better get started. *Byee*—'

I suppose it was a compliment that Graham simply assumed I could do what he asked, but I wasn't sure it was possible. With about eight thousand words already recorded and allowing two thousand or so as a buffer so they could keep rolling in the studio, the task before me was to remove about thirty per cent of the twenty thousand words that remained. I got stuck in with a red pen out in reception, doing what I could to shave a phrase here, cut a description there, while trying not to nick the many connective arteries that supported any le Carré narrative but particularly this one, which carried the blood-flow of the whole Karla trilogy through its veins. And I had to do it at a gallop, to keep ahead of the recording, all the time staying mindful that my new cuts would have to pass the scrutiny of the writer himself. I had to stop every few pages to make three copies of each re-edited section and pass them back in, only to have them get through the pared-down pages a lot faster, so that I had to make the next new cuts faster still.

I kept grimly at it until the two of them emerged laughing from the studio just before noon. Graham kissed the top of my head as I sat surrounded by pages of script, and blithely announced that they'd decided to break for an early lunch at La Capannina, to give me time to work on the rest of the cuts in peace. *So order a sandwich or something, honey, and see you when we get back. Byee—*

Something rankled as I watched them go. It wasn't being denied the company of the Great Man over lunch, though I felt I'd more than earned a break at the Italian tratt on the corner of Frith and Romilly that Graham used as the staff canteen. It was that I'd been working my allegedly lovely arse off against the clock all morning in the clear understanding that it was entirely down to the Great Man that the script was over-running and entirely down to me that it would come out on time, yet I hadn't received a single appreciative word from him in return. My first instinct was right. There *was* something going on with this guy about working with women, or at the very least about working with *me*—

A considerate touch on my shoulder interrupted these discontented rumblings. It was the receptionist asking whether I wanted egg and cress or prawn salad when she went out to Marks & Spencer for sandwiches.

Though there seemed no scope for further deterioration, things grew actively worse when the session resumed in the afternoon. By three o'clock, I'd only managed to cut the script down to about twenty-eight thousand words and some seventeen thousand of them were already in the can. It felt as if I were careening downhill without brakes as I tried to wrest every last spare word from what was left. The final straw came when Graham poked his head out of the studio door, decided at a cursory glance that the *receptionist* was too busy to be disturbed and asked *me* if I wouldn't mind bringing them in some coffee – two white-no-sugar for him and Frenchie and one black for the reader, sugar requirement unknown.

'How many teaspoons of powdered glass do you take in your coffee, David?' I asked brightly as I brought in the tray.

If he realised I was playing one of his own lines back to him he showed no sign, but Graham caught my tone and cut in.

'D'you know what, David? I think we may have overworked our girl here today.'

He stroked my arm fondly, but I was unapologetic for being snippy.

'Listen,' he went on. 'I think her Oxbridge brain is probably getting a little overwrought with the task in hand. We've got about three-quarters of the show in the can already, but she still has a major chunk left to cut from the rest. Do you think we could call it a day and come back for another short session tomorrow morning, to finish up? That would give her overnight to remove the last of the deathless prose before her MA runs out. What do you say?'

The Great Man considered this for a moment.

'I don't see why not,' he said at last. 'Yes, I think we could manage that.'

Graham checked the studio log in reception and booked a ten-thirty start. That's all settled then, he announced, I could go.

It was all I needed to hear. I scooped up my script, called out to an actor I recognised to hold the lift – a *real* reader who had just finished a session in one of the other studios – and I was out of there. *Byee—*

Some other guy turned up at the studio the next day, without the bad suit and briefcase. The Fuller Brush man must have sent his younger brother.

I left my flat as late as possible, part of me hoping to find the session cancelled, and reached John Wood at the stroke of ten-thirty, not a second before, with my defences raised. Graham and the Great Man were already there, talking like they'd been pals forever and both dressed more casually; the writer wearing a russet-coloured soft suede windcheater over an open-necked shirt and slacks, Graham minus his jacket and back in his standard soft checked shirt, knit tie and cords. They looked up as I came in and straight away I picked up on an odd buzz of excitement. It felt as if someone were about to open a bottle of champagne, though nothing special appeared to be going on.

'Hello, *Sue*! How *are* you?'

This, against all conceivable likelihood, was le Carré, eagerly greeting me like a long-lost and much-missed friend. He was actually smiling, not a thing he'd done once in my direction the day before. In fact, his whole demeanour had changed. His eyes were brighter and seemed to have new colours in them, sparks of amber and green that I would swear weren't there yesterday. His voice, previously restrained in conversation, if not downright clipped, was warm and filled with enthusiasm. And all of it was directed at me.

This was another man.

After yesterday I might have suspected a set-up of some kind, a practical joke pre-arranged between the two of them, but that wasn't Graham's style. He only greeted me in his usual bluff and cheery way.

'Hi, honey – how'd it go?'

'It went,' I said neutrally, not yet on board with the prevailing mood, and produced three freshly minted copies of the end tranche of the script – the all-time *final* edit of *Smiley's People*. 'Finished word count as requested.'

'Oh, goodie, you managed to cut it down,' Graham said, taking the copies and already chuckling at a gag he couldn't resist. 'Does Karla still defect?'

And to make a start on another happy day on the farm, he set down his copy on the desk, handed a second one to the author and flipped the third unceremoniously over to Frenchie, who, as ever, raised a thumb and got on with setting up.

But the writer wasn't quite so ready to start. He was scanning the new pages closely, fingers held pensively to his lower lip as his eyes darted over the lines. I waited for the verdict, ready to counter anything he said. If he wasn't happy with what I'd spent my whole evening working on – even going back to the book to search for more nimble passages that better suited the shorter cut – then he could damn well fix it himself. I might even have suggested where he could put the rolled-up pages if he found them unsatisfactory. It took him a while to say anything as he studied the text, but when he did there was a very gratifying trace of awe in his voice.

'How *wonderful*,' he said. 'You've done it. I didn't think it possible but you've actually *done* it. How clever of you. Thank you so much.'

And with another smile of what seemed genuine appreciation cast towards me, he took the final cut into the sound booth and we were once more ready to rock and roll.

The rest of the recording went off without a glitch, and in barely an hour and a half we were all done and dusted. The very first commercial production of le Carré reading le Carré was in the can.

'*Alors – fin d'histoire*,' Graham said heartily, in his favourite phrase of Franglais, as the writer let himself out of the booth for the last time. 'Thanks, David, and well done for sticking with it. I'll let George know when we've got a release date from the client and I'll make sure they send you some complimentary copies. I expect you'll want to be off now.'

'Well, I'm happy it's done,' David said, and for the first time he did actually seem happy. 'But what I really want to do is ask your lovely co-producer if she'll have lunch with me. Will you, Sue? I'd be so pleased if you would.'

And he turned to me with an expression of such keen yet wistful anticipation that I could no more refuse him than disappoint a puppy.

We started giggling on the stairs – again, for some reason, he didn't attempt the lift – seven flights spiralling dizzily downwards. It wasn't anything specific that made us laugh or decide to race each other down, except that it suddenly felt like Finals were over and we had both passed with flying colours and anyway why not and who cared?

By the time we spilled out onto the street David had wrapped my arm in his so that we had to walk closely side by side, weaving in step through the Soho backstreets while we talked breezily about a million things at once, kicking at dropped fruit from the nearby vegetable market as we went along, two kids out on a spree. We were exactly the same height, with me in my not very high heels and him in his enormous desert boots. We moved along together fluidly, hip to haunch, matching our strides in a mutual gear. We felt – unaccountably – like a *pair*.

A surge of something deliciously exciting had taken me over. Had taken *us* over, apparently, since David's excitement seemed to mirror mine. An irresistible fizz had bubbled up between us, that champagne-cork-about-to-pop atmosphere I sensed when I first arrived. I could no longer remember what I so particularly didn't like about the man less than twenty-four hours earlier and had absolutely no idea how the transformation had happened.

La Capannina was a proudly unreconstructed 1960s Soho trattoria, with white rough-plastered walls hung with lumpy amateur oil paintings and fake-rustic ceiling beams festooned with straw-cased Chianti bottles and lengths of plastic vine. Graham used it as the regular lunch place for productions, and John – Giovanni – and Linda, the couple who ran the restaurant, began to glad-hand us the moment we stepped over the threshold. They knew me from being there so often with Graham, but I don't think they had any idea who the reader *du jour* was. John showed us straight to Graham's usual table in the corner by the bar.

'Will Mr Goodwin be joining you?' he enquired, asking me.

When I said that he wouldn't, the third place-setting was regretfully removed. But being considered part of Graham's gang evidently didn't sit well with David. For a man who made such a point of keeping his identity largely unknown, it seemed also that he didn't like travelling on anyone else's coat-tails. To set his own seal on the proceedings he immediately declared that we must have champagne.

John dispatched a waiter to bring a bottle, asking courteously, 'You are celebrating?'

'Yes!' David confirmed, giggling like a wayward fourth-former. 'End of term! We want everything on the menu twice over and still have room for *gelati* after!'

'Certainly,' John nodded with his knowing maître d' smile, and ducked discreetly away as the champagne bucket promptly arrived.

'That got rid of *him*!' David said in a conspiratorial stage-whisper across the table, while the waiter deftly poured.

Then the mood shifted again, becoming calmer and more intimate as we sipped our drinks and affected to study our menus. I already knew the Capannina offerings by heart and at that point didn't care what I was going to eat. For David, too, the menu seemed mostly a prop. Something was clearly happening here and food, if not the champagne, was the least of it.

'Tell me, Sue, were you actually at Oxenford?'

He'd picked up on Graham's remark yesterday. But – *Oxenford?* 'I was.'

'Which college?'

'Somerville.'

'Ahh, *Somerville*—' he repeated, tilting his head back judiciously, an intellectual Bisto Kid savouring the aroma of whatever it was this told him about me. (W. Somerset Maugham, the original spy-turned-novelist, had given his secret agent Ashenden the cover name Somerville, which may have contributed to David's reaction. And in one of his own novels he'd had the daughter of a hotel night waiter go there …)

'And did you wear a long gown?'

He was asking, albeit rather affectedly, if I'd been given an award. The university offers two kinds: exhibitions and scholarships. They seldom carry much money with them – mine was a princely £50 a year, barely enough to buy my books – but bestow academic status. Scholars rank higher than exhibitioners, but both are entitled to wear long gowns. The remaining bulk of undergraduates wear short gowns and are known as commoners. David had himself been a commoner at Lincoln College.

'A scholar!' he exclaimed when I told him. 'How marvellous! What subject?'

'English Language and Literature,' I said. 'Course Two, starting with *Beowulf*. Course One pretty much ends with it.'

'And did you take a brilliant first or a debauched fourth?'

We seemed to have slipped back a few decades in our terms of reference. Perhaps John should have left the extra place-setting for Sebastian Flyte's teddy bear Aloysius, or John Betjeman's original, Archibald Ormsby-Gore. The university had dispensed with fourth-class degrees long before I got there.

'Neither,' I told him. 'I got a sleepwalking second.'

He took a moment to absorb this detail, though I couldn't quite see the problem. I imagined that would be the end of the topic, but he regrouped.

'And what did you make of your dons? Were there any great heroes, any good friends?'

He looked taken aback by my mirthless snort.

'Didn't you care for any of them?' he asked.

'Not much.'

'But didn't they inspire you to love your subject?'

I tried not to gag. 'On the contrary.'

Generally speaking, I'd had to protect my love of the subject *from* my dons.

David was looking mildly horrified now so I expanded my position, gently pointing out that the tradition of dons becoming friends and mentors was as lost to the overall picture of Oxford by the time I got there as the traditional skyline of dreaming spires was lost to the developers. At least for me. I went up anticipating that sort of dynamic, everyone does, but didn't find it with any of my tutors. Nor they with me, I'm sure.

'I see,' David said, but I didn't think he did. From his reaction he appeared never to have encountered the idea before. He took another moment, then asked, 'So did you only have tutes in college?'

Ah. I could see where this was heading. The man who elbowed me – the *girl* – out of his working environment yesterday was ready to believe it was my all-women's college that must have let the side down.

'We did,' I confirmed, and caught the *thought as much* glint in the back of his eyes. 'But we also had seminars with a don at one of the men's colleges. I didn't like him any better. He wore corduroy suits.'

'The fiend,' David said supportively, though wanker had been the settled opinion at the time.

'But how disappointing for you,' he concluded.

'Not really. I dare say I was far more disappointing for them.'

'But why? They must have considered you an alpha-plus mind, surely, to have awarded you the scholarship?'

'Of course. Alpha-*plus*-plus, actually.' This was the top *women's* college we were talking about, I reminded him. Because of the historically disadvantageous ratio of female-to-male admissions at the time, Somerville was multiple times harder to get into than any of the top men's colleges. *Let alone Lincoln*, I forbore to add. 'It's just that I soon developed a gamma-minus attitude to go with it.'

'But surely you wanted a first?'

'Not really,' I said again. My achievement, as I saw it, had been getting *into* Oxford – with a *scholarship* – in the first place. After that, it was axiomatic that I was going to come away with a degree *from* Oxford. I appreciate this wasn't the attitude 'my dons' expected of me, but they really were an unappealing lot, so frankly, too bad. Or, as my Classics mistress at school was given to remark, *dolendum est.* The books would always be there – and have been, in all aspects of my life since – but everything else Oxford had to offer would be gone in three short years. So I put my energies into enjoying all the rest of life at the university instead, which was as much an Oxford tradition as any other. As Christopher Hitchens once put it, 'I wasn't going to piss away my time at Oxford studying.'

Much as people seem ready to be impressed by an Oxford degree – and I claim no false modesty to suggest they shouldn't be – it's mostly the fact that you went there at all that carries the weight. I've only once been asked to prove I actually graduated and it wasn't for work, but for documentation when I almost emigrated to Canada some years ago. David is still the only person who ever cared what class of degree I obtained. To employ le Carré terminology, I could just as well have invented the 'legend' for myself all along. So, no, I didn't want a first; not for the kudos then and not for bragging rights afterwards. If a second was good enough for Graham Greene – as just one example – it was more than good enough for me. Hitchens got a third.

But David had taken a first, in German (though, as I later discovered, after a year out before his final year and with his first wife as a full-time study-buddy). He couldn't seem to take any of my attitude in. He seemed to have a built-in regard for the institution itself, something I only ever partially acquired. I was quite a recent graduate, but Oxford already seemed distant to me, while for David, who had graduated decades before me, it seemed still to occupy a very vibrant place in his mind.

'What was your special subject?' he asked. 'Old English?'

'God, no.'

It was Classical Greek Literature, in fact, which I had loved at school and which even another unedifying college tutor couldn't spoil for me. I would tell David this another time, but right then he so badly wanted me to join him on the academic-purity-test high-ground that wild horses wouldn't have made me say so.

'No,' I told him. 'My special subject was balls.'

His chin shot up. 'Balls?'

'Big Commemoration ones, mostly. And all the Winter Balls at Merton. Even one May Ball at Cambridge. About a dozen altogether.'

'I think you're amazing—'

'Thank you.'

'Have some more champagne—'

'Thank you.'

'And you're so beautiful—'

'Thank you.'

'Not at all. It would be rude not to mention it. And so clever with the script in the studio. I think I shall appoint you my Recording Angel, do you mind?'

Beating the watchful waiter to the ice-bucket, David refilled my surprisingly empty glass, which I was sure was full only a few minutes ago, then replenished his own. I realised I was keeping pace with the writer, who appeared to have gills to be able to drink and talk so efficiently at the same time. As he talked, his vocal range remained as flexible as it had been in the studio. Just now his voice was delicate and light. Deceptively light, I was beginning to think, since I was vaguely aware of being debriefed – if not vetted.

There was a break while the waiter took our orders and then the close questioning resumed.

'Tell me – did you have lots of handsome young squires when you were at the university?'

Still with Oxford – and *squires* now?

'Not lots. Just one lovely Canadian doctoral student the whole time.'

'Canadian! Beast! It was all that deep snow they have out there.'

'What was?'

'His treating you to such spectacular balls.'

I laughed. It was cute of him to play back my own joke.

'And what was his college?' David persisted in mock fury. 'Not that I care. I hate him.'

'He was in the MCR at Christ Church. My second home.'

'A House man! Ha! I hate him! And what was he doing his DPhil on? Apart from female anatomy, the beast.'

'I doubt I ever really knew,' I confessed. 'I remember it was all Old Norse sagas and runes. *Irregular Verbs in Heimskringla*, or something.'

'Well, you would think there'd be enough. So how did you come to know Graham?'

How funny. Just when he'd got me laughing over all this Oxford nonsense, he dropped that question out of the blue. I'd only read those two of his books, so was hardly a maven in le Carré trade-craft at the time, but it crossed my mind even then that this was all interrogation technique. In which case, it was just further nonsense, because he only needed to ask me straight out whatever he wanted to know.

So I told him how I met Graham through his best friend, the comedy writer Jeremy Lloyd, whom I'd dated when I first arrived in London (after Jeremy picked me up in the Picasso café on the King's Road ...). Jeremy and I went out briefly, were even more briefly engaged, and the three of us had been great friends ever since.

'So you and Graham are chums?'

'Enormous.'

'And he's married?'

'To Audrey.'

'No kids?'

I shook my head. The notion of Graham with offspring didn't compute.

'Just Millie, a big red Irish water spaniel. And a manor house and sheep farm in Wiltshire bought with Audrey's money.'

'I thought you were his bird at first.'

'Did you?'

That seemed an odd reading. Graham and I were always happy and schmoozy with each other in the studio – exactly as we always were outside of it – but not in any way that would particularly suggest we were involved. Was it the kiss on the top of my head yesterday that did it? Perhaps people were usually more formal around the Great Man. Perhaps those wrist-watch and microphone brush-offs were supposed to sober us up. *Dolendum est.*

'Is that why you were so mean to me yesterday?' I asked.

'Oh. Was I mean to you? I'm sure I didn't mean to be – mean to you, that is.'

This was as close to an apology as I was going to get, I felt, so I let it pass. In any case, the man sitting opposite me bore virtually no resemblance to the previous fellow. The two personae appeared to be on non-intersecting orbits, the contrast between them like the light and dark sides of the moon. David was even physically different. He was just six months younger than Graham, something they established yesterday, and it was easy to imagine them in the same class at school; Graham a little taller and bolder, David a little more reserved. But now David seemed far more youthful, with a sharpened vigour about him that dispelled the years. Yesterday he'd seemed bland and nondescript, a figure cast in bare plaster. Today his features were coloured in and glazed. His sandy fairness had a gingery sparkle, his skin and eyes had a heightened tone; his whole bearing was buffed up. Today he was positively *glossy*.

He reached out across the table and gently began to stroke the back of my hand. Moments before the waiter brought our food, he lifted my hand up, leaned in and kissed the tips of my fingers.

*　　*　　*

After lunch we stood outside on the pavement in the breezy September sunshine and looked at each other. We were talked out for the moment and needed a different venue for the next episode, if there was going to be one.

'Let's go to a movie or something,' David offered, moving a strand of hair from my face. 'What shall we see?' he mused, then answered himself. 'I know – *Bambi*!'

'No, not *Bambi*,' I countered, matching his mock-solemn tone. 'I know – *Rambo*!'

'No, not *Rambo*. I know – *Bambo*! Let's see where it's showing!'

We laughed and walked on, David's arm once more snaking through mine. We wandered down to Piccadilly Circus, managing to linger over the exotic *affiches* covering the windows of the Raymond Revuebar on the way, before finally stopping on the pavement opposite Eros, where we stood looking at one another again.

'Well—' David said.

'Well—' I echoed.

I couldn't see his expression properly because his hand was over his brow against the sun. I smiled back, but something in me told me suddenly that I was going to decline whatever might be coming next. David dropped his hand and smiled too, but he had read my inner prompting and it was a different, rueful little smile.

'You'll get those books I mentioned, won't you?' he pressed. 'They're important to me. I'm sure you'll enjoy them.'

I confessed to forgetting the titles he told me about over lunch, we'd talked about so many different things. He took a note card and pen from inside his windcheater and wrote them down, then gave me the card. His address in Hampstead was printed along the top and underneath he had written: *The Good Soldier* – Ford Madox Ford, *The Horse's Mouth* – Joyce Cary. Titles which had somehow escaped my reading up till then.

'Do read them,' he pressed again. 'Particularly *The Good Soldier* – it's the book of my life.'

'Thanks,' I said. 'Yes, I will.'

He hailed an oncoming taxi, which promptly drew up. Then, without prelude, he kissed me urgently on the mouth, turned to the taxi, heaved open the door and got in. As the black cab pulled away, he looked back at me from the rear window for as long as he could, until the curve of Shaftesbury Avenue carried him out of sight.

So that was how my life was when David first walked in. I was a tall, blonde city girl not long out of college and generally up for anything. (I was happy to consider myself *a* girl, just not to be designated *the* girl.) I lived in Chelsea, worked in the West End and shopped in Knightsbridge, albeit in the sales. I saw friends, dated great guys and took frequent trips to the continent and the States. I had a happy, exciting career in audio with Graham and in television as a freelance programme researcher. In short, I was the confident, striding media-girl-about-town that I had always envisioned myself being. Everything in my world was wonderful.

David simply offered to make it more wonderful, by an order of magnitude, with that fizz of extra-super-special excitement and intensity he supplied and the way he insisted it was all just for me.

To this day, I don't know what barely registering impulse made me deflect the start of it; what transient misgiving David saw at the back of my eyes, or felt reciprocated at the back of his, that ensured we parted in front of Eros that blowy sunny afternoon. Perhaps on some inner level I knew, perhaps he did too, that I needed another year of life BC – Before Cornwell – another year under my own control, on my own terms and territory, before I surrendered to David, the perfect spy, and let him run me.

Second Encounter
August 1983

Soho Zurück

For ... there is no man who loves a woman that does not desire to come to her for the renewal of his courage, for the cutting asunder of his difficulties.

Ford Madox Ford, *The Good Soldier*

It was almost a year after our first encounter with the writer and Graham and I were once again waiting for him to arrive at John Wood Studios. It was the start of a leisurely three-day session that was sure to go well, so this time Graham had no nerves. This time, the apprehension was all mine.

During the eleven months since I watched David get into that taxi at Piccadilly Circus, I had wondered more than once what I might have missed by not picking up on his suggestion that we 'go to a movie or something'. He didn't push the notion and I didn't really decline; we just let the possibility of what might happen linger a little, then drift away. But the notion kept drifting back. I'd already known some lovely, special men, all stars in their own right, but I had the feeling that David was in a constellation of his own. As this next recording approached – of *The Little Drummer Girl*, the latest le Carré international bestseller – I caught myself hoping that unspecified 'something' would still be on offer. I knew I wasn't going to pass on it a second time.

But as before, the abridgement was not without its difficulties.

In January I'd cut a proof copy of *Drummer Girl*, which wasn't yet published, down to a very workable twenty-six thousand words, four thousand short of the standard length to allow for our reader's rather stately pace, and sent off a copy of the finished typescript to George Greenfield for author approval. This was a contractual obligation, customarily only a rubber stamp, and since we weren't going to be in the studio with it until the end of the summer I thought no more about it. The novel was published to great acclaim at the end of March and was seen as a timely treatment of the Israeli–Palestinian conflict, with the atrocious days-long massacre at the Sabra and Shatila refugee camps in Lebanon having occurred less than six months earlier. When the American Embassy compound in Beirut was subsequently devastated by a terrorist truck bomb on 18 April, just weeks after publication, the book was seen not just as timely but as extraordinarily prescient. Barely two weeks after that, at the beginning of May, I received an unexpected phone call from Jane Cornwell, the Great Man's wife.

She began by complimenting me on the abridgement, then added, 'But you have left rather a lot out.' She made it sound as if this were something David had just noticed, though he'd had the script for four months by then.

'It's a twenty-six thousand word abridgement,' I replied, as tactfully as I could while stating the obvious. 'That's really all I could leave in.'

'Yes,' she said quickly. 'We appreciate that. But we feel there's rather *too much* missing. For instance, right at the beginning – the girl who delivers the bomb in Bad Godesberg. We feel she should have more of a presence …'

Jane continued with a long list of the many scenes that would improve the script by their inclusion and, when she gave me the chance, I said I agreed with every one of them, but pointed out that every addition would necessitate the subtraction of something else. I asked for suggestions, but she had no views about what could be cut to make way for the extra scenes. Evidently that wasn't in her brief.

'Well, you see, it's a big, complicated book,' she told me finally, as though that were something I might not have appreciated.

Actually, even judged by previous le Carrés, it was an extraordinarily complex narrative. Charlie, a disaffected young British actress looking for a cause to believe in, is recruited by Mossad and elaborately trained – virtually re-programmed – to infiltrate the cell of a Palestinian terrorist so that the Israelis can locate and kill him. And that was just the core story. There were layers and layers built around it to reinforce the whole.

'We want to be sure we do it justice in the recording,' Jane continued. 'What we really feel is that it needs longer to tell the story. Would that be possible, do you think – for you to make the abridgement longer?'

'Certainly,' I replied. 'I can *cut* it to any length you like, but we *record* to three hours. Graham will need to square it with the client if you want to change that. You'll really have to talk to him.'

As is usually the case with someone who tries to tell you your job, Jane retreated once I held my ground. She attempted chit-chat next, but it was still about the Great Man's work. She began to tell me about the Hollywood film that was going to be made from the new book. She said that David had started working on the script with the director, George Roy Hill of *Butch Cassidy* fame. I forbore to ask whether the girl who delivered the Bad Godesberg bomb had much of a presence in the screenplay.

'They're casting now,' Jane said. 'We understand Meryl Streep is keen to play Charlie.'

'Great,' I said. 'She's terrific.'

'Oh, yes, of course. But we feel she might be a little *icebergy* for the character. What do you think about her?'

What did *I* think? Who cared? Although, since she asked, what I thought about actors in general – after working with so many in audio and television and having a number as friends – was that they seldom pursued parts they weren't up to playing. No actor wants a pratfall unless it's in the script. What I thought about Meryl Streep in particular was that they would be lucky to have her. Le Carré movies hadn't yet proved to be Oscar-winning material, but Streep was already an Oscar-winning actress. As for *icebergy*, I couldn't see how her portrayal of the frail and damaged heroine in *Sophie's Choice* warranted that judgement, or her double role in *The French Lieutenant's Woman*. Both films were based on bestselling quality novels and Streep seemed able to suggest that in her acting, bringing a subtle sort of literary undertow with her. In short, what I thought was – how can you *not* want Meryl Streep?

But I didn't see the point in saying any of that to the writer's wife, who was only making a poor fist of being nice to me after putting her foot in it before. I simply remarked that I thought Streep would be great for the part. The conversation drew to a close with Jane saying that David would speak to Graham about getting a longer reading and with me not saying that was what should have happened in the first place. David must have known that was how to sort the issue if he felt so strongly about it, so I couldn't see why he'd directed his wife to speak to me when it wasn't my shot to call. She'd had to phone Graham in the first place to get my number. Finally, I was left wondering what it must be like to live your life in complete surrender of the personal pronoun. In the fifteen minutes we'd been talking, Jane Cornwell had said 'we' about thirty times but hadn't once used 'I'.

So David did speak to Graham and Graham did square it with the client. Now there was going to be a special six-hour, four-cassette pack of *Drummer Girl* and my next task was to make the new cut. Graham, in best bishop-to-actress mode, said he was sure I'd agree that longer was always more satisfying than shorter, especially since he was going to pay me a full second fee, given that I had to include all the specific extra scenes that David wanted, listed in a closely typed eight-page memo I promptly received from Jane. It appeared she was the Great Man's secretary – his amanuensis – as well as his wife. The passing image I had of her was as one of the uncharacterised 'Mothers' who looked after the 'boys' on the fifth floor of the Circus. I took another week to finish the second version and it received the rubber stamp without further comment. I'd never had that kind of run-around over an abridgement before – and never did again, not even when I worked on the latest Frederick Forsyth and cut a hundred and forty-eight pages out of the first hundred and forty-nine – so it puzzled me why David had suddenly become so picky about this one. There was a reason, as things turned out; I just didn't have enough clues at my disposal yet to work out what it was.

David arrived at John Wood wearing a different zip-up jacket, this one in cream leather, over the same sort of soft checked shirt and dark corduroys that Graham favoured. He looked as if he felt at home in the studio this time, even seeming somehow relieved to be with us, as though he'd reached a safe mooring after a choppy sail. He slapped Graham solemnly on the back and then, before saying a word, without even a smile, wrapped his big arms around me and hugged me right off my feet. After only a very few mild pleasantries he took his script into the sound booth and sat down at the mic. Once again, we were ready to rock and roll.

As before, his microphone level was bang on, the only difference being that David requested slightly more volume in his headphones. His hearing was going, he said, adding woefully that he might soon have to start wearing a hearing aid.

'Oh, magic,' Graham muttered to me, as the engineer – not Frenchie this time – made the adjustment. 'Talking books – read by the deaf, bought by the blind …'

* * *

The new reading was quite as faultless as its predecessor. With no need to push ourselves we soon took a break, but when David came through to the control room to join us for coffee he already seemed rather washed out. The downbeat vibe he'd brought with him when he arrived didn't seem to have lifted. Even Graham noticed.

'Are we working you too hard, old love?' he asked, not very seriously, since he'd booked three full studio days for what was barely two days' work.

David took a deep breath and expelled it slowly.

'It was a rough summer.'

'Counting the money?'

Graham was incorrigible.

David smiled wanly at the joke and knocked back a gulp of black coffee as though it were neat Scotch. 'The thing is,' he said quietly after a moment, with an odd sort of throw-away solemnity, 'the thing is, I don't think I'm going to write again.'

Well, here was news. One of the world's most successful, most renowned, most admired authors, at the very summit of his career, had just told us he was thinking of jacking it all in. And the way he said it was strange. This wasn't Hillary planting the flag at the top of Everest; nor was it Alexander lamenting the want of fresh worlds to conquer. There was nothing either triumphant or regretful about David's manner. It was just flat, without affect. It was as if, since I'd last seen him, something had knocked the wind clean out of him.

As usual, Graham saw it from a different angle.

'Well, it's not like you *have* to write any more, my dear, is it?' he said. 'I mean, you can't need the money. You must have a few mill stashed away by now.'

Although it was entirely unwitting, there was nevertheless something therapeutic in the high sweep of Graham's misapprehension. David managed a slightly stronger smile and played along.

'Yeah,' he agreed mildly. 'I suppose. A couple.'

'Right.' Graham was confident he'd hit the nail of the situation right on its head. 'So why not chuck it in? Go out at the top.'

'Um, well—'

'Why not? Just fuck 'em, I say. Leave while they're still wet for more.'

'Mmm – that's certainly one approach,' David agreed mildly again. 'Shall we make a start on the next reel?'

The whole three-day recording was such a walkover it was really just one marathon boozy lunch with a few reel changes between courses. On day one, Wednesday, David treated Graham and me to a champagne lunch at La Capannina. In our tender care he seemed to have perked up over the course of the morning and was cheery enough to regale us with an account of being invited to lunch at Buckingham Palace, putting us into uncontrollable hysterics with his impression of HMQ, which he executed in a respectful but scrupulously accurate falsetto.

He also told us about the film, which had just started shooting.

'Who's playing Charlie?' I asked, wondering who they'd eventually decided to cast.

'Diane Keaton,' he replied.

Ah. From my studies in Classical Greek literature, I recalled that this was what happened when the gods offered their best thing first and you demurred.

'I think she'll be really good,' he went on. 'She's got a quality about her that I like.'

Well, yes, indeed. There were her wonderful performances as the doomed free-loving Theresa in *Looking For Mr. Goodbar* and as the neurasthenic wife of the next Don Corleone in *The Godfather*. Woody Allen's two most memorable (and most misogynistic) films are unimaginable without her. But for the feisty, maladjusted Charlie, who has to hold her own with a bunch of Mossad heavies while they train her to go after some Palestinian terrorists, perhaps you'd want an actress who could pack rather more of a punch. Maybe Meryl Streep?

But again I said none of this and Graham only said what he always said about actresses, which was to name the performance he fancied them in most.

'I thought she was magic in *Annie Hall*. But why didn't your sister get the part? You based it on her, didn't you? I fancied her madly in *Rock Follies*.'

David's sister was the actress Charlotte Cornwell; *Rock Follies* was a seventies drama series about an all-female rock band, made by Thames Television, where I'd worked myself as a researcher some months earlier.

'Well, you know how it is in Hollywood,' David answered with a diplomatic shrug. 'They don't know the English talent. But I think it's a really strong cast with Keaton heading it. And Klaus Kinski playing Kurtz—'

I continued to hold my counsel. Who cared what *I* thought? *Icebergy* – hah.

Day two, Thursday, and lunch was again, at his insistence, David's shout. He certainly loved a bash. This time the three of us went to L'Escargot in Charlotte Street and drank even more champagne than we did on day one – shampoo, as David invariably called it – and soon, in Graham's favourite phrase, were feeling no pain.

'So you've finally come out with it, then,' Graham noted. He had genned up on the massive coverage David had been receiving for the new book. 'You finally confessed that you were a spy.'

'I thought it was time to stop pretending otherwise,' the writer replied lightly.

'And great publicity.' Graham wasn't going to let that pass.

'I suppose. The conspiracy theorists had me down for a cross between Mata Hari and Himmler's aunt, so I thought now would

40

be as good a time as any to come clean with the rather more mundane truth about my career. Frankly, I only ever had a worm's eye view of the trade.'

Immediately after playing down his espionage career, David then dropped the biggest name in the annals of 'the trade'.

'I was in Bonn, of course, when the news broke about Philby.'

'You mean over the Burgess–Maclean affair?' Graham asked keenly.

It was funny. David's astonishing announcement that he was planning to give up writing for good held far less interest for Graham than this insider tid-bit about a decades-old story of Soviet-run British double agents. It made me think that if David really did intend to forsake writing he ought to take up the lecture circuit. He had Graham on the edge of his seat as he continued with his foray into the history of Cold War treachery.

'If you recall, after their joint defection to Moscow in 1951, the hunt was on for whoever it was who had tipped them off – the person the papers were predictably calling the Third Man.'

David was sounding rather donnish now, that elevated and somewhat godly tone which was working on Graham because he hadn't met with it before. I was paying close attention too, but because David piqued my interest as a man, not because of all that spy stuff, which rather left me cold.

'So there was an enquiry,' he went on, 'a trial of sorts, and by 1955 we have so august a person as the foreign secretary, one Harold Macmillan, telling the House of Commons that he had – and I quote – "no reason to conclude that Mr Philby has at any time betrayed the interests of this country".'

David nailed Supermac's patrician drawl perfectly. Then his voice changed again, slip-streaming from lofty lecture to music-hall banter on the turn of a phrase.

'Now, I ask you, ladies and gentlemen – who briefed Macmillan?'

'The Foreign Office?' Graham guessed.

'Correct. And who briefed the FO?'

'Your lot?'

'Correct again. Give the man a bun.'

Reverting to his standard narrative voice, David continued to breeze through his topic, every detail as readily at his fingertips as a copy of Bradshaw's to a Victorian traveller. 'It *had* to be Kim, of course,' he concluded. 'No one else had the connections to all parties, no one else could have tipped off Maclean. The simple truth was that none of us wanted to *believe* it was him. Here was someone at the very heart of *our* counter-espionage operations, who controlled everything *we* knew about the Russians. If he was the Third Man then there was no Tooth Fairy, no Santa Claus and Dumbo never could fly. If it really was Kim, then it was the end of the world as we knew it.'

'So how did you find out, in the end?' Graham asked.

'I was duty officer the night the coded wires started coming in, about the sudden disappearance of one of ours in Beirut. No name, of course. Then two messages came in together. First: *Identity of person now confirmed, see my next.* Second: *Find a word of six letters, first letter P.*' David spread his hands and raised his eyebrows to convey his astonishment at the time. '"Christ—!" I said. "It's Kim!"'

Graham's mouth may actually have been open. The quality of the voice and the skill in the delivery was what storytelling was all about.

In the hiatus between courses Graham spotted someone he knew at a nearby table and got up to exchange a few words. While we were briefly alone David asked me softly, 'Will you have supper with me tomorrow, Sue?'

'Yes,' I answered in a sudden mild daze, 'of course.'

'Good. I'll pick you up at your flat at seven.'

There was no time to say anything more before Graham rejoined us and David moved smoothly on to another topic of conversation. I'd never had a secret from Graham before. Now I did.

We wound up the session on Friday by late morning, with the whole six-hour recording securely in the can. To mark the occasion, David presented us all – including the engineer, which was a nice touch – with boxed presentation copies of *The Little Drummer Girl*, very grand, ornately tooled volumes that he called the 'human skin' edition. He quickly wrote little dedications in the copies for Graham and the engineer, then paused elaborately to chew on his pen before writing in mine.

'Now, what shall I write in this one—?' he mused stagily, getting a laugh all round. 'Ah – I know!'

He scribbled furiously on the title page, slapped the book shut and handed it to me with a little bow. I took a look inside at the fresh inscription while David watched my reaction, apprehensive that he'd overstepped the mark. I gave no sign but passed the open book to Graham, who read it out loud.

'*For lovely Sue, who shortened it …*'

The Great Man must have worked all night on that one. Graham guffawed and cranked up the double entendre another notch.

'Well, she's certainly performed the service on enough grateful authors, so she should be pretty good at it by now,' he said. 'And I'm sure she particularly appreciated your extra length, David – or was it the thickness?'

In the general mirth that ensued, David seized me in another whole-body hug and whispered fervently in my ear – 'I adore you!' – before we both joined in the next wave of laughter.

In return for the previous two days of sybaritic feasting courtesy of David, Graham was going to take us to Harry's Bar for our third and final lunch and we were all gussied up for the occasion. I was wearing a dress featuring buttons from the hem to the upper thigh – quite all of which, for reasons of public order, Graham insisted I didn't keep undone – and he and David had ditched their casuals for suits. If David's wasn't the same suit as last year, then it was another one that looked just slightly less off the peg. This wasn't my observation alone. Graham's sartorial verdict, while David was in the loo during a break, had been that although the writer doubtlessly spent the earth on bespoke tailoring, he nevertheless managed to look as if he had just stepped out of a Marks & Spencer menswear department. It was a brutal observation, though not brutally meant (and intending no offence to M&S), but it wasn't wrong. Beside Graham's easy man-about-town suavity, David – trying his best – passed for a suburban accountant. It seemed a personal blind spot, at odds with his ability to draw the appearance of his fictional characters with such detailed precision – though, ironically, it quite closely matched his most characteristic description of Smiley.

The clubby sophistication of Harry's Bar soon ran to riot once the three of us were installed. I lost count of the bottles we up-ended as we ploughed our way through the menu, laughing and raising lunatic toasts to ourselves and generally becoming the sort of table that our fellow diners didn't want to sit next to, but would rather have liked to sit at. Our camaraderie was at its convivial post-wrap peak, particularly between the two men. When they discovered they had skiing as a common passion, David promptly offered him the use of his chalet in Wengen in the coming season and Graham promptly accepted.

As for me, David was just so hugely attractive it was as if he had an industrial magnet inside him, drawing me close. It wasn't too different for Graham. We were both smitten. We both wanted as much of him as he would give, and he appeared ready and willing to give us his all. There was such beguiling candour in his manner towards us, as though we had been specially selected for his confidences, were specially qualified to be the secret sharers of his domain. Yet even so, even with his opening up to us and drawing us to him, it was clear that this was just the headland. The greater part of him, like a land-mass shrouded in mist, was still held in enigmatic reserve. This man, I now knew, was going to become my lover.

Hampstead

We met at seven as planned, but not at my flat. David called me a little before six, the phone ringing just as I'd stepped out of my bath.

'You do still want me to turn up, don't you?'

'Yes, of course.'

'Suddenly I wasn't sure.' He sounded as nervous as a youth. There was a faint tremor in his voice, coupled with a sense of urgency under restraint, which I felt too. 'So we're still on?'

'Yes – of course.'

Standing naked by the phone I realised we couldn't possibly meet here, because I would simply wait like this to greet him at the door and we would never leave the flat. There was no shortage of nearby places for a more conventional, not to say more conventual, meeting. I mentioned one, a New York-style cocktail bar and restaurant which had recently opened in the Pheasantry, a storied old building with a triumphal arch to its forecourt and caryatids holding up the main portico, just a little way down the King's Road from my flat.

'It sounds perfect,' David said. 'I'll be there. Till seven, then. Gosh.'

We sat in a corner booth while our waitress brought us our drinks. More champagne, but this time as cocktails. As she set the tall sparkling glasses down on our table David tipped her a large note as an inducement to look after us with special care.

'We may need some more of these,' he told her confidentially. 'I think a pretty steady flow would work best.'

She cast a professional eye over us and sussed the situation at a glance. Smiling sweetly, she nodded at David, palmed the note, tucked her tray under her arm and left us with a suitably American 'Enjoy!'

So – here we were at last. But for the immediate moment we seemed to have no conversation. We were like tongue-tied teenagers at a school dance. I couldn't bear the suspense.

'We are going to spend the night together, David, aren't we?'

'Oh, yes – yes, please.'

'Good. Excellent. Now I can relax. Phew.'

'Phew. You're amazing, did I tell you?'

'You did. And the rest, as Frenchie would say.'

'Yes. *And* the rest.'

We raised our glasses and half-emptied them at a single draught. The tension was broken, or at least the nervy first-date worst of it, and now we could just schmooze. Talking and laughing once again – David lightly dropping in and out of topics, receiving anything I said as if it offered a fresh vista on his own thoughts – we soon got through a couple more glasses each. Or it might have been more. Excitement and anticipation gave us the edge over the alcohol and no one except our waitress was keeping count. After a little over an hour, David checked his watch.

'Do you think it might be time we moved on to solids?'

'Why not?' I said. 'There's a restaurant upstairs here.'

'Let's move somewhere else, shall we? I always like to venture on from first places. In fact, I booked us a table at Daphne's for ten minutes ago.'

'Wonderful. I love Daphne's. Let's go.'

'Yes, let's – only – not right this minute.'

'Why not?'

'Because I have an erection.'

Perfectly aware that it wouldn't speed our departure, I nevertheless leant over to kiss his cheek.

'That's all right,' I told him. 'So do I.'

At Daphne's we ordered everything on the menu and, with the debauch of Caesars, tasted it all and finished nothing. Given our blow-out at Harry's Bar barely six hours earlier, this was hardly surprising and, anyway, just as at our first lunch a year ago, food was the least of what was going on.

'Tell me,' David said, apropos of nothing we had spoken about so far, 'where does a girl go for a holiday in the late summer sun these days?'

It was funny he should ask the question, uncanny in fact, because friends of mine had just offered me the use of their holiday home in Greece that autumn.

'Mainland or one of the islands?' he asked when I told him.

'One of the islands.'

'Which one?'

'Lesbos.'

We both failed to resist the Pavlovian snigger. My friends Priscilla and John always pronounced it with a 'v'. A Lesvian holiday home probably didn't invite the same run of gags.

'When were you thinking of going?'

I hadn't thought about it at all yet. Priss had only mentioned it recently, saying they were going out for one final late-summer trip and that I was welcome to use it any time after that.

'They claim the weather is always fine till the end of October,' I said, 'even for swimming.'

'Ah. That's good,' David said sagely. 'I'd consider it a great shame otherwise.'

'Why's that?' I asked. Jeremy had taught me never to do feed-lines, but I needed to know.

'Because I want to imagine you walking naked out of the sea. Venus rising from the foam.'

'Aphrodite,' I corrected him, laughing, though David had seemed to speak quite seriously. 'Since it's Greece.'

'Yeah. But walking naked out of the sea.'

'Aphrodite Anadyomene, then.'

'Yeah. That too. As long as it's with lots of foam.'

*   *   *

It was miles up to Hampstead from Chelsea and the taxi seemed to take forever to get us there. We could have been at my place in five minutes, but something told me all along that David wanted to be on his own territory that night. While we were dining, a pale balmy evening had turned into a silky black night. All the long journey north I stared out of my window and David stared out of his while on the seat between us our hands were locked together. We didn't face each other or speak. The physical anticipation was too intense, too achingly fierce for words or looks.

Finally, a private roadway sign slipped by and our cab drew us round the circumference of a communal garden. I thought I caught a glimpse of a tennis court among the shrubs. David told the driver where to pull up and swiftly paid him as we got out. He made a show of putting away his wallet and fishing for his latchkey until the ticking cab circled away, then immediately dropped the pretence and took me by the hand and walked us a little further along. He hadn't let the driver pull up in front of his exact address or see us walk towards it.

'Come into my *Schloss*,' he said, as the house rose up out of the darkness, solid and massive in the night. A fleeting vision from Bram Stoker came to me as he stood on the unlighted threshold and beckoned me inside.

Few places are deader to the senses than an unfamiliar unlighted house at night, but this house felt particularly dead right then. David didn't turn on the hall light until he had shut the front door securely behind us, so I couldn't immediately tell why it was so. When he finally flicked the switch, the answer became apparent. The light fixture was covered with a cloth and cast a dim eerie glow over a hallway full of what looked like lurking stage ghosts. Heavy dust-sheets were draped over everything.

'I've got some workmen in,' he said apologetically.

'But not right this minute?' I asked – stupidly, since it was close to eleven o'clock on Friday night. Over his shoulder, in the uncovered hall mirror, I saw a dimly reflected face filled with an edgy mix of anticipation and apprehension. It took me a moment to realise it was my own.

'No, not right this minute,' he reassured me. 'And they won't be here in the morning either. It's quite safe, everyone's away, we're quite alone.'

He took my hand again and led the way upstairs.

'I thought we'd use Tim's room,' he said. This was the youngest of his three grown-up sons from his first marriage, who he'd said during one of the lunches was an undergraduate at his old Oxford college. 'I made sure he'd be staying at his girlfriend's pad over the weekend.'

It must have been my apprehensiveness that made me mark the quaint expression. His girlfriend's *pad* – like a line from a fifties film, where someone was about to fix a pink gin.

'Just in case, of course,' he added quickly. 'Don't worry, I changed the sheets when I came back from lunch. Strictly on the off-chance, you understand.'

David was apprehensive too, these little explanations catching in his throat as he attacked the stairs in twos and even threes while I followed in different shoes, trying to take each step quickly in order as he hurried me up behind him, still holding my hand.

'Here—'

He threw open the door to an unremarkable studenty room, dark-painted, with wardrobe doors hanging ajar, books scattered across a desk, and posters held up with Blu Tack. A newly made double bed, rather too big for the room, took up most of the floor space. An Anglepoise lamp was already on, shining over the desk, but David turned its head to face the wall, as if even the lightbulb shouldn't know we were there.

'We're here at last,' he said, turning back to me. 'I can't believe it. Oh, my *darling*—!'

*   *   *

Our clothes lay in an incontinent heap on the floor, fastenings gaping wantonly, arms and legs tangled together, a tumbled conundrum of hotly vacated shapes to which our bodies on the bed were the answer. It was as if we had always been lovers. There was no shyness between us, only an infinite familiarity. Everything about us formed an inextricable physical union. This was sex as I had never encountered it before, the sex I had determinedly pursued all my adult life, the sex I truly believed I had always been enjoying, until then. But this was different from anything before, by an order of magnitude. This was sex that only the hero and heroine can have; sex for the cameras, sex for the Olympics, sex for the gods.

'There's not a spare inch of you, Sue, not one anywhere,' David claimed, marvelling, and it was the same for me, looking at him. He was strong and muscled and quite beautiful. 'And your legs,' he added. 'They simply don't stop. They go all the way up to heaven—'

Some time later I was lying on my stomach – between rounds – and David was lying behind me, tracing his fingers over my skin. He had huge workman's hands but his touch was feather-soft.

'I'll do anything for you, my darling,' he said softly in my ear. 'Anything to please you, anything you want. Just tell me.'

So I whispered two words over my shoulder; something he hadn't attempted thus far. He made no immediate reply but there was a thoughtful pause as – so I imagined – he planned his best route forward. I anticipated being gently turned over on to my back, my knees being moved up and parted. Instead, I received a hard smack as the full flat of his big hand landed sharply on my rear.

'What was *that* for?!' I yelped, sitting up in bed and rubbing the offended part, completely confused.

'You asked me to do it,' David answered, now totally perplexed himself.

'I absolutely did not,' I objected.

'Yes, you did – you said *beat me*.'

'No, I did *not*!' I told him again, but I was already laughing and David's hand shot to his mouth as he realised his mistake.

'Oh!! Oh, I know what you said now! Oh, my darling—! Oh, my Gawd—! I *knew* I needed a hearing aid!'

At first I thought I was dreaming the noise. It was early morning and we'd been sleeping at most for a couple of hours. The rest of the night had continued as it began, until the extraordinary blitz of erotic sensation left us both finally incapable of more.

Then I heard the noise again and knew it was real; a faint rustling clatter coming from downstairs, as though someone were trying to move around quietly. David was asleep, but when I gripped his shoulder his body instantly translated my touch and he came awake in the same second, fully alert. He rose on one elbow, listening intently. The gentle clatter started again.

'Christ,' he said under his breath, 'it's Tim—'

He was out of bed and at the bedroom door in one movement. Leaving me with the superfluous gesture of a raised finger – as if I were likely to make any noise myself – he took the stairs naked, calling out ahead as he descended.

'Timo – that you? Tim? Hullo—?'

There was about a minute's silence, long enough for me to wonder how my new lover's legendary talent for compelling narrative would get us out of this one. Then I heard another brief burst of the same erratic noise, a little louder, followed by a deep laugh from David.

'Hey, Sue – it's all right,' he called up. 'Come downstairs. We've got a visitor, but it's not what you think.'

Since the master of the house had just taken the stairs buck naked, I felt authorised to do the same. By then I was sure it couldn't be the son, or indeed anyone else higher up the food chain. If it was the builder, who'd turned up to do some overtime first thing on Saturday morning, then it was his lucky day.

I tracked David's voice to the kitchen. He was standing by the window at the sink.

'Come on,' he beckoned. 'Quick.'

The tiles were cold under my feet as I crossed the floor. Everything was new and shiny, but designed to look old and Italian-farmhousey. A high-end Hampstead kitchen. David indicated a row of herb pots on the windowsill.

'Here's our intruder, look—'

I looked, but could only see parsley and basil and chives. Then something fluttered madly among the leaves and shot up to the corner of the ceiling. A tiny black eye shone down at us like a spot of liquid terror.

'Oh, David—' I looked up at the minuscule creature clinging for its life to some invisible flaw in the decor, a bundle of dun feathers the size of a large moth. 'It's a wren—'

'Is that what it is? Well, he's a clever sod – he got in past my security. MI5 probably trained him to shit micro-listening-devices into concealed areas. I think it's time we encouraged him to go back to base and file his report.'

David opened the window and we both stood back. The bird took a moment to gather itself and dropped back to the cover of the herbs. But when it tried to escape, it flew against the closed side of the window, too disoriented to make the simple sideways move to freedom. We watched it repeatedly hit the glass, with more desperate force at every attempt, each time falling back again into the herbs. I never could bear the sight of an animal in distress and couldn't stand to watch.

'It'll kill itself if we don't get it out,' I said.

'I should think he'll definitely go home with a headache. Here—'

David made to shoo the bird with his hand, but I stopped him.

'No – you'll frighten it to death. Let me—'

I grabbed a glass towel from the side of the sink and threw it gently over the wren as it skimmed frantically up the window pane yet another time. The bird dropped to the windowsill and lay unmoving beneath the cloth. I scooped up the cloth in a soft bundle, held it still for a second, then shook it lightly out of the window. A moment later I was relieved to see the wren fly away.

'That was a good trick,' David said, wrapping his arms around me. 'Where'd you learn that?'

'MI5,' I replied. 'Advanced wren-wrangling. Course Two.'

'You're amazing.'

'*You* are. *We* were – last night.'

'I know. Phew. Hey, Sue, we're standing naked together in my kitchen. How about that?'

'Yes, hey, how about that. But you are sure the builder's not coming now, aren't you?'

If I had to wrangle a workman, I was going to need a bigger cloth.

'Well, if he wasn't coming already, he soon would be, looking at you. Wow. Talk about Venus rising—'

David held me closer.

'Something's rising—' I noted.

'I know, like Lazarus from the dead. But let's not attend to him right now. I've got a better idea. Why don't we get dressed and go for a walk on the Heath, then come back and take our breakfast upstairs and see if he still wants to play?'

'Sounds good to me,' I agreed. 'We'll probably spot our wren.'

And like the comic double-act it behoves all new lovers to become, we instantly chorused together, 'If he doesn't spot us first!'

Hampstead Heath appeared to open up almost immediately through a gate at the end of David's back garden. It was still early and joggers and dog-walkers were our only companions, but already the sun was beaming down on the grass and trees. The Heath should have been looking a little tired and worn at the height of summer, but the pathetic fallacy had beaten us to it and everything was fresh and spring-clear, bright with new possibilities.

I wasn't dressed for a ramble, but last night's cocktail shift didn't look too morning-aftery and I found I could manage the grass pretty well in my shoes. David had thrown on his Graham-ish cords and a casual shirt. He took slow, heavy strides at my side, his hands thrust deep into the pockets of his trousers. Just as he had many voices, he seemed also to have many walks, perhaps many moods to go with them. He was more pensive now, as though some temporarily dismissed trouble had crept back upon him. I felt it must be what he'd told Graham and me earlier in the week.

We continued walking for a while, stopping when we got to the crest of the Heath. A hazy-bright view of London appeared in the distance. Hampstead has always been known for its writers, and many have walked the Heath and written about it. But in those years, with Smiley in such ascendancy on page and screen, David had managed to make it his own. It was impossible to stand there and not half-see the elderly spymaster walking along the winding lamp-posted paths in his expensive ill-fitting clothes, stopping to polish his glasses on the fat end of his tie. Yet his creator had said only three days before that he might never write again.

'Were you serious on Wednesday?' I asked.

'About not writing anymore?'

'Yes. I've been wanting to ask you ever since.'

'Mmm,' he said after a pause. 'I think I might be.'

'You looked all-in at the start of the session. What made it such a bad summer?'

David scanned the horizon from under a furrowed brow.

'We should've gone to that movie, you and I,' he answered obliquely. 'We really should.'

I realised he meant the extra step we didn't take after our first lunch a year ago. But it looked as though we'd taken that extra step now. I couldn't see how the delay might have caused a problem.

'Last year, you mean. Why?'

'Because I met someone after you, out in Lebanon, when I was researching *Drummer Girl*.'

'Oh.'

I hadn't stopped to think about it, but of course David must have had other girlfriends, despite being permanently married. He was too good at it with me to be a tyro.

'Did you have a bad break-up with her?' I asked him. 'Is that what upset you?'

No other explanation crossed my mind. For all that David was self-evidently unfaithful to his wife, I intuitively knew he would be entirely faithful as a lover. He had given so much more of himself to me last night than just the extraordinary physical element. Whatever relationship he'd had in Lebanon, I was certain it was over. But with a thousand guesses I could never have imagined why.

'No,' David answered, still looking out at the view, his voice expressionless. 'She died. In the embassy bombing in April. Blown up. Gone.'

He made a strangely dispassionate '*Boom*' gesture with his hands, then picked up his dogged stride and began to tell me the story.

It had been late in the day for research, but following the massacre at Sabra and Shatila in September, he'd gone back to Lebanon. He'd felt he had to, after an atrocity of such terrible dimensions. Wanting someone to show him around the camps in the aftermath, through his CIA connections at the US embassy in Beirut he met an American journalist named Janet

Lee Stevens, a Middle Eastern Studies graduate working with Amnesty International.

'She took me around,' he told me. 'Showed me where the authorities sent in the bulldozers after the massacre. It was appalling, what had happened. Bodies mutilated, women raped, pregnant ones disembowelled. The clean-up made it worse.'

They soon began a relationship. 'She was just a little plain bit of a thing,' he remarked, 'not tall and blonde and beautiful like some. But she was a wonderful lover.'

'Did you love her?' I asked.

'Yes,' he replied. The word seemed to come out of him from a distance. 'She had a fierce heart and was passionate about so many things – I loved her for that. She was devoted to the Palestinians, especially the refugees and their children. And they loved her.'

We walked on for another while before he stopped again to tell me more.

'We'd planned a holiday in the middle of April, to celebrate the end of the book. She was taking leave and coming from Lebanon, so we agreed on Cyprus. So I'm waiting for her at Larnaca airport when a couple of uniforms come up and ask me if I'm who I am. I thought, hullo, Jane's on to me. They escort me to a back room and some official sits me down and tells me that the person I'm waiting for has been killed in the embassy bombing.' He paused again before adding a final detail. 'She wasn't supposed to have gone in that day. She went back for something for me ...'

David was telling me the story exactly as it had unfolded for him, in real time, and I couldn't ignore the irony that this was exactly how he would have written the scene himself, for maximum impact on both the character and the reader. The very novel he had just set in that region, which took him there for research, began with a bombing and then the new relationship, which had arisen out of that research, ended with one. It seemed unbearable that his own life had so cruelly played back a facsimile of his own art.

He'd gone over to America afterwards, to attend Janet's funeral and meet her family. She had a twin sister, he said. Her 'double', I thought automatically.

What he didn't say was how the authorities had known to find him; how they'd known who he was waiting for and that she'd been killed. How they knew any of it so quickly, in what must have been utter chaos in Beirut. The bombing was breaking news worldwide, yet they located David before he'd heard. *They who?* I should have asked, of course, but didn't. It was hardly the moment to request clarification, but I'd already begun to notice how he always left so much to inference, how there were always so many possible interpretations to anything he said. I was trying so hard, even at that early stage, to catch them all, and somehow already knew that asking him anything directly wouldn't work. There was, in fact, one huge detail he was leaving out, something I wouldn't discover until years later. But on that blameless sunny summer morning, standing on Hampstead Heath next to my new-found lover, it was as much as I could do to register the impact of his sad story, made all the more moving by his unadorned and expression-less telling of it. Who else had he been able to unburden himself to in the months since it happened? Clearly not his wife, possibly no one in his family. Did he have a trusted friend to confide in? It seemed likely that I was one of just a very few to whom he'd been able to open up. But imagine how many people he *couldn't* have told, how many he'd had to keep it *from*. How many times in all the publicity for his new book must he have been asked about the embassy bombing and had to respond as though he saw it only as a consequence of inexorable geopolitics, not also as a source of terrible personal loss. Consider how many times he must have had to force a modest smile after being congratulated for writing so presciently about the very conflict which brought it about. I was beginning to see why it had been such a rough summer for him. It was my first glimpse into how entirely constructed from secrets David's private life was and the emotional price he paid for it.

And there was one specific secret aspect he could only share with me; the notion in his mind – and now in mine – that it might never have happened if we'd begun our own relationship a year earlier. If we'd only gone to see that movie.

David stood like a sentinel, still looking out at the hazy cityscape on the low horizon, his hands deep in the pockets of his cords. Was he remembering her? Reliving the moment he heard? Recalling her funeral and meeting her twin? I slipped my hand into one of his pockets and threaded my fingers through his. We went back to the house, breakfast forgotten, and spent another long session in bed. This time it was gentler and quieter, though no less intense. It felt like a requiem for a young woman who had died before her time.

David called me at my flat at nine fifteen on Sunday morning. Scaling the north face of the Eiger couldn't have left me more exhausted than the events of the previous four days, and after coming home from Hampstead on Saturday I could have used an early night. But I had a supper date that I didn't want to cancel – with the friends who were letting me use their holiday home on Lesbos – and went out again that evening. It was good to see John and Priscilla and I was glad I made the effort, but I was running on fumes. I fell into bed once I was home and was still sleeping at a depth of some fathoms when he called.

But David's voice didn't have a trace of weariness. He was bounding with energy.

'You're a miracle worker, my darling,' he exclaimed. 'You've got me writing again! You've swept away the cobwebs. It's all wonderful and it's all you. Go back to sleep. I've written you some lovely letters, you should get them on Tuesday. I'll call you very soon and we'll make some dates.'

He rang again on Sunday afternoon. I was just about awake by then.

'Is the Lesbos holiday promised to anyone? Because if it isn't I wondered whether we might go there—'

'Together?'

'Well, yes. Honeymoons are usually more fun that way. I figured we needed one. And George Roy and the crew are going to be on location on Mykonos, so after our trip I might go and see how they're doing.'

He didn't call again until Wednesday.

'Did you like my letters?'

'They haven't arrived yet.'

'Really? They should have.'

'Well, they haven't – sorry.'

'No – I'm sorry. They were lovely letters and I wanted you to read them. Hmm. I wonder—? Tell me your address again.'

I told him and heard pages being hurriedly turned.

'Oh, Gawd! Hang up your boots, Cornwell. You know what I've done, don't you? I gave you a coded entry in my master address book and I've only gone and misread my own bleeding code! I've sent two very long and graphic love letters off to you at the same number King's College Avenue, SW3.'

'Oh, dear,' I said. 'I don't think there's any address like that near here.'

'I *know* there isn't. I put you down as King's College Road, NW3, up here – only I was too stupid to decode it the right way!'

Later on there was a courier at my door handing me an envelope. Inside was a single sheet of notepaper; David's chalet address in

Wengen was embossed at the top and it was closely written on both sides. He wrote that he was ashamed of himself for having misread his own code and felt he must hurry to write to me again to make everything real, in case the things he whispered to me that night were only dreamed. He said he turned my body over and over in his memory, marvelling in the recollection, yet not quite believing it. He told me that I had roused him from a time of terrible self-doubt, given him back his manhood and his confidence, and that he felt as if he were writing with my hand on him, telling him, *You can, you can.* Admiration, tenderness, sweet gratitude; the words were like a rarefied ether as I breathed them in. My astonishing new lover, this massive talent, this writer of international estimation and renown, was thanking *me* for restoring him to a belief in his life and work. And he was telling me that he loved me.

He ended by saying there was much more in the originals and it was a shame that I would never see them, but at least the lads in the lost-letter department at the Post Office would have a good time going through them, looking for a return address.

This episode with the letters was so perfectly emblematic of David's whole life, it seems to me now. That he encoded my address to keep it secret in his own home, hiding it out of a lifetime's habit of secrecy whereby he instinctively treated his domestic environment as enemy territory. That he mangled the deciphering of his own code because he had been too long out of the field, away from the real world of secrets, even though the compulsion to create secrecy was as strong as it ever had been. That there was never any real need to encode my address in the first place, since his wife already had it to send me the *Drummer Girl* memo and would most likely have thought nothing of it even if she had seen it in his own 'master' address book (presumably he didn't keep a separate 'mistress' one). That the very first letter I received from him, of the many dozens that would follow, was actually a 'double', a hasty copy rushed out by courier to testify to the existence of the lost originals that he'd sent to what he called 'a non-existent address' – a 'dead letterbox', one might say. And yet at the same time, because he never did relay the 'much more' he had originally written – despite his facility for recalling every word – the 'double' managed also to become the 'official version'. I see all this now as a reflection of how entirely fractal David's life was, how each separate part was just a smaller replica of the whole. The perfect multifaceted reflection of the perfect spy.

Zurich

'I very badly want to fuck you,' David told me earnestly, as we sat together in a low-lit corner of the airport bar, his hand below the table, earnestly between my thighs.

He had raised our departure to 'operational status' and there was a high-alert buzz about him. His eyes were constantly scanning the sight-lines of the room, the entrances and exits, watching who came, who stayed, who went. He was in the field, where he operated best. The married man eloping with his new mistress. The lifelong spy for whom everything was a matter of cover. I hadn't seen this version of him before. I was beginning to understand there were many versions of David.

It was late September and we were on our way to Greece. We were in Zurich because David seemed to fly everywhere by Swissair. The city was where his European agent, Rainer Heumann, had his offices, making it a useful cut-out for covert onward journeys like this. The AmEx credit card he used for our trips and treats was in the name of his Swiss-based company, Authors Workshop, which Rainer oversaw, so his extracurricular running costs were rerouted there too. This was already our second trip away together. The first was also in Switzerland, at a grand hotel in Vitznau on Lake Lucerne. Our delightfully *fin-de-siècle* room opened on to a stone terrace with wide-stretching views across the water to the mountains beyond. A vast canopied bed held us in a luxurious embrace while we drank champagne and made love in almost continuous rotation throughout our three-day stay, David passing the first mouthful from his glass to me in a kiss and giving me the first of many pieces of jewellery. 'Have some flowers,' he said sweetly as he laid the small red box in my lap. It was an antique piece from a Bond Street jeweller, a gold necklace set with garnets arranged as petals. We took walks by the lake, found wonderful local cafés and restaurants, and on Sunday morning let the Rigi cogwheel train take us up the steep rise to the top of the world – or so it seemed – as we sat on its articulated wooden seats among local passengers who sang folk songs to the impromptu accompaniment of an old man with a ukulele. We found a grassy slope to eat a picnic of *Bündnerfleisch* and chèvre and Swiss white wine, before taking the Rigi-Bahn back down.

Once we returned I received deliveries of huge bouquets and more letters and two more books: Malcolm Lowry's *Under the Volcano* and Budd Schulberg's *What Makes Sammy Run?* As with the titles he'd recommended last year, David seemed to be suggesting that these also held parts of the puzzle of his own character for him. I didn't know whether he wanted to have me work him out for myself, or just to share his own puzzlement at the way he was, as he put it, inside his own head.

It was only about forty minutes till our Athens flight, but David had ordered a bottle of Krug and directed me to open the fresh-cream Sprüngli truffles he'd bought while he was waiting to meet my flight from London. He explained that one would go down better with the other and wasn't wrong. By the time the flight was called both the shampoo and the chocs were gone. I pointed to the empty packaging as we left the table.

'The truffe,' I said. 'The whole truffe and nothing but the truffe.'

David laughed as we headed for the gate, but it was a tight, nervous laugh. He had a lot of nerves near the surface. The Krug he'd downed hadn't touched the sides. If anything, his watchfulness was even keener. We hadn't made our destination yet and in David's lore, as he'd explained it to me, *they could still get us before we do*. (And indeed, before we got home, they very nearly did.)

At the time, I dismissed this as a little paranoid. I didn't understand why he couldn't shed the perpetual secrecy, couldn't see what he had to lose by openly owning all the parts of his life. He was a big famous guy with a secure place in the world and all the money he could possibly need to meet any contingency in this and another dozen lifetimes. Yet so often he acted like a man on the run.

I had a lot to learn and it would be a long lesson learning it. It would take me years to arrive at even a partial answer to the one elementary question that was so central to his existence. What was he so afraid of? What was he so worried would catch up with him? *What made David run?*

This second trip could already have been our third, all in about a month and a half of being together. He'd wanted me to join him on a trip to Munich, but at the last minute decided to go alone. I went with him to Heathrow, so we could spend the night together at an airport hotel.

'Where you off to then, guv?' the cabbie asked in the time-honoured formula, as he drove us out along the Cromwell Road.

'Oslo,' David replied without missing a beat, then whispered the explanation of his tradecraft into my ear. *If you're going south, tell them north.* A simple but effective technique of inversion.

Ah. So if your girlfriend lives in SW3, put her down in your address book as living in NW3, in case your wife goes looking to find you out. (Chances were, if you couldn't decipher your own code, then she wouldn't be able to either …)

All our other meetings since that first night in Hampstead had been ad hoc at my place, whenever his schedule allowed. My own schedule frequently allowed, since I had given up two other lovers for David. But then, I wasn't a famous writer, married with encumbrances.

For this trip, the big one, David had left for Zurich a day or two ahead of me. More business with Rainer, ostensibly. He called me from the city to check everything was in order at my end.

'It's going to be wonderful, my darling,' he said, with a sort of joyous reverence in his voice, like a young groom-to-be in a

Victorian novel. 'It'll be our honeymoon, I can't wait.' Then his tone switched to business-as-usual. 'Now, did my spook travel team send you all your documents?'

'Spook' was a word David used liberally, long before it was popularised, to indicate someone with an Intelligence background (or foreground, I was never sure). He had previously told me that the private travel agent he used was an ex-operative of some sort. He'd also said that George Greenfield had been with Military Intelligence in the war. *Uncle George was a spy? Well, I never.* My first thought was, *I must tell Graham.* But then I realised I couldn't tell Graham, because I hadn't yet told him about my relationship with David. (George always denied it, by the way.)

I confirmed that the tickets had arrived. 'Don't worry, David,' I said, 'the lamplighters made the drop.'

'Good,' he answered. 'So they should have. They know I like my covert operations to run by the rules.'

'Moscow Rules?' I asked, thinking he was just playing along with my use of le Carré-speak. But he was deadly serious.

'Naturally. No one can know about us. I've made that plain to them. They have my instructions.'

I heard him exhale forcefully at the other end of the line, sounding for all the world like a wanted man who'd been holding his breath against a threat of detection that had just passed. I realised then that there was no irony or playfulness in David's use of his own argot. He even insisted next that we have a fallback.

But first he asked suddenly, 'You will be there, won't you?'

A strange question out of the blue. What on earth made him think I might *not* be there? Was it because of the woman in Beirut? Did this remind him of the last time he had waited for her?

'Of course I'll be there,' I assured him. 'Of course.'

'Good,' he said, and breathed another great sigh into the phone. 'Good. A chap doesn't want to go on his honeymoon alone.'

'David, don't worry. You know I'll be there.'

'Yes, I'm beginning to – know things about you. We can get to know each other properly, can't we, when we're there. Stretch out by ourselves, just the two of us.'

'Yes. On the beach in the sun.'

'Anywhere, as long as it's away. Away from everyone.'

'It will be. My friends tell me all the tourists should have gone by now – even the German lesbians who are always the last to leave.'

'I'm glad of that,' David said, still immune to any kind of humour. 'I shouldn't want the competition. So now, listen, my darling, about our fallback. Take Rainer's number—'

Rainer, as I've said, was David's main man. If he wasn't technically another former spook, then he had lived a life that was definitely spook-friendly. (He was German-born, half-Jewish, and as a young man during the war had escaped from a Nazi labour camp.) Which meant that all three of David's agents about whom I had any information so far – his British agent, his European agent and his UK travel agent – had probably been, well, agents. This went a long way to explaining why we had to have a fallback, why the lamplighters had to deliver my tickets and why our affair had at all times to be conducted under Moscow Rules. David's own spy rubric appeared to be as indispensable to him in his life as in his writing; perhaps more so in his life. Was I in a relationship with David Cornwell or John le Carré? Right then, I had no idea if there was any clear difference between the two.

So our fallback, should my lover not be there to meet me in Zurich, was for me to call Rainer, who was presumably briefed on all contingencies. David had already couriered me a thick wad of Swiss francs – probably from the reptile fund – which was more than enough to put me up in the bridal suite of the most expensive hotel in the city while I awaited his arrival or further instructions.

The simple notion that I might go on to Lesbos by myself and start the holiday as originally planned, with David joining me when his life let him, didn't enter the discussion.

I didn't need to call Rainer. David was waiting for me at the connecting flights area, the box of Sprüngli clamped under his arm. He was wearing his favourite zip-up leather jacket and casual slacks with desert boots underneath. I had already noticed how he seemed to get a much better look about him whenever he was in Switzerland. He even brushed his hair a different way, straight back from his forehead, instead of the less flattering parted-the-way-nanny-did he favoured in London. He could have passed now for a savvy, good-looking Swiss professional leaving his apartment in the city for a long weekend in the mountains; a photo-journalist perhaps, or the kind of cool university lecturer that lithe young female undergrads work especially hard to earn good grades from. Regrettably, the kind I never had myself.

But despite the cool-guy gear, David's body language exposed him at fifty yards as an anxious suitor. It hadn't occurred to me that he might actually have *meant* the whole 'honeymoon' thing. I'd thought it was just his way of joking about our first long trip away. But I was gradually coming to understand something. For all the genuine good humour he could generate, David didn't ever really *joke* about anything; not about his life and work, not about the spy stuff and not about whatever it was that this relationship we'd started meant to him. I had to get it into my head. This was a man who took everything in his life – even our love and our laughter – in deadly earnest.

Seeing the look of extraordinary relief on his face, the sudden release of strain in his expression when he saw me, I realised he truly *had* worried that I wouldn't come. Christ – didn't he know? How could he *not* know? As if anything could have *stopped* me.

*　　*　　*

The flight to Athens was long enough for yet another bottle of Krug and quantities of smoked salmon pressed on us by the smiling Swissair cabin crew, who intuitively treated us like newly-weds. The ongoing flow of champagne eventually overtook any reserve I had left – never a great deal to begin with – and I quietly suggested we might attempt post-prandial membership of the Mile High Club. Our section of the plane was nearly empty and the Swissair onboard loos were immaculately clean. Short of a private jet – *and where was his, I'd like to know?* – this had to be the ideal scenario.

David took a moment to digest what I'd said, then regretfully declined, giving me an odd sidelong look.

'You've done that before, have you?' he asked.

The way he posed the question told me he wouldn't be happy with the answer either way. If I said no, he wouldn't like failing the challenge to be first. If I said yes, he wouldn't like knowing someone had beaten him to it.

'I have,' I confirmed.

At this, his eyebrows knitted together in hilarious mock fury. It seemed the truffe wasn't always easy to swallow.

'Lots of times?' he pressed, demanding the whole truffe now.

'A couple.'

He said nothing for a while, but looked thunderously at me out of the side of his eye. I trusted it *was* mock-fury. It wasn't terribly easy to tell.

'Have you any idea how much I hate him?' he fumed in a stage whisper.

'Hate who?' I asked back. Again, I knew from Jeremy never to do feed-lines, but I was laughing too much not to oblige.

'The swine you did it with. It was that Canadian, wasn't it?'

And nothing but the truffe! My mind flashed back to a Wardair flight to Ottawa and the inevitable effect of copious amounts of free Seagram's upon two students.

'Yes,' I confirmed. 'It was.'

'Well, *fuck* him, the swine,' David growled out of the corner of his mouth. 'Him and his runes.'

The more he fumed, the more I laughed. It was as well I didn't mention a more recent incidence, on a Christmas trip to New York with the television exec I'd been dating immediately before him, or he might have blown a fuse. But what a memory the man had, to remember not just my Oxford boyfriend, but also my passing remark about his doctoral thesis. Our conversation at La Capannina had happened over a year ago. But I would learn that about him too. David remembered everything.

For the last hop to Lesbos we left the safe charge of the Swissers, as David always called them, and boarded an aircraft that looked as if its original purpose had been crop spraying. We landed at Mytilene airport without event and the moment we stepped out of the spindly little plane the sweet, soft local air washed over us in welcome. We'd arrived on Sappho's fabled isle and were going to be there for twelve whole days, just the two of us. It already felt like a trip to heaven.

Was I in love with David? Oh, yes, to be sure. But was it true love or simply the most wondrous fling? Could it even be both? I was too enveloped in the thrilling up-close magic of it all to know the answer. But then, as I think David had already planned, that was what the honeymoon was for – so that I would find out.

Plomari

As Exhibit A in defence of David's insistence on the perpetual need for cover, we found that our taxi driver knew exactly who we were and where we were heading. He was just the next in line at the airport cab rank, but recognised the address in Plomari straight away. He lived there, he told us over his beefy shoulder as we slid onto the hot black leather of his back seat, and knew very well the lady Priscilla and her husband, the nice man John. Sure. They had even left his number for us at the house. They were good in England, yes?

Yes, they were very good in England, I said, mildly amazed at the coincidence, while David gave me a *You see?* look.

We must call him Tony, our driver said, and while David leaned forward over the back of the front passenger seat and made an instant chum of him, expertly feeling out all the pressure points of trans-European male bonding, I poked my elbow out of the window and watched the dusty countryside wind by, as the passing air flushed up smells of hot stone and straw.

The road twisted and turned for some miles, climbing and dipping over the hills, until after a good hour Plomari rose up to greet us, its streets running higgledy-piggledy between the last hill and the sea. As we entered the town on the long harbour road, passing locals stirring out for their evening promenade, David laid a hand on Tony's shoulder. Could he let us out here so we might have a drink and something to eat? Maybe he could take our bags to the house and come back for us in a couple of hours?

'Sure. Is good idea. Is no problem.'

Excessively large Greek banknotes exchanged hands as we got out. David seemed to be a compulsively heavy tipper. As I handed over Priscilla's house-keys, he asked Tony to recommend a restaurant.

'Sure. Costas'.' He pointed up the street to where the local stores were pulling up their shutters ahead of the coming evening's trade. 'Is best place in town.'

'Let's find a place for a snoot first,' David suggested as Tony drove off with our luggage.

Not to over-patronise first establishments, we found two, both facing the harbour about fifty yards apart. We downed large cloudy ouzos in each place and sweet black coffees thick enough to chew. Before heading to the restaurant we took a few moments to lean out over the harbour wall and watch the low red sun dip finally out of sight, Apollo riding his chariot into the sea, turning the sky into an impossibly lovely purple streaked with gold.

David stared into the darkling view as if somewhere in its far reaches a searchlight had finally gone out. He put his arm around my shoulder and pulled me tightly to his side.

'We made it,' he said, in barely a whisper.

Leaning into him as he held me close, I could feel coils of tension leave his body, the disengagement of inner cogs that had been running in high gear for far too long. I wanted to believe that this release was down to our being there together, was down to *us*, and that was a big part of it, no doubt. But there was another factor in play as well. It wasn't only our arrival that had brought him this relief. It was what he'd left behind. David gave off the unmistakable scent of *escape*, of having *made it*, as he'd said. But escape from what?

Costas himself showed us to a little marble-topped table for two in the corner of the terrace of his busy taverna. Our fame had gone before us, not David's at all, but ours, as Priscilla's chosen guests. Tony must have tipped him off. We were brought further ouzos on the house, to be followed, at David's request, by a bottle of the best red Costas could find in his cellar. My own request was for a bottle of spring water. I had schooled myself not to keep up with David's monumental capacity for alcohol during this trip, but I'd been doing just that, pretty much glass for glass, since arriving in Zurich.

'Don't you ever drink plain water?' I asked, as he filled my tumbler but not his own.

'Not usually as a first choice of beverage, no. You know what W. C. Fields said about water, don't you?'

I shook my head and gulped down the clear contents of my glass, while David executed a perfect impression of the old deadpan actor.

'Never touch the stuff. Fish fuck in it.'

As David was finishing the last of a generous snifter of brandy, Tony drew up on schedule to take us up the hill to the house. It must have been all of three hundred yards. When we got out he refused any further payment from David and handed the keys back to me.

'*Kalispera*,' he said to us respectfully and drove off.

'Oh, my darling, *look*—' David said wistfully, his arm circling my waist as he scanned the front of the little brick house with its green shutters. 'It's our first house.'

We made a swift recce of our new quarters. The stone-flagged front hall led to a shower room and loo and a storeroom behind. Next floor up were the living room and kitchen, with all kinds of provisions got in for us by a neighbour as Priss had promised. And finally, above that, was the bedroom, where a big double bed lay under the rafters.

'Come here,' David said softly, pulling me on to the bed. 'I must have you now – now and forever after. Happy honeymoon.'

Our first day should be spent exploring, David declared next morning. But before that we had to shop, *so let's get a move on.*

Right-o. *Poop-poop!*

'What are we shopping for?' I asked as we headed down the sunny street, thinking there couldn't be much more than fresh squid to buy on the whole island.

'Beach gear, for me. I didn't bring any.'

'Why not?'

He looked at me as though I'd asked a very stupid question – which of course I had.

'I thought it inadvisable to be seen packing any.'

'Oh – yes, of course.'

It was strange, given the circumstances of our relationship, but for long tracts of time when we were together I managed completely to forget that David was married. Since his infidelity didn't appear to trouble him, it didn't trouble me, though frankly even had it troubled him, it still wouldn't have troubled me, since I wasn't the one who was married. But sometimes, as just then, the reality would intrude.

'Doesn't she know you were coming here?'

'No. Certainly not the beach bit of it. And naturally not the tall blonde bit of it either.'

I was almost entirely incurious about David's relationship with his wife. I understand this isn't how many women in an equivalent situation would feel, but it was nevertheless true for me. I never had the nesting instinct, I suppose, or much of the coupling-up one either. A voluntary union of two individuals for as long as it works has been about the scope of my ambition with any man. As one subsequent lover felicitously put it, I have no tentacles. Regarding David's marriage, it was axiomatic that it had its limitations or he wouldn't have been there with me, or indeed, wherever he'd been with those who had preceded me. By then I was sure that the woman who died in Beirut wasn't the first by a long way. (About a year and a half later, David would actually introduce me to another of my predecessors.) But I couldn't help wondering what tale he'd spun for his wife. A research trip, most probably, so naturally he couldn't be seen packing a pair of trunks. Swimming in the sea off a Greek island wasn't anything a fellow needed to do for research, not even the famously meticulous John le Carré. It explained why he was still dressed like a Swiss weekender; it was how he left Hampstead. If you're going somewhere warm – as I now knew the inverted operational reasoning went – let your wife see you packing for somewhere cool. I assumed Jane believed what he told her, because God help her if she didn't, the suspicion would surely eat her alive. David called her every day while we were away, for ten minutes or so. Checking in with base, he termed it, but it was one-way signals only. In exchange for his uxorious diligence, she wasn't allowed to call him. I expect he lied very effectively.

This set me thinking about the phone call I'd had from Jane myself back in May, about making the *Drummer Girl* abridgement longer. It must have been on David's instructions, though he knew I had no say in the matter. I began to see now that it was for cover, to put her off the scent of what he was really planning, which was his second approach to me. I could even imagine the sort of thing he would have said to her, to seal the false narrative. If you're going south, tell them north. If you plan to seduce another woman, make sure your wife thinks you have no regard for her. *Give that tedious abridger a call, will you?* I could hear him telling her. *See if she can sort the script out before they get me into the studio this time. I can't go through the nonsense we had with Smiley's People again.* Something like that; something off-hand and plausible and just deadly enough to kill any suspicion. For cover, to get what he really wanted, which was more days in the studio to be able to cast his spell over me. All of which, I also began to realise, carried one further implication – that he'd already been lining me up then, with that other poor woman not even a month dead.

I've thought about this a lot since then and I believe I'm right. I don't think David ever had a problem with the first *Drummer Girl* abridgement. Most probably it was lying dormant on his desk while he pursued his new love interest in Beirut. Perhaps the Cyprus holiday was already planned. The truth for me, meanwhile, was that almost immediately after we parted at Piccadilly Circus – in front of Eros, for goodness' sake – I'd seriously regretted not taking David up on his offer. I looked him up in *Who's Who*, wanting to find out more about him, and when I discovered his birthday was coming up I decided I would try to re-engage him by sending a card. I spent ages selecting just the right one from the endless array at Paperchase, then carefully honed what I'd put inside – something crafted to be witty and appreciative about the books he'd recommended, particularly *The Good Soldier*, and just sufficiently appealing and open to inference without tipping off anyone else who might open it first. I wanted him to know that my hesitation had been only momentary and that I still wanted to go to that movie. I posted the card to Hampstead, hoping to hear back, and was hugely saddened when I didn't. I couldn't know he'd returned to Lebanon by then and had probably already met Janet ...

Then on 18 April, *Boom*—

When I received the phone call from Jane, David must have just arrived back in Hampstead from the funeral in the States, full of secret grief and guilt – *She'd gone back for something for me* – and feeling as though he might never write again.

What we really feel is that it needs longer to tell the story, Jane had said to me.

It was only after I'd confirmed that I could cut the book to any length required – as if it needed saying, though possibly David needed his wife to *hear* me say it – that he called Graham to arrange things. And when it came to fixing the studio dates, he made sure Graham booked three days in the studio for what was only an easy two-day read. Wednesday to Friday, furthermore, so that we would finish in time for the weekend. The instructions Jane sent me were dated 16 May, not even a month after the bombing. She wrote a covering paragraph, stressing that if I didn't think I could manage to fit in all the extra scenes into the new abridgement *exactly* as he requested, then David felt we should probably call it a day …

Given the state he must have been in after the bombing and the funeral, I think he hadn't wanted to risk turning up at the studio for a single day's reading, only to find that I was no longer interested in picking up where we'd left off the year before. So he turned the whole thing into a subtle sort of test. Very subtle, in fact, because I quite failed to realise I was taking it. I only knew that if he did 'call it a day' then I might not see him again and the possibility of that hit me hard. That single stark phrase galvanised me to make sure I delivered the second script exactly as his notes directed – no small feat, I might add – so that he *wouldn't* call it a day. Because I really *did* want to see him again. He must have told himself – *If she makes the effort, I'm in with a chance.*

So yes, what I began to realise on our holiday is what I sincerely believe now; he *was* lining me up then. Not selfishly or cynically and by no means heartlessly, but simply in desperation to mend what had been so broken in him – beaten up, as he wrote in that first letter – and to restore his faith in his creative life. I don't think I flatter myself. There was an extraordinary bond between us, which we both felt from that first lunch – which David, whose life had been a constant search for love, perhaps felt even more forcefully than I did. After Beirut, I think he knew he needed something that strong to pull him through. A few days into our holiday he would call me his last love. I didn't fully understand this claim when he made it, but subsequent events would prove him more right than even he knew.

There were only two local shops that sold swimming gear, the first one we tried catering predominantly for scuba-diving, with goggles and snorkels and flippers hanging around the walls.

'They can do me a wetsuit or a pair of Speedos,' David announced after a close conversation with the proprietor. 'You'll be pleased to hear I'm only going to try on the latter.'

As he edged himself into the cubbyhole changing room, drawing a shabby curtain behind him, I could hear Graham's voice in my head irreverently asking why he hadn't popped into the men's department at M&S on his way out to Heathrow for a pair of their swimming trunks to complete his wardrobe.

After a couple of minutes he drew back the curtain and stood with his hands cupped over his crotch, looking acutely embarrassed and appearing to be naked below his shirt. He huddled next to me and removed his hands. He was wearing the Speedos, in fact, but there was so little of them – and such a pleasing amount more of him – that one might hardly have known. David's build leaned more towards yeoman farmer than athlete and the streamlined trunks had some stretching to do, leaving absolutely nothing to the imagination. Anyone curious to know whether John le Carré was circumcised wouldn't even have had to guess.

'I can't wear *these*—' he told me in an appalled whisper, as the cottage-loaf-shaped Greek wife who ran the shop with her barrel-shaped Greek husband craned over the counter to cop an eyeful. 'They show my bush!'

I said I rather liked them, but agreed there was definitely nowhere for him to keep his sandwiches. David made his apologies to the proprietor and hurriedly changed back into his sensible German slacks. We went along to the second store, a dingy little lock-up with children's day-glo tiddler nets on long canes hanging up outside, which had precisely two pairs of trunks on offer, one in school-uniform black nylon that were a size too small and another in mustard-coloured cotton that were a size too big. David promptly told the shopkeeper he would take both.

'What about some tops?' I suggested.

We looked along the rails. From a sorry end-of-season selection, David picked a standard cotton T-shirt that was either dark green or sun-faded black and a completely weird top with short sleeves and a soft collar, made of nasty shiny synthetic fabric with hideous broad horizontal stripes.

'This one was too ugly even for the German girls to buy,' he lamented. 'They kept it specially for me.'

As the shopkeeper cheerily made a neat paper parcel of four items he'd thought he would never off-load, David asked him where the main beach was.

'Ah, Katerina's beach,' the man offered helpfully. 'Down there, please, and turn right.'

'Thanks very much,' David answered genially, taking up his parcel. Once we were out of sight of the shop he turned us around and we headed off in the opposite direction.

We walked a small distance, leaving the main part of the town behind and following a cliff path, until a little secluded bay revealed itself like a bite out of the shoreline. It was completely deserted.

'That's our place,' David declared. 'Come on!'

We clambered down, scratching up yellow dust as we descended to the pebbled beach. David swiftly changed into his new cotton trunks and I took off the shirt and cut-offs I was wearing over my bikini. We swam lazily for a while, the water warm and buoyant under us with the heat of the whole summer stored in it, and then got back to the beach to dry off.

'We're tarts,' he said, as the ticklish autumn breeze found our wet skin. 'That's what we are, stupid tarts. We didn't bring anything to dry ourselves with.'

'Or anything to lie on,' I added, sitting on my shirt. 'Or anything to eat or drink. Yes, I know.'

'Then why didn't you say something?'

'I assumed it was all part of the master plan.'

'Knowing cow.'

This was my first visit to any part of Greece and fragments from my classical studies were coming back to me. Sitting on the shingle and looking at David sprawled on his back beside me – sand and tiny pieces of shell clinging to the lines of his body, the mustard-coloured trunks clinging too, beautifully translucent from the water – I chased a scene from Homer through my mind.

'What're you thinking, Sue?' he asked me with his eyes closed. 'It's salacious, I'm sure.'

When it came to detecting a private thought process, David was more than a little uncanny.

'I was thinking of Odysseus when he washes up on the shore somewhere around here and wants to approach Nausicaa. But he's naked, so he has to break off a large leafy bough with his great hands to cover his manhood.'

'I can see why a girl might remember that from her studies.'

'I definitely remember his "salt-grimed nakedness",' I said, looking at how well the description fitted my own lover now. 'And that he had huge hands and needed a large bough.'

'Well, naturally,' David agreed matter-of-factly. 'They're renowned for their donkey-knockers, these Greeks. But can you tell me one thing, my darling – I'm sure you'll know. Was this Homer's island as well as Sappho's? I mean, did she come here to write poetry because it was already famous for him?'

I gave him a squinty look – which he didn't see because his eyes were still closed – at his implication that a woman writer would need to have been inspired by a man.

'No,' I told him. 'Homer was from Chios, by tradition. This was Sappho's own patch.'

'She lived here?' he asked.

Again, I had to chase the details for a moment.

'I know she was born here ' I said, groping for the rest from some long-forgotten essay. 'But if I remember, she became an exile. Plenty did in those days. I think she died in Sicily.'

'I see,' was all he said, thereby drawing our discussion of the island's world-famous female poet to a close. 'So I was making you think of Odysseus, was I?' he went on. 'An older version, I suppose.'

'Not so much, I don't think. Let's see – he was ten years away fighting in Troy, then another ten on his travels and he was already king of Ithaca with a wife and son before he went. He must have been quite close to your age now by the time he got back.'

'Such scholarship!'

'Not really. It's all in the text.'

'And why did he go on his odyssey after the Trojan war in the first place? I don't think I've ever known. What was he doing all that travelling for?'

That too was in the text, and though David's classical studies were considerably farther behind him than mine were behind me, it struck me as another peculiar blind spot.

'He didn't mean to go anywhere,' I explained. 'The gods were against him. He was only trying to get home.'

'I see,' he said again. I imagined he'd be pleased to have the answer at last, but his tone suggested I'd rather spoiled the plot. He turned over on to his stomach and put his chin on his folded forearms. He was looking at me now. 'You'll let me write while we're here, won't you, my darling? It won't get in the way, I promise.'

I asked him a question in return.

'Why do you imagine I would want to stop you?'

'Well, this is your place, your holiday.'

'You can write and make love in the same day, can't you?'

'With you, yes. Several times every day. All night, too, if pushed.'

'Well, then – what's the problem?'

'Don't have one. You're amazing. Beautiful. Funny. Knowing. I think I'll make you my Muse as well as my Recording Angel. I'm sure you can be both.'

'I'm sure I can, too, but you don't get to choose us, I'm afraid. We're appointed.'

'Then I'll apply for appointment.'

'Ha! Take a number and get in line.'

'I adore you, my darling. I really do. And I want to fuck you right now something rotten.'

As David began to stroke my thigh and the salt waves lapped against the shore, another well-learned line came back to me from my studies:

> ἔστιν θάλασσα – τίς δέ νιν κατασβέσει;
> (Here is the sea – who will drink it up?)

It felt like we lived there. It was the little house, nudging us into the sort of unassuming domestic routine that no grand hotel or big villa ever could, but it was David too. He seemed to have an innate capacity to turn native wherever he was. I saw this first in the studio, the way he just slotted in like one of the regulars, then at my flat where he moved around as much like a room-mate as a lover. He had a way of automatically adapting to his environment, becoming instantly familiar with it. He could fit into a new situation with the ease of slipping on a pair of old shoes. It was from years of living his cover, I imagined, first in his spook years and later in his personal life. In fact, first of all in his personal life, as he would soon begin to tell me, for sheer survival as he grew up in the ever-shifting crooked sham world of his father.

All the same, there was an undeniable process going on between David and me, something he was constantly urging on: the establishment of 'us'. The word was one I hardly used in the normal way and was cautious of its application then, but David's conversation was peppered with the joint pronoun in all its forms. And the more he said things like '*they love us*' when the waiters at Costas' extended special favours, or '*we live here*', or indeed '*our house*', which he said all the time, so the more it began to feel as if there might be something to it.

David's days began – as they probably had for more than twenty years before I met him – with writing. I would feel him stir around five. He would get out of bed and steal downstairs, leaving me to turn over and finish sleeping, which was just as well since, after strolling home from Costas' around ten the night before, we usually didn't finish what we did best any time before midnight, often later. By around eight I would lean over the edge of the bed and look down through the inch-wide cracks in the old floorboards, to see him sitting at the dining table, fixed in concentration, his pen flying over the sheets of white A4.

'It's about my dad,' he told me. 'I'm writing about me and my dad.'

While he was still writing, I rose and showered and went out for milk, or yoghurt, or honey, or whatever other item we'd run short of at the house. There was a local daily English-language newspaper that I always bought at David's request. It was no more than a couple of sheets folded to tabloid size but I noticed that it usually carried a piece about either attempted or successful Turkish espionage. I supposed – erroneously, as it turned out – that it was his way of keeping his hand on the local spook tiller, in the same way that he always seemed to have a little short-wave radio with him in his suitcase wherever we went, perhaps, though I never caught him listening in, so that he could tune in to the BBC World Service at a pre-arranged time for a message in code. He had brought a serious-looking Zeiss camera with him as well and took endless pictures of me, usually half-dressed or completely naked, and frequently from the rear. Much as David never tired of telling me how beautiful he thought I was – a compliment I never tired of hearing – I was coming to think he considered that to be my best side. In his defence, I had forbidden him ever to take a picture of me when I was wearing my glasses, so perhaps it was just his way of getting a candid shot.

'Why don't you get contacts?' he asked me as I shied away from his camera yet again in my specs.

'Funny you should ask. I was just going to make an optician's appointment when this big famous writer chap came along and whisked me away to a Greek island.'

'Really? Are you really going to? I mean, I love your glasses because it's such pure but-Miss-Jones-you're-beautiful when you take them off. But I do worry sometimes,' he said wryly, 'that you can't properly see the full extent of my manhood when we're in bed.'

'I'm short-sighted,' I assured him. 'I can see things close up perfectly well.' This provoked a purring sound from the writer at the recent memory of just how close up close up could get. 'But if you're worried,' I said, deciding he needed teasing on the subject, 'you can always get me a magnifying glass.'

'Cow. Shan't. But just you be sure to get those contacts when we get back. And tell them to give you extra-strong bifocals so as to enlarge your lover's microscopic member.'

We shared a mutually appreciative smile. I loved him when he was being ironic.

'And you'll let me pay for them, of course.'

When he finished his morning's writing, David always went out by himself for a while 'to radio base', meaning use the payphone at the local post office to call his wife, choosing not to use the phone in the house. UK landlines didn't have incoming number display or last-number redial then, but I shouldn't have been surprised if he already had that kind of advanced tech and more at home.

Either that, or he just didn't need me around when he lied to his wife, though it wasn't as if I had any desire to listen in. There was always an unnatural brightness about him when he came back from calling home, a deflecting veneer over something brittle underneath. 'Decompression', he would call it, after a few more trips. But his dealings with his wife were none of my concern and I asked no questions.

Then one morning he went off for a longer spell.

'You don't mind if I go off for a while, do you, my love? Just for a walk and to read the paper? I won't be long – an hour at most.'

He tipped me an odd artificial little salute with the folded newspaper, then tucked it neatly under his arm like a pace-stick, for all the world like a retired half-colonel getting his pass from the little woman before heading out for a pint at the village pub.

'That's yesterday's paper,' I said, noticing an article I'd read on the front page.

'Doesn't matter,' he said breezily. 'I'll catch up. See you.'

He came back after an hour, without the day-old newspaper and looking happy, elevated even, but still in an odd unnatural way. I even thought I heard him humming – for the first and last time ever – as he came in downstairs. I was quite oblivious to what he was doing. I hadn't yet cottoned on to his act-it-first/write-about-it-later creative process, but the whole performance would end up in his new novel. He would use snatches of our conversations, too, filleting elements from them like a sushi chef extracting the edible part from a blowfish, taking a single turn of phrase, a random observation, anything that drew his ear. At this early stage of his book he seemed to be a sort of Autolycus, snapping up all manner of otherwise unconsidered trifles.

Then we headed out for the day, with David offering his usual mild admonishment for what we should have been doing by now – getting air, going for a walk or a swim or an explore – even though our timetable was entirely of his making. He had this habit of rebuking one scenario with another and was always keen to move on to the next thing whenever he deemed any particular activity to be over. Consequently, we did a lot of moving on to the next thing, even when the current thing should have been about relaxing and doing nothing much at all. We never really relaxed, even after sex. We either did something else afterwards or had more sex to the point of exhaustion. Satiation had a strange way of making David restive, as if he were resentful of having his desires met, of letting consummation take away his want of whatever he'd just had his fill. And so we moved on.

Poop-poop!

We bought fresh-baked bread and fabulous local cheeses and fat olives and ate lunch on the beach, or sometimes up in the hills if we decided to hike inland. And vino. And vodka. David sank both like there was no tomorrow, but neither ever seemed to touch him. He never got that soft focus of the happy drinker. For every coil that unwound in him when the alcohol hit there seemed always to be another, just as tightly compressed, that it didn't reach. Then we'd head back to the house for more of what we liked to do at least three or four times a day, frequently more. David's powers of recovery were prodigious. I'd known some fine lovers before – and would again – but never one quite like him.

After we showered and changed we made for Costas', who welcomed us like family and kept the same table for us every night. We'd take ourselves for a walk along the harbour on the way, to 'have a snoot' at one of the promenade cafés first, David scribbling in his notebook as the locals strolled by.

I respected his writing time in the morning as sacrosanct – I slept through most of it anyway – but at this end of the day I felt we needed to keep it light. One evening I took photos of him as he huddled over his pen and pad, just to let him know he wasn't to get too immersed. The beginnings of a smile crept in at the corners of his mouth, but he kept jotting. Then I saw something I couldn't resist and pointed to the long arm of the harbour wall that stretched out into the water.

'What do they call that then, David?' I asked.

He still didn't want to be distracted, but he looked up to see where I was pointing. Despite himself he laughed.

'It's a *mole*,' he said appreciatively, as if I'd scored an unexpected point in a game with rules of his own devising, and closed his notebook.

Once or twice in the evening we stayed in and made something simple for ourselves, salad and omelettes or the like, puttering around semi-naked in the kitchen. We only ever seemed to dress our top halves in the house – each of us wearing one of the two sweaters David had packed, ostensibly for the cooler clime of Zurich – preferring to keep the lower parts ready for action, which indeed could happen at any time.

And one time, when we were half-dressed in that way and I was getting ice for our drinks from the top of the fridge and David was squatting down below me looking for something in the larder section to add to the salad dressing he was making, I ducked down behind him and put an ice cube on his scrotum. Everything was just hanging there in free suspension and I simply couldn't resist. I'd only planned to give a glancing touch and pull the ice cube away the moment he flinched – only he *didn't* flinch. Not believing his reaction – or rather, his astonishing lack of one – I kept the ice cube *in place*, even pressing it *more firmly* in place. But he only continued looking for whatever it was he wanted in the fridge. I was mystified.

'Can't you *feel* that?' I asked.

'Well,' he replied steadily, 'it's not the most agreeable sensation in the world, I'd have to say that.'

But he still didn't flinch, though his testicles had definitely decided to come in from the cold. He just coolly (well, yes) located a jar of mustard, while in glassy disbelief I continued to hold the ice-cube against his ever more tightly shrivelling sack.

'Do you think,' he said after another few seconds, 'we could say that this particular experiment is over?'

I finally took the ice cube away. I even sucked it, to make sure it was as cold as it should have been. The laws of physics failing to pertain to Priscilla's freezer seemed altogether more plausible than David's unflinching control over what should have been his autonomic nervous system.

'*Training*?' I asked after another moment or two. It was the only thing that made any sense.

'Mmm,' he confirmed lightly and went on with fixing the dressing.

Gradually, David told me things about himself and his life, and he began by taking me through his rather large family. I was an only child and my parents chose not to have a great deal to do with either of their own large families, so I hadn't much personal experience on that front. My various aunts and uncles and grandparents and cousins were perfectly kind to me whenever they appeared, but essentially mine was a family of just three. What I had noticed about people with large families, however, was that they only ever seemed to want to tell me about them when things weren't to their liking. But David said he wanted to tell me about his family and so I listened. We were having a mid-day 'snoot' at one of the harbour-side bars and he began by telling me about his four sons, the oldest three of whom were now grown young men. Simon, the eldest, was already married and lived in the Far East with his Thai wife. 'He's a mystery to me,' David proclaimed, as though that were explanatory. Stephen was 'the middle one', a birth detail he presented as an intrinsic difficulty, though he added, 'He seems to have found photography, thank God.' George Roy Hill had given him the job of official stills photographer on the *Drummer Girl* shoot and I'd already noticed his credit underneath David's author photograph on some of the books. Timothy was the youngest of the first three and an undergraduate at David's old college. Tim, he said, was 'the sensitive one'. These were by his first wife, Ann, whom he'd divorced a dozen years ago and who, I learned next, was definitely *not* the model for Smiley's Ann.

'No – Smiley's Ann isn't *my* Ann,' he corrected me quickly when I suggested it. 'Not at all.' He pointed out a standard-looking Greek woman who was walking away from us a little further down the road. 'There—' he said. 'That's like my Ann. Short. Long back and low saddle.'

David watched the unwitting woman walk out of sight before letting his gaze drift out across the bright noontide sea.

'I think *his* Ann,' he said dispassionately, but quite affirmatively, 'may be *you*.'

He didn't turn to me when he said this, but kept looking out – and it was as well, because I was momentarily without the capacity to sensibly respond.

'Oh, yes,' he said in the same factual tone, intuitively reading my silent astonishment and dismissing it as an invalid response. He might have been expanding a point in a lecture on his work. 'Yes – beautiful, intelligent, self-motivated, sexy. Even admiring. My dream woman. The girl on the beach I can't have.'

'But you can,' I said after a moment. 'You can have me.'

'No,' he corrected me again, still staring out. 'Like this, yes. But no, not now. You're my last love, you see. I know that now. You should have come to me earlier. Years ago, before I married again. Before I got myself banged up for life.'

'I was still at school,' I said meaninglessly.

'Yes, I'm quite aware of that. It's all your fault for being so young and so perfect.'

The fourth son, he continued, seamlessly resuming his original discourse after this diversion, was Nicholas, by second wife Jane.

He was presently a pupil at University College School, an independent day school in Hampstead. All his sons were *marvellous*, he insisted, in case he might have given me a different impression. He said it a second time with greater emphasis, managing to sound a little like Connie Sachs. *All wonderful, marvellous boys.* He mentioned his younger half-brother Rupert, the journalist, Charlotte's full brother by their father's second wife, Jean. He had an older full brother himself, Tony, who lived in the States, was an advertising executive and had been a promising cricketer in his youth. David didn't speak about either of his wives, though not, I felt, out of any delicacy towards me. It was as if he were primarily concerned with giving me the Cornwell bloodline, to which the women who had borne its members were auxiliary at best, ancillary in general.

(This may seem rather a harsh observation on my part then, but it was backed up – indeed reinforced – by what I subsequently saw in the books. All women, but particularly wives, get a very rough ride in le Carré. One way or another, they invariably bring about their husband's or partner's downfall. Elsa Fennan's treachery gets her husband killed in *Call for the Dead*. Stella Rode, the murder victim in *A Murder of Quality*, is the bar to her husband's ambition, while another schoolmaster's wife, Shane Hecht, is described in far more vicious terms than the unrepenting paedophile who is the murderer of the piece. Liz brings about Leamas's death at the very end of *The Spy Who Came in from the Cold*, just as Riemeck's girl brings about his right at the start. In *The Looking Glass War*, Turner's wife constantly derides the value of his work, and in *Tinker Tailor Soldier Spy*, Ann Smiley's affair with Bill Haydon is what blinds Smiley to the fact that his colleague is the double agent. His eventual success in getting Karla to defect in *Smiley's People* derives from his exploitation of the Soviet spymaster's only weak spot – the deranged daughter his wife bore him. Even in the book David was writing then, the wife of his hero would reveal his secret hiding place to the authorities, thereby bringing about his suicide. Meanwhile, blood relatives in le Carré, even of the women, are almost invariably male. Ann Smiley has a male cousin or two and Connie Sachs has a genius father and a string of brainiac brothers, but there is no mention of either woman's mother. Both of his directly autobiographical heroes, like David himself, only have sons. I could go on …)

David sighed heavily after going through this roll call, assuming a sort of noble weariness at the responsibility of such a large encumbrance, as though he'd been achieving greatness under superhuman strain. A literary Atlas weighed down by the burden of the related world. Poor David, I half wanted to say, half guessed I was supposed to say, but resisted. He had the means to make his life how he wanted it, if it wasn't currently to his liking. If he didn't want to be 'banged up' then he shouldn't have married for a second time. There was rather more to his use of prison terminology than I realised at the time, however, so it was good that I held my counsel. In any event, commiseration would have been superfluous, because he next began to talk about Ronnie, his late father and present subject, and at a stroke his whole manner revived. The weariness lifted, the weight of the world was shrugged off. He was suddenly bursting with Ronnie.

'He was a conman, you see,' David explained, his enthusiasm renewed. 'He'd set up companies, dozens and dozens of them, with nothing more than string and sealing-wax, and promise investors the earth, then cheat them out of their money. He did time for it, on and off, at their various Majesties' pleasure. Olive, my mum, ran off when I was about five – she couldn't stand it anymore. Tony and I were sent off to school, but we'd never know if the school fees were going to be paid or where we'd be spending the holidays or who we'd be calling our new mum. So the book's about Ronnie. I've called him Rick, Rick Pym. My hero's Magnus, his son. I've been trying to write about him for years and failing to for even longer. Now I *am* writing about him and it's got a lot to do with a tall and lovely girl. You've made it possible, Sue. You've helped the process come alive. You see, my darling, you *are* my Muse – appointed or not.'

'I'm just a writer, you know?'

This was another tone I hadn't heard before. Laid back. Cool with things. 'I'm happy if people like my stuff,' he went on. 'It's just good when they get it.'

We were sitting on the beach after a swim, alone on another deserted little bay with just the ever-present Greek look-out patrolling the bluff above us for company.

'Ten books,' he went on. 'It's not nothing.'

He made the claim prettily and quietly, but with a touch of *Weltschmerz* in his voice, as though his underlying wish was to be understood at rather lower cost to the self.

'They should give you the Queen's Award for Industry,' I said, attempting to jolly him gently away from what sounded like a little patch of the blues on the horizon. But I should have learned not to do that by then, because he took my suggestion quite seriously.

'Mmm. They offered me a K this year. I turned them down.'

'Really?' No Sir David Cornwell, then. But it was a little incongruous, I thought, after he'd just said he liked it when people 'got his stuff'. Wouldn't a knighthood have been an acknowledgement of that?

When I asked him why he turned down the honour – and he didn't specify whether the offer had come from the Palace or from No.10 – he only shrugged gnomically. *Of course you did, David*, I think I was supposed to say, *quite right*.

'It's just not my scene,' was all he said.

The uncharacteristic sixties expression didn't ring true. The older pink-gin vernacular from the fifties that I'd heard him use before suited him better. Something didn't square. Before I could think what and why, he added, 'It wasn't the first time.'

I heard a touch of something else in his voice now. Surely not *pride*?

'You mean you've turned them down before?'

'Mmm.'

'And they asked you again?'

'Mmm.'

I nearly said, *Well, next time you'd better make sure you mean it*, but I could see he still wasn't up for the funny side. His expression as he sat on the pebbly strand, holding his knees and staring fixedly out to the horizon, told me that we'd reached a new level of high seriousness. For a man who could giggle like a schoolboy, make love like a god and write like a demon – and who had clocked up twenty years at the very top of his chosen tree – David seemed nevertheless to have the sensitivity of a virgin (to borrow his own phrase for Smiley) when it came to his status in the literary world.

He looked my way, waiting to see if I would ask anything else, but I didn't. I was treading cautiously that afternoon, having already fallen foul of David's touchy sensibilities first thing in the morning. The events of the previous evening seemed to have set it all in motion.

After another long schmoozy supper at Costas' we'd somehow got into a joke-swapping contest, which started when David asked me if I knew any good ones. I've never been especially keen on the set-piece joke, preferring humour that arises spontaneously, but I did have one special favourite, which I told him. It was the gorilla joke, with its great punchline: *He never calls, he never writes …*

'I was going to tell you that one,' David said, with a slightly peevish pout.

'Well, then,' I replied, as one does with little boys who want to be thought cleverer than anyone else, 'you tell me another one.'

So he did, and it went on from there. David's best effort was pretty good, but I think I won in the end, because the punchline of my last one – originally told to me by Jeremy – had David rolling on the floor.

But then, next morning – and there was no way to see it coming – he suddenly claimed that I was without proper seriousness in how I lived my life.

'You have great intellect, great capacity, many strengths, but you lack *gravitas*,' he declared, from a donnish height he must have scaled in his own mind overnight. Losing a joke-telling contest was obviously no laughing matter for the Great Man. I concluded that I really should have let him tell the one about the gorilla.

So, in the context of our present conversation on the beach, if he wanted me to take what he said at face value – even though it all seemed some little way up his own lower orifice – then that's what I'd do. It was a lucky decision, coming not a moment too soon, because after a pause he added an extra detail.

'And I've told Rainer I don't wish to be considered for the Nobel.'

I decided David's special subject at Oxford must have been Advanced Cognitive Dissonance, because basic logic didn't seem to enter anywhere into that last statement (although *gravitas* looked as if it already had, all the way up to the third joint).

Would that be the Nobel Prize for Literature, David, I so badly wanted to ask, *or for World Peace?*

But I gave no voice to this dissent. By then, I was certain I wouldn't see my lover for dust if I did. Once David pronounced on a matter it seemed to go straight onto the statute books, at least in his own mind, after which it would be treason to demur. The cast was *really strong*; his sons were *all wonderful*; and now, I *lacked gravitas*.

I had to bite down hard to stay silent, all the same. Why on earth did this extraordinary man, with his talent, his fortune, his fame, need to give himself such ridiculous conceits? Not that the idea of his being awarded the Nobel was ridiculous; far less likely candidates had been chosen over the years. But to make specific provision to head them off at the pass, just in case they did? That definitely *was* ridiculous. How did it work, anyway? Had Rainer sent a pre-emptive letter to the committee? *Dear Sirs, My client wishes me to let you know that under no circumstances are you to consider him as a recipient for your prize ...* Or was it more of a standing instruction, that Rainer was automatically to turn them down if – sorry, *when* – they did? In which case, how the hell did *that* work? Did he enclose a note with the Authors Workshop annual report – *FYI, David, just to let you know they didn't nominate you again this year ...*? It was all too farcical to contemplate, either the whole or any part. I don't know how I held my tongue.

But David was untroubled by my silence. Far from suspecting me of harbouring thoughts of such outlawed *levitas*, he had clearly taken my lack of response for what he expected to receive, what he must actually *have* received from other quarters, in order to feel free to come out with this stuff with me – namely, full assent. *Of course you did, David, quite right*. But it was just so ludicrous. And if I applied his go-to technique of south–north inversion here (which he shouldn't have explained to me if he didn't want me to do just that), then stressing he really didn't want these awards must have meant, in fact, that he really rather did ...

As he sat beside me on the bay he absently clawed up a handful of pebbles and began strafing them into the waves. In that unconsidered action, I started to see the beginnings of an answer to the conundrum. Somewhere deep inside the vast and, so one would think, impregnable edifice that was John le Carré, there was a little boy named David sitting in splendid isolation, king of his own self-built castle, and he was letting the big boys of the world know that he wasn't coming out to play – just in case they weren't going to ask. He got up and waded out hip-deep into the water, which was beginning to grow dark – wine dark, as the poet said – under the slanting sun. He skimmed some more stones for a while, not very expertly, they didn't bounce much, but perhaps he needed to try and show me he could. (Alternatively, perhaps it was only for cover, so that he could go back into the water to pee.) Then he left the water and did a clumsy cartwheel back up the beach.

'Come on,' he said, regaining his tone of cheery admonition. 'We're dallying. The look-out will think we're waiting for a Russian sub disguised as a Greek trawler. Let's grab an early supper at Costas' and go back to our place and fuck all night.'

Next day was our last full day on the island and the moody atmosphere David had started to generate remained inexorably on the slide. At first I suspected my continued though now certainly chastened *levitas* was to blame – the unpardonable crime of enjoying myself on holiday – but gradually I came to see it wasn't that. Whatever was going on with him now was nothing of my making. It was a downbeat purely of David's internal drumming.

That morning we hiked inland until we reached a local peak, the highest place it was possible for us to get to without Tony taking us halfway there by taxi first. It was David's idea, a joyless yomp; I had no say in the matter. We'd brought our lunch with us and ate it without communion, hunched on separate tussocks like marines chowing down K-rations. Without any words being spoken it was suddenly wretched between us and it was David who had generated the change. His mood was powerful enough to drag both of us down to whatever depths he had decided to plumb. We were in it together but only one of us had any idea of what was going on. It was like a dark dream version of being in the studio, with David hermetically sealed in his own communication-proof zone. I could see him right in front of me, but my talk-back had cut out and he wouldn't look at me through the glass. Staring resolutely out to the horizon, he was wilfully oblivious to any reality except his own. He had retreated to some point of internal geography to which I had no map, focused on who-knew-what bleak vistas; Xerxes looking at his troops laid waste; Prospero contemplating the disaster of his island universe. There was a storm coming. The atmospheric pressure was building up and a dark cloudbank was following the wind-line, heading onshore. David's mood was so palpable, the weather felt like his creature, a thing of his summoning.

Something told me not to say anything. His mood was too intense. My voice would be discordant to his thoughts however gently I spoke, my words rejected and derided as inferior to his own however carefully I chose them. I sensed I mustn't touch him, either. My lover's willingness seemed to have shrivelled up into itself, like a slug in salt.

Writing. It was the only way in.

His ever-present notepad and pen jutted out of his shirt pocket and I reached over with cautious fingers, feeling like a cutpurse at work. But he let me take them.

Tell me, I wrote, and handed pen and pad back.

It took a long minute – it may have been three or four – but then he began to respond. He turned to a clean page.

The problem, he wrote, *is with David as the writer and with Pym as the man.*

Then he stopped cold. I took the pen from him and drew a ring around *Tell me* as he held the pad, then offered the pen back. He took it, but with an odd look, a suspicious lift of the lip as though I had laid a trap, then he started to write again.

How to continue caring about the destiny of others after entering a contract to renounce one's own.

The neat little epigram was sewn up tightly, but meant for me to unpick. I'd made sense of oblique lines of prose before, I'd spent three years doing it at bloody Oxford; I had to be up to understanding *this*. The key word seemed to be *contract*. His marriage had to be what he meant; how he was 'banged up' in Hampstead.

He began to write something else.

Only course of action is to break the fucking contract. But then the problem—

Nothing followed for a long while. When I couldn't stand to wait any longer I took the pen again.

Don't want to enough? I scribbled despairingly, hoping against hope to be contradicted.

Grabbing the pen from me this time, he wrote *Must*. My heart lifted madly until I watched two more words appear in large capitals:

MUST RUN

I felt hot tears on my cheeks before I knew I was crying. Run from me, did he mean? Run from us?

But suddenly he smiled – for the first time all day – and was once more busy with his pen. I was no longer watching. I couldn't stand to see the blue-ink words emerge and couldn't have focused anyway. Everything was just a blur. Now it was my turn to look out to the portent-laden horizon, where the clouds were still advancing in a slow smothering swarm.

I felt a sly nudge in my ribs, the sort of surreptitious poke that always came before you were slipped a note along the back row in class and, sure enough, David was passing the pad back to me. He had drawn a little cartoon rabbit, bug-eyed, running for his life across the page. Underneath he had written a new line,

Rabbits get scared when they have to run in new fields.

And beneath that, as my heart lifted again,

They need Sues.

*   *   *

To test David's new resolve, the storm followed us home. Trying to beat the rain back, we thumbed a lift in the back of a clapped-out Toyota pick-up truck and were rattled to our bones as the driver took the rocky downhill run at full throttle. We could finally laugh, now that we were on this breakneck descent, and our laughter was as fierce as the battering we were taking. Our driver was a madman, damning himself as only a Greek could by challenging the gods who commanded the weather to race him back to town. And we were every bit as crazy as he was, trusting life and limb to his maniacal driving, and knowing it made us laugh all the harder. It was all just a desperate divine joke and if death or injury were to pounce out at us from behind a sudden rock or tree, then it would only be the punchline hitting us where it hurt.

By the time we were dropped off at the harbour we'd been shaken clean out of our senses and could only continue to laugh like fools as we struggled to get our legs back under us for the last climb up the road to the house. But by then it didn't matter how hard we laughed, because the dark clouds – and the ancient beings who directed them – knew where we lived. Hubris, and all that.

First Rule of taking a secret honeymoon with your married ex-spook lover in Greece: Don't talk about making it safely home.

Inside the house the electricity supply had blown, but the static continued to build, charging us both. Somehow we made it through a thrown-together candlelit supper without ravaging each other, but when the storm finally broke David threw us both onto the living-room couch and drove himself into me like a ploughshare.

Afterwards, we climbed the stairs without speaking, hand tightly in hand, as the storm hurled itself around us. Priscilla's thin floorboards creaked wildly and the hastily fastened shutters heaved on their hinges as we lay in bed, huddled like refugees in each other's arms, staring blindly up at the rafters while we waited for the first heaven to pass away.

Within the hour things seemed to quieten down, but the storm hadn't passed, only retreated somewhere to regroup. The present lull was just a fake-out.

'Shall we say it's over?' David asked, in the trick of the calm, and at first I thought he meant the storm. 'Shall we call it the best holiday in the world but say it's over? And just stay friends?'

'No!' I cried out, rejecting the awful meaning of his words, 'God, no!'

I sat bolt upright in bed with the shock. I didn't believe he could be saying that. He'd just spent the last fortnight talking about us, us, us, making it all so lovely and so, so real. I was certain of my feelings for him now. I loved him more than I had ever thought possible. David had buried himself deep inside me with his love and his love-making. He had imprinted himself indelibly on to me in his pale blue ink. Yet *now* he wanted to give it all up?

'No,' I insisted again shakily, trying to gain some modicum of control over my voice. 'No, David – why on earth should we do that? Why on earth would you want to?'

'Because it won't ever get any better than this, my darling. And it won't get any easier. This way we'd just have the fun of it. We wouldn't have any of the pain.'

Not have the pain? I already felt as if I had a steel bolt through my ribs. How much more painful could it get?

'I thought you loved me?' I said.

It was either the stupidest thing to say or the truest. Perhaps both.

'I do, my darling, I do,' David protested. 'I've never loved anybody more and I never will. You're my perfect woman. The most beautiful, the most desirable, the wittiest, wisest, the most loving – ever.'

'Then why end it now? It's madness. I won't let you.'

'You want to go on then?'

'Of *course*. Of *course* I do. We've only started – *of course* I want to go on. Don't you?'

'I want to badly, but I don't know if I can. If we stay together I should have to get out.'

'Out?'

'From Hampstead. From the slammer I've made for myself there. I'm a born architect of slammers.'

Break the fucking contract. It *was* what he meant. He had returned to the language of escape. Our trip had begun with it and now was ending with it too.

'So do it,' I said simply. 'Find a way. I'm sure you can.'

'Will you be there if I do?'

'Of course – *yes*. I'm not going anywhere, David.'

'It may take a while.'

'It doesn't matter.'

'Really?'

'Really. I love you, David.'

'And I love you, my darling, but—'

'I'll be there. Before and after. And during. Just do it. Just do whatever you have to.'

'It's a rocky path you've chosen, you can't know.'

'Then I'll find out. But let's not cross any bridges before we have to.'

'Or burn any boats.'

'Particularly not tonight.'

'No. Not tonight. You're so wise. Much more than me. I get such blacks. Such dreadful thoughts. I'm just a scared rabbit, you see, and I need my girl.'

He was scared and needed *me*? Dear God. Where was the reassurance for *my* fears, from the sudden whiplash of 'let's just be friends'? Or was this it – the new commitment to escape? Was David set on his course now, regarding his marriage? Did he really mean to 'get out'?

Athens

We woke up next morning to find that a pair of Priscilla's shutters had blown away in the night.

'They're probably in Ephesus by now,' David remarked. 'We'll leave some of the folding stuff with the neighbours before we go and ask them to get new ones put up.'

I was a little groggy from last night, I couldn't remember when or if we ever stopped talking or drinking or fucking. As I packed I couldn't quite get the exact run of our storm-tossed conversation in my head. Did David say he was actually planning to leave his wife? Did I get that right? The possibility of our being able to meet up whenever we wanted to, go away whenever we wanted to, without his having to lie to anybody about it and without his fear of discovery dictating how we conducted our relationship – well, it put a spring into relinquishing the house and the island, that was for sure. Two weeks earlier this had been the big trip to look forward to. Now it felt like just the start of the journey.

Actions, however, still had to follow words. As I checked round the house to see if we'd overlooked anything, I noticed both pairs of David's swimming trunks lying on top of the bag of kitchen rubbish waiting to be thrown out. He had jettisoned the incriminating evidence and kept the rest, including the hideous stripy top. Clearly he still preferred to be suspected of bad taste than adultery.

As a farewell gesture to the house, David picked out the one le Carré paperback that had been lurking between all the Jeffrey Archers and Frederick Forsyths and Jackie Collinses on Priscilla's holiday reading shelf – a sun-bleached copy of *The Honourable Schoolboy* – and wrote a little dedication in it to her and John. He had already said he would send them a case of something nice and a big tin of caviar when we got back.

We locked up the little house and left the keys and a wad of money for new shutters with the people next door and piled into the back of Tony's taxi to take us to the airport.

'It was good, your holiday?' he asked with a big proprietary smile.

Yes, I answered. Yes. It was very good.

As we re-crossed the spice-coloured countryside, Tony tried to engage David in the same sort of man-to-man chit-chat they'd enjoyed on the way in. But David politely deflected each attempt. We were leaving now and he didn't need an instant chum on the way out.

David had given up the idea of going on by himself to join the film crew in Mykonos. The plan now was for us to spend the last night in Athens before leaving for Zurich together in the morning. When our flight got in we moved straight to the carousels for our luggage and stood chatting amiably while we waited. There was a nice easy calm between us. It had been a really good trip and, after our big conversation during the storm, we knew there was a lot more good stuff to come once we got back.

Second Rule of taking a secret honeymoon with your married ex-spook lover in Greece: Do *not* talk about making it safely home.

I'd been about to put my hand through his arm as we waited, with David making his habitual scan of the area, when he suddenly turned on me.

Don't touch me! he whispered sharply.

The out-of-the-blue severity of his tone made me pull back automatically, as if I'd brushed against a live wire. I felt him stiffen inexplicably at my side and when I looked at him for explanation all identifiable expression had vanished from his face. I had no notion what was wrong.

Then he told me, in another harsh and now also appalled whisper.

It's Steve and the whole fucking crew. They've just arrived.

Of all the airports in all the world … I glanced over to the far side of arrivals, where a group of folk had gathered by another carousel. Now that my attention was drawn to them, I could see they were surrounded by stacks of heavy black equipment cases that some burly biker-looking guys were off-loading from the conveyor. I could vaguely discern the wispy outline of Diane Keaton and a gnome-like figure who might have been Klaus Kinski. I didn't know what George Roy Hill looked like, but he was probably there too. The only one looking our way was a pale expressionless young man who had to be David's son, Stephen; 'the middle one'.

After our long secret holiday by ourselves, I could see why David was so shocked. It was a shock for me too, but mostly because of David's response to spotting them. That *Don't touch me* had a vicious edge.

'I have to go over and see them,' he declared, adding another nasty warning shot. 'Wait here.'

'Hi, Dad. Did I see you with someone over there?'

'Mmm? Oh, yes. Some tedious girl who started talking to me on the plane. Her boyfriend deserted her, so I said I'd help her with her luggage. Probably thought she was in with a chance with me. Ha-ha! So, Steve – how's the movie—?'

Something like that. It wasn't hard for me to imagine some further exposition of the fiction I was fairly certain he'd initiated with Jane over the recording of *Drummer Girl*. More south–north inversion technique. If you've been caught in the company of your secret dream woman who you've been balling night and day for nearly two weeks on a Greek island hideaway, make them think she's just an inconvenient stranger.

After a few minutes he came back to join me at the carousel. He said nothing, but the mood he brought with him was off the barometric scale. He fetched a trolley and started loading our bags onto it, acting as if it was all a royal pain in the arse – acting as if I were one too, taking any piece away from me as I attempted to lift it, the way you remove your valuables from a meddlesome child.

'What did you tell them?' I asked shakily. David's impenetrable and frighteningly cold volte-face towards me was beyond unnerving. I'm sure I'd gone pale, despite what only that morning my then enthusiastic lover had so admiringly called my 'end-of-honeymoon light-honey tan'. He offered no reply, just continued to treat me like an inconvenient stranger, maintaining his steely method acting for the benefit of the distance shots, since the others were easily thirty-five yards away.

'I'll check you in to the hotel and leave you some money,' he said curtly. 'Get room service or something. I've said I'll have supper with George and the crew. I'll stay over with Steve and come back for you in the morning—'

For one split second – the kind that has 'irreversible' stamped on it – I very nearly said, *Don't fucking bother*.

But I didn't and I wish I could claim this was because my better senses prevailed. But it wasn't the case. In that moment I had no better senses. I was completely off balance, out of kilter with any true sense of my own core self. David had seen to it that I was. He had suddenly breached all the terms we'd been operating under up till then and I'd simply lost my bearings as to how to act at all. It was brilliantly effective. He must have passed-out from Sarratt with another first: How to Keep Your Joes in Line, Course Two.

So instead of telling him where he could shove his money and exposing his rotten little charade to all present, I submitted to 'the carousel brush-off'. Once again, David had reduced me to 'the girl' – though, unlike my namesake who delivered the Bad Godesberg bomb, I suddenly had almost no presence at all in his new screenplay. Maybe I was just 'some girl' this time. But even as an extra, without a line of dialogue to my name, I still had to take direction.

'And let's have less of the marooned body language, shall we?' he told me out of the side of his mouth.

To be clear, I wasn't expecting an introduction. But I was blindingly furious with him all the same. This was a man who had lied fluently to his wife on the phone every morning of the 'honeymoon' he'd been enjoying with me for twelve days straight. A man who only a few weeks earlier had managed to manipulate another of his adult sons clean out of the family home for the weekend so that he could fuck me for the first time in that same son's own bed. A man who less than six months earlier had grieved undetectably for his *last* lover while he continued to share the marital home – and presumably the marital bed – and drafted his all-unwitting wife to help execute his plan to line me up as his *next* lover. A man whose own *nom de plume* – lest we *ever* forget – was an international byword for intrigue and plot construction on the most labyrinthine scale. Yet *this* man couldn't find a way to handle the unexpected situation decently all round? Had all the fabled subtlety of tradecraft by which he'd conducted his life and work for decades suddenly deserted him? Or had it only deserted *us* and moved on to the next scene; the one where the hero dumps the incriminating baggage (that would be me) and so manages to maintain his cover.

I had no issue with the fact that David had needed to come up with an instant cover story. I understood only too well that I was in a secret relationship with a famous married man. I hadn't even told Graham about it, for Christ's sake. But he so easily could have been sweet to me about it. It would only have taken a few words. *I can't get out of this one, my darling. We're blown if I don't go with them. Just make out we're strangers for now. Don't worry, I'll make it up to you, I promise—* Anything like that would have been fine, just to acknowledge the obvious need for subterfuge and to include me in it. But David didn't seem willing to play *that* double game. Perversely, he'd decided to start living the cover he was going to use for being caught with me *with me*, dishing out this shitty treatment to limber up for the part he was going to play with his son and the rest of them. If this was the first test of his resolve to 'get out' of the 'slammer' he'd built for himself in his second marriage, then he'd flunked it abysmally.

'I must go and look after my baby,' he announced, jamming the last of our bags onto the trolley and heading for the taxi rank, sounding less like a concerned parent than a Norland nanny under the delusion she was in charge of national security.

Even when we were out of sight of the crew, there was still nothing in his tone of voice for me, or in his face. Nothing at all in his self-serving 'theatre of the real' acknowledged the truth of my existence. I hated his putting me through this performance, but cravenly raised no objection. David's psychological hold over the scenario was so complete that the words wouldn't come and I knew I couldn't have withstood the response from him if they had. *Of course you must, David*, I might as well have been saying, like the rest of the Greek chorus he was so used to having around him in his life. *Of course*.

The farce continued to the hotel, David insisting I take a cab by myself, even separating our luggage though no one from the film could still see us, while he followed in another behind. I was trapped in David's movie now – the Saturday twelve noon first show – and there was no longer any 'us' in the scene that was playing. All the magical powers of 'us-ness' that he could summon had been moved on to the next scene, with the cast and crew. Our 'us' was a literary fragment abandoned on a Greek island.

I only wish it had occurred to me to order a large tub of caviar and any bottle of extortionate vintage from room service that night, just to make a point. David picked me up from the hotel next morning and we had a surprisingly un-moody and upbeat journey home. Without any reference to how he had left things between us, he gleefully told me everything about his evening; how wonderful Steve was, how marvellous his stills were, how splendid the cast was, how brilliantly the film was going. I listened, answering intermittently with variations of the only authorised response – *Yes, David, of course* – as he rattled on, oblivious to how the evening had been for me. At one point, as though the thought had just struck him, he paused to say, 'Do you know, my darling – I think you'd probably make *quite* a good continuity girl if you wanted to work in the movies.'

It was no use even contemplating anything to say in reply. At Heathrow he saw me into a black cab with a breezy wave. No *It was wonderful*, or *I can't wait to see you again*. Just – *Byee*.

Chelsea

It is very difficult to give an all-round impression of any man.
Ford Madox Ford, *The Good Soldier*

David sent me a bleak letter a couple of days after we got back from Greece, to let me know that he was 'progressing' in his efforts to extricate himself from his domestic situation. It surprised me, after Athens, that he still intended to 'get out', but the whole episode at the airport appeared to have passed from his mind. Perhaps the two things were only connected in mine. I wasn't usually given to overthinking relationships – it's usually never a good idea – but there were so many elements to David's behaviour, so many moving parts to him, that overthinking barely kept me abreast.

He said in the letter that the plan was for them all – meaning him and Jane and their son; 'poor all', he actually wrote – to go down to the house in Cornwall over half-term, after his birthday, 'and hammer something out down there'. It sounded pretty grim. But he said the writing was going really well and still claimed this was down to me. He asked me to give him time and space. He said he knew I would. He called his marriage 'indescribable' and said he couldn't see me any time soon.

Well. Less than two months earlier I'd been perfectly happy – deliriously happy would be no overstatement – at the prospect of becoming David's mistress. Without giving it too much thought, if any at all, I'd assumed he would be keeping his life and I'd keep mine and, whenever circumstances allowed, we'd meet up at home or abroad to blow the walls out in bed and generally have great times together. That, to me, would have been the perfect arrangement. But since our last day on the island those no longer appeared to be the terms of engagement. Perhaps for David they never were, right from the start.

Recording Angel, Muse, Best Girl Ever – I was fine with all that. A new lover's hyperbole can hardly ever go too far and who wouldn't want to be claimed as all those things by one of the foremost writers of our time? As for getting out of his marriage, however he envisioned achieving it, it was likely to have been something he'd been considering long before I entered the scene. For myself, I've never quite understood the notion of marriage. I'd already had two proposals before I met David, from really great guys whom I sincerely loved, so I wasn't looking for a third from him. To borrow the phrase he'd used regarding a knighthood, it just wasn't my scene. I might have taken a different view had I wanted children, but procreation wasn't my scene either. Despite my glimpse of how ruthlessly his fear of discovery could make him act, I loved David with a hitherto un-guessed-at and all-but-inexpressible intensity. I knew he loved me back, just as truly and just as passionately. But none of that meant our lives had to be integrated on any other level.

Except now – to believe the import of this latest letter – in six weeks flat I'd also become the sole repository of his hopes for the immediate future, for the resurgence of his writing and of his fantasy of the perfect woman, the 'girl on the beach' he'd claimed he couldn't have but now identified as the key to unlocking his way forward. And since he'd declared I wasn't going to see him 'any time soon', he seemed to expect me to be and to do all of it while waiting for him like a faithful war bride. I was only in my mid-twenties and hadn't long cast off from the moorings to embark on the journey of my own life. I wasn't at all sure if I had the sea legs to navigate my way – or even stay afloat – on the choppy waters of his.

But then, as he'd made such a dispassionate point of telling me on the island, it was all my fault for being so young and so perfect …

*   *   *

I was in John Wood Studios later that week, recording nursery tales by myself – that is, with Frenchie and the actor who was reading the script, but minus Graham. Now I was back he felt free to stay down in Wiltshire on the farm, as he told me in his own inimitable style when he rang to give me the session.

'Tail it round to Woodsie's for ten on Friday morning, will you, honey? I've got better things to do than listen to some poxy actor read me *The Three Bleeding Billy-Goats Gruff*. I'd rather de-louse the sheep. How was the holiday?'

'Fabulous,' I told him truthfully, though I was still maintaining the fiction that I went with a girlfriend. Moscow Rules, David had said. 'Just fabulous.'

'I expect you're golden brown all over,' Graham remarked, his voice going treacly down the phone. 'Gorblimey, a tall blonde brainy bird with demon specs and a tan – it's just as well I'm staying on the farm till it wears off.'

When I told him that the demon specs were about to be swapped for contacts I heard a throaty groan.

'Oh, do me a favour, honey, don't get contacts. I know we've kept it clean so far, but if you get contacts I won't be answerable. I'll be all over you like a rash. And keep your legs crossed in front of the reader. The client wants a recording that's suitable for the under-fives, so no heavy breathing, OK?'

I loved Graham.

David called me at the studio late morning, which was clever of him given we hadn't spoken since Graham gave me the booking. He managed to time the call on a reel change too. He sounded chirpy, but for all the reasons above – and the fact that I was working – I was feeling the need to sound a little cool towards the Great Man.

'I guessed you were there,' he said. 'What are you recording?'

'We're just about to start on *Red Riding Hood*.'

'Crikey. Weighty stuff. Well, just you be sure not to let the wolf eat you, my love. That's my job.'

'I'll tell the reader. He's an obliging chap.'

'I hate him already, the lucky swine, having you there to make encouraging noises and laugh with him all day. I miss you, my darling. I miss your smile – and, of course, the rest.'

Had I been at my flat I most likely would have said *I miss you* back, my coolness evaporating under the appeal of David's voice and the persuasive spell he could so effortlessly cast when he was happy, when things were fine with him. (And how come things *were* fine with him anyway? What happened to 'indescribable' and 'poor all'?) But with Frenchie within earshot it was easier to maintain the hint of frost. If he'd heard me saying anything remotely lovey-dovey down the phone it would have licensed him to do Pepé Le Pew impressions for the rest of the session. I told David that we'd just got the next reel up.

'Yes, of course. I don't want to keep you. I really only rang to say I feel very mature about our relationship and it's all wonderful and is a girl having lunch with me next Tuesday and maybe a movie after?'

I noted the date. His birthday was next Wednesday. I hadn't expected to see him anywhere close to it and he'd already told me not to get him a present. Seeing him the day before would be an unexpected treat, though I managed to say, 'Sure, great,' nonchalantly enough for Frenchie to pay no attention.

'Good,' David said, sounding very pleased. 'Tuesday then. I'll pick you up at twelve thirty.'

Graham called from the farm that evening for an update on the session.

'By the way, David rang me down here and asked for your number at the studio. At least, he asked for the studio number and I assume he wanted you, 'cos Frenchie's not that kind of girl. Did he offer to play the Big Bad Wolf?'

'I told him the part was taken,' I said, going along with the joke, 'but if he was interested we were still auditioning for Humpty Dumpty.'

'As long as he brings his own wall – hardy-har.' Graham left it there. He probably wasn't overcurious, but even if he had been he still wouldn't have pressed. He was just the perfect friend in so many ways; Gooders by name and Gooders by nature.

'We've just signed Jacobi for *1984*,' he announced. 'He's going away skiing in the middle of December, which means we've got to book him in well before then. So cut the Orwell straight away, will you? The full thirty-thou, as per. Makes a difference having a pro lined up to read your stuff, doesn't it? Hardy-har. Catch you later, honey.'

David took me to Odin's, the famous Marylebone bistro, where the lunchtime crowd was made up entirely of expense-account suits. I wasn't quite the only woman there, but I was very likely the only side-order girlfriend and, except for staff, definitely the only person under thirty.

'I thought this might be fun,' he said confidently as we were given menus the size of pillowcases. While I looked down the list of fashionable offerings, thinking none of them had half the appeal of Costas' simple nosh, David made one of his oblique sidelong remarks.

'Don't think I don't notice when a girl swallows on her disappointment and says nothing.'

Were there three negatives in that construction or only two? And did he mean in regard to this self-conscious watering hole he'd decided to take me to for lunch – I didn't think my nose had actually turned up – or did he mean Athens? Was that a sly acknowledgement of his ditching me for his son and the crew?

I know it might seem the simplest thing to have asked *what do you mean?* But it wasn't at all. Querying what David, John le Carré, *meant* – asking him to clarify his characteristic ellipsis – would have been offering a challenge to the very essence of the man. Besides irritating him profoundly, the question would probably have received only another riddle of the sphinx for answer anyway, so I let the remark pass. Viewed from a certain angle it might have been an apology, or at least an acknowledgement of my not having demanded one myself.

After we gave our orders he made his habitual scan of the terrain.

'Hah!' he said with a slight lift of his lip. 'Do you see Pinter at his usual table?'

I followed the direction of his nod and recognised the black-browed playwright lunching with another suit. He didn't look over our way, but had probably seen us when we came in. (It was *years* before I realised that David had taken me to that restaurant precisely *because* Pinter would be there; a new twist on literary rivalry!)

'The Great Poet,' he said coolly, in reference to Pinter's most recent publication. From his impeccably balanced tone, it could equally have been thinly veiled irony or thickly veiled praise. 'He's a great fan of Charlotte's.'

I could not have said the same myself. I found David's sister quite unwatchable, which may well have been why Pinter thought so highly of her.

'Graham fancied her madly in *Rock Follies*,' was all I could think to say, knowing David had heard it before. (Though in fact, as I subsequently discovered, it was actually Julie Covington Graham fancied; he'd confused Charlotte's character with hers in the credits …)

'Yes, so he said. Though I doubt she'd go for him. My sister says she loves you very much, by the way.'

'Me? Why?'

'Because she loves me very much and you make me happy. She said so. And she wants us to go round to her place for supper sometime soon. She really wants to meet you. Shall we do that, my darling?'

'Any time,' I answered. 'Tell her I'll look forward to it.'

So. David had written that he couldn't see me any time soon, yet here we were having lunch a week later. He'd insisted we conduct our affair by Moscow Rules, yet was openly displaying me 'on the Town'. He'd disowned me in front of one member of his family, yet told another all about us. A theatre of the absurd play came to mind, where all the chairs are shifted around for no discernible reason, when there's not even a discernible reason for all the chairs in the first place. Perhaps Pinter could have explained.

'Now, on to far more important matters. First, I thought you should know I'm buying a flat. I've told my chief scout in these matters that I want a pad where I can write and get away from my family to entertain my bird. I said I needed a small but elegant bolthole far enough away from the *Schloss* in Hampstead to create some space between me and it, but close enough so that I can get back in a hurry if so required. He thinks he's found me a place.'

Not giving me a moment to process what he'd just said, which was simply *huge*, he continued.

'And second, I thought a girl might like something for her birthday.' He reached into his jacket and withdrew a red jeweller's case. 'Here,' he said, passing it across the table. 'Happy Birthday for tomorrow.'

'But it's your birthday tomorrow,' I said, 'not mine.'

'I know. Happy Birthday. Open it.'

'You told me not to get you anything.'

'I know. Happy Birthday. Open it.'

I lifted the lid and saw a delicate cage-link gold necklace lying on a satin cushion.

'It's late eighteenth century,' he explained. 'They made things to last in those days. I got it for the clasp, look—'

I looked. There was a little gauntleted hand, set with a tiny turquoise, valiantly clutching the last link of the chain.

'It's to say hold on, my darling. It's not going to be easy and it's not going to be quick. I'm like poor old Odysseus, the gods are against me. But I'm heading for shore. Just hold on until I can get out,' he urged me. 'Can you stand it? Can you wait?'

'I said I would,' I managed to say. My eyes were brimming with all that I felt for this extraordinary, paradoxical, unlike-any-other man. I loved him desperately and desperately wanted to under-stand every aspect of him, as much the parts that hurt him as the parts that I already knew would hurt me. 'I suppose I can spin thread like Penelope,' I said, trying to hold my reactions back. 'I love you, David. Happy Birthday. I love you so much.'

'And I love you too. Massively. But don't make me blub in front of Pinter or he'll think I've read his latest volume.'

After lunch, David said he couldn't make a movie. Jane had to attend to an unexpected situation with her mother, so he'd have to collect their son from school. He must have known this before lunch, since he'd been nowhere near a phone while he was with me. He asked would I instead please help him shop for something for Timo's twenty-first?

'I'd an idea to get him a gold ingot with his signature engraved on it,' he told me in the taxi. 'But I was advised that if you put any markings on them it devalues the bullion. So I thought I'd take a look around Phillips in Bond *Strasse* instead. You won't mind coming with me, will you?'

The gold necklace I'd just received was in an S. J. Phillips box, as was the flower-petal one he'd given me on our trip to Vitznau and which I'd made a point of wearing to lunch. My first ever job in London was as a temporary sales assistant at Asprey in Bond Street. (I was dating Jeremy at the time, who had used his own early experience as a sales assistant in Simpsons of Piccadilly for his long-running BBC comedy series *Are You Being Served?* He took great delight in strolling up to the pens-and-diaries counter where I was stationed to ask me 'Are you free, Miss Dawson?') Asprey is super-chic now, since its 2004 revamp, but then had an old-style elegance, with acres of pale green carpet, brightly lighted display cases and a cohort of courteous well-spoken staff, to which I had happily, if briefly, belonged. I was rather shocked, therefore, to see the inside of S. J. Phillips, with its dark wood floors and panelling, and with every available inch crammed with what seemed, to my Asprey-trained but otherwise untutored eye, to be a load of old stuff. There appeared to be no staff on the premises; the only person inside when we entered was the proprietor, Nicholas Norton, who was busy attending to something in a cabinet. He looked over briefly as we came in, offered an informal 'Hullo!' and resumed what he'd been doing. Compared with the ultra-polite greeting all customers received at Asprey, this was the Bond Street equivalent of 'You again!' to David. Were they pals? Was Norton another ex-spook? Or was David such a frequent shopper there that they treated him like family?

We poked around for a bit, but nothing looked particularly promising. There was something a little strange about the process, too – the father's secret mistress helping to pick out a gift for the son – though David didn't appear to see a problem. Then I spotted a two-inch length of slim well-turned arm protruding from the clutter of *objets* lodged on top of a high cabinet. Taken down, it proved to be an art deco statuette of a golden near-naked sylph posing athletically on a plinth.

'Oh, my love, how clever of you,' David declared. 'You get a lot of Brownie points for that. Look at her, she's perfect. Timo will love her.'

The piece was set aside and we left. I assumed it would be boxed and delivered, though David left no instructions. He didn't even leave his signature, another huge contrast to Asprey. Even James Goldsmith had to sign his account there.

Once again, it was *years* before I realised David had no intention of buying his son a birthday present from Phillips, the least likely shop for the purpose in the entire West End. The statuette was merely a fortuitous find and who knows whether he cancelled the purchase later. Or he may have just added it to what he was already getting him. Whatever mark-up Norton had put on it would have been peanuts next to what David had been prepared to shell out for a gold bar. He must have bought the necklace for me there just before lunch – it's the only way to account for the '*You again*' welcome – then took me back on the birthday present ruse expressly to show Norton who it was he'd bought it *for*. I was even *wearing* the other one he'd bought there! I had no idea. Was that his plan all along, once he knew he didn't have time for a film? Or had it occurred to him only when he saw that I was wearing the first necklace at lunch? (I can't believe he would have been so crass as to have me wear the one he'd just bought.) Did he get a secret kick out of my being so oblivious to his manoeuvring? How would he have reacted if I'd been able to tell him I knew what he was doing? The possible permutations of his thinking can make my head spin even now – though I have to concede he was paying me quite a substantial compliment, albeit in a characteristically covert way.

We went straight back to my place next, for what David had taken to calling *a full and frank exchange of views*, apparently one of his father's expressions. We ought to go away again soon, he said before he went an hour or so later, leaving me to try and digest the main take-away from our lunch date. Was he really getting a bolthole where we could meet? Was this his first step towards getting out of the slammer?

David rang at ten to nine next morning.

'I'm fifty-two, my darling. I just rang to say Happy Birthday.'

He sounded thin somehow, stretched out on what he'd given me to believe was the rack of his life at the other end of the line in

Hampstead. It was the school run just then, so he was alone in the house. It was a detail from his domestic life I could have done without realising, but I loved him for using what were probably the only free minutes he'd have to himself that whole day to call me.

'Happy Birthday,' I said back.

'Thanks,' he said with a small sigh.

'I'm picking up the contacts today,' I told him, trying to cheer him up.

'Oh, how wonderful. That's the best birthday present ever.' It probably was, all things considered, but he didn't sound even a little bit cheered. 'I'm just so much older than you and it's terrifying,' he went on. 'Do you realise that in thirteen years I'll be sixty-five?'

'Then you can come and see me on your OAP bus pass.'

'Cow. Shan't. I love you.'

I told him I loved him back. David said he really rang to ask if I would spend the weekend at the end of half-term with him at the house in Cornwall. He said his wife and son would have gone back to London by then. They would have 'had their talk', would have 'hammered something out'. He said he'd really need me after that. He wanted me to meet some of his friends down there too. So Saturday to Tuesday inclusive, then, in ten days' time, if that worked with my schedule.

I checked my diary.

'That would work,' I confirmed. 'Graham doesn't want me again until Thursday.'

'And I want you now,' David replied. 'So that's perfect.'

That weekend I received my first-class rail tickets by courier from the spook travel agent. Next Saturday morning I was to take the 'Cornish Riviera' train from Paddington to Penzance, arriving mid-afternoon. David's wife and son mustn't have been due to leave until after lunch, or else I could have taken the Friday overnight sleeper and got there first thing; another domestic detail I didn't need in my head, yet found myself calculating. David said he would be waiting for me at the station. The fallback this time, should anything go wrong and he not be there, was for me to take a taxi to Sancreed House, a few miles away from his own place at Land's End, where the painter John Miller lived. Miller was his best friend, he said, and one of the people he wanted me to meet.

Not long after the tickets arrived, there was another courier at my door, this one bearing a diva-sized bouquet from an exclusive West End florist. The card read *Hurry up, love David*. The flowers filled all the vases I had in my flat and I had to run across the road to Habitat to buy more.

Land's End

David picked me up from Penzance station and we drove to his house at Land's End. While driving he held my hand on his knee, pressing it, kneading it, as if he couldn't quite believe in its reality. He was so glad to see me here, he said. This was where he really lived, he said, not Hampstead. This was his real home.

As an urban type living in the heart of London, I could never see the benefit in travelling for hours just to end up somewhere else in 'the country' for the weekend, especially when Heathrow was so handy for a real getaway to so many other wonderful cities. I'd never visited this last tip of England and the end of October was not the best time for a favourable first impression. The sky was low and grey, the sea was flat and grey, and the light was already falling as we drove. Everything seemed wind-blasted and bare. Shortly before we reached the house we passed through a bleak little village built of colourless local stone. I paid it no attention until I saw the sign saying St Buryan, which rang a distant bell for me, though I couldn't have said why. As if he'd read my mind, David filled in the connection.

'Peckinpah filmed *Straw Dogs* here,' he told me.

In regard to how the visit was going to go, that should probably have been my first clue.

David's house, Tregiffian, stood virtually on the cliff's edge facing the vast waste of the Atlantic. Originally a row of derelict workmen's cottages he'd bought in the waning years of his first marriage, it had been knocked into one dwelling and completely refurbished, with the suitable gentleman's additions of sunroom, terrace, an extra wing and landscaped gardens. His two dogs appeared in the hallway as we arrived – Whisper and Mach, a father and son pair of whippets – and introduced themselves by rolling over for belly rubs. I bent down to oblige, but their master told them to stand down, saying they'd have to wait their turn if they were after that kind of attention from me. He took my coat, set it with my bag on the stairs, then put my arm through his to guide me round the house.

'Do you like it?' he asked, gleefully showing me around, and once again I could see the little boy in him, this time the one who wanted to parade his stuff.

I said it was lovely. And it was. But the moment I crossed the threshold, I was assailed by the same sensation that confronted me in the *Schloss* at Hampstead. There I had ascribed it to the dust-sheets and building work, but I couldn't see evidence of builders here. I thought perhaps it was the last of the daylight reflecting eerily off the ocean, but when David switched on the lights it didn't make much difference. There was a heavy colour scheme, a lot of deep red and dark wood, grey flagstones and more lifeless local stone. But I knew what I felt wasn't really down to the decor or fading coastal light, or even the pervasive Cornish damp. It touched me the minute I was inside.

David particularly wanted to show me his workroom. (This was the word he always used, not office or study.) It was down a corridor from the main body of the house, in a part which seemed more recently built. His attitude changed as he eased open the door. Gleeful became reverential. It was a privilege, his body language seemed to be saying, to be admitted. I followed him into a large lofty room with more than a little of a chapel about it. A wooden lectern stood pulpit-like against the back wall and at the other end of the room, by a tall narrow window with a long view of the sea, lay a writing desk the size of Robinson Crusoe's raft. Like surf left by a receding wave, pages of David's blue-ink handwriting drifted across it, along with other desk jetsam – some pens and a notepad and a small cushion for his non-writing arm to rest on as he worked. Apart from his work chair, the only other item of furniture was a long pale sofa against one of the walls. The room seemed austere and comfortless, but must have been how he liked it. Perhaps comfort hindered David's writing. Perhaps not only his writing.

'I've made it lovely, don't you think?' he asked me again when the tour of the ground floor concluded. Again I answered that he had and it was. But I couldn't shake the feeling that for all the money he must have spent, all the evident time and careful effort to get everything just the way he wanted (he never once mentioned input from either wife, by the way), the whole place felt desolate.

We would be sleeping in the master bedroom, he announced, but right now we had to go back into the main sitting room, which he'd only let me glance at on the tour. I'd caught a glimpse of large comfy sofas, upholstered in a red chinoiserie pattern, all arranged in front of a stone fireplace with a log fire blazing in the hearth. Now I saw what he'd done. Before coming to pick me up he'd laid out a picnic on the rug in front of the fire; feta and stuffed vine leaves, olives and hummus and crusty bread, yogurt and honey, with a bottle of extremely serious red wine warming on the stone hearth.

'I thought I'd do us a Greek,' he said. 'And by the way, aren't you ever going to have sex with me? You've been here five whole minutes—'

We were happily post-coital and post-prandial, sitting on the rug with our backs to the sofa and our feet to the replenished fire, drinking the last of the wine, when David asked me lightly, 'Have you been calling the house, my darling?'

As was so often the case when he said things out of the blue, choosing the most incongruous moment, I didn't immediately take his meaning. I thought he meant *this* house, Tregiffian.

'You didn't give me the number here.'

'Not here. Hampstead.'

I did have that number. Jane had supplied it with her notes for the longer *Drummer Girl* abridgement, cautioning *not on general release*. I began to see what David was suggesting.

'No – I haven't been calling the house in Hampstead. Why should I?'

'Jane's been getting calls,' he continued, sidestepping my question. 'Somebody ringing and not speaking when she picks up. She lives in terror of kidnappers.'

'Then maybe it *was* kidnappers,' I returned smartly, 'because it wasn't *me*.'

He gave me a steely look. If I couldn't be condemned for nuisance phone calls, he might consider pressing charges for flippancy. Over the lunch at Odin's, he'd told me of a recent bomb scare at the Hampstead house. *Jane saw wires hanging underneath the car and a smashed tail light*, he said, *and she called Scotland Yard*. The police had cordoned off the area, apparently, but it was a false alarm, so he made light of it in the telling. *While the Bomb Squad checked it out, we had the regular bobbies hiding in the bushes, as if, by not being seen, they wouldn't be blown up!*

With factors like that in play, I didn't care for the idea that he considered me a possible suspect for the silent calls.

But for David the moment had passed. He went straight to what I would come to learn was always his next move after he'd knocked me off balance.

'I think I need to fuck you some more,' he said, nuzzling in.

Next day we drove over to Sancreed for Sunday lunch with John Miller and his partner Michael Truscott. Miller was David's best friend and a well-known artist; prints of his stylised local beach-scapes were immensely popular at the time. David said that Michael was also well known as a local potter.

The two men seemed to share a joshing closeness with David and were both very sweet to me. Miller was David's age, a spare, silver-haired, almost ascetic figure with a wry humour to his conversation. Michael was younger, slim, dark-haired and quietly spoken, also with a clever wit. It was good to meet them and it was all happy enough.

But still—

It didn't *feel* right. Something about the lunch rang hollow. I don't mean to suggest that either of them was insincere or inhospitable or ungracious. I had a really nice time in their company. But somehow they were both in performance mode. David was too. I'd already spent too many hours working with actors and performers not to recognise the element of *show*, however subtle and polished, and the lunch was a well-paced three-hander. They seemed to have gone into girlfriend-drill, a sort of coded understanding between the three of them. I wondered, and instantly doubted, whether it was different when he brought Jane over. Perhaps it was wife-drill then, the performances just as polished, but with a less lively script. Or perhaps he didn't bring Jane over.

Despite the continuously maintained 'anyone for tennis?' patter, Miller did let one thing slip right at the end. After we finished the leisurely meal at their long refectory table, Michael suggested we take coffee in the sitting-room. No thanks, David replied; he had to get back to make some calls. Seeing us to the door, Miller said to me, 'David always has to have a reason for leaving.'

Back at the house, after I'd been equipped with a spare waxed jacket – David seemed surprised I hadn't brought one with me, as if I owned such a garment myself – we walked Mach and Whisper on the footpath along the edge of David's own mile of cliff. The dogs rocketed through the bracken, tearing off at mad tangents on their master's attack command – 'Critics!' – in search of kill.

'So how did it go at half-term?' I asked pleasantly after we'd been walking for a while. He'd previously made such a big issue of telling me how he and his wife would 'talk' then, but so far hadn't made any reference to it.

That probably was clue number two.

Suddenly a tangible chill descended over him. I might just have asked him how much money he had in the bank, or the consistency of his last bowel movement.

'What do you want to know?' he asked me back.

I suppose I ought to have said *never mind* and brushed it off, though most likely the damage was already done by my having had the temerity to ask. But I felt entitled to. He was getting out, he'd told me – he was getting a bolt-hole, he'd told me – 'Wait, my darling' and 'Hold on' while he 'hammered something out' over half-term. If he was going to be so touchy about it, he shouldn't have told me anything at all. I didn't want a blow-by-blow re-enactment, he didn't have to betray any confidences. I was simply asking whether he felt he'd made progress with what he set out to do. So I repeated what I'd said.

'Just – how did it go?'

He let the silence set in again for a long minute as we continued walking, then finally answered.

'We talked.'

He said nothing more for the rest of the walk. He still issued commands to the dogs, who were unperturbed by their master's sudden drop in body temperature. They probably thought he was in search of kill, too. This barren heath wasn't my kind of place to begin with, but now it felt like an alien planet. Other than the dogs and any unlucky rabbits they might find, there was no sign of warm-blooded life for miles around, though my lover was only paces away from me. I might have been walking along his damn-awful cliff top, wearing his damn-awful hacking jacket, going back to his damn-awful house entirely by myself.

David didn't speak to me again until we got back inside. As we sloughed off our coats he told me oh-so softly, 'I don't need you here, you know, if you're going to be moody.'

Maybe I didn't need to be there at all.

*   *   *

The tension continued through most of the next two days. The tripwires I'd witnessed David laying around himself towards the end of our stay in Greece, which I'd managed mostly to avoid, were much more sophisticated devices on his own turf. He seemed to have a cat's cradle of invisible sensor beams strung all around him, regulated to his body readings, to his moods and sensibilities, whatever they happened to be. But the alarm they triggered was silent, so not only could I never see which wire I'd tripped, I never knew when I had. I only knew that I'd done or said something to set off the alarm when David would freeze me out at random intervals. But with no way to tell what I'd done or said, there was no way for me to know what to do or say next, what not to do or say again. Even so, I kept trying and must have succeeded some of the time, because just as randomly he would wrap me in his arms and draw me close with a smile, as if I'd passed some undisclosed module of his ever-escalating test. Sex was the only constant, the only point of true contact. Everything else was in ever-shifting flux.

The bed in the master bedroom was rock hard and about ten feet wide, the sort you acquire either because your nights are given over to copious amounts of acrobatic sex or, more likely, you want to sleep five feet away from your wife. I'd have preferred we were in the guest room, but perhaps the laundry considerations were too tell-tale. Or perhaps David wanted to be reminded of our acrobatics next time he was sleeping five feet away from his wife.

He took little sleeping pills every night but they didn't seem to be much help to him. I'd noticed he was an uneasy sleeper in Lesbos, but he was far worse in this house, where he moaned and talked in frantic mumbles in the night. Was it the foghorn that racked his dreams, droning like a beached whale, or the beam from the nearby lighthouse strobing relentlessly through the blinds? Both disturbed *my* sleep. I didn't see how he could think of this place as a haven. It felt to me like a site of banishment and exile.

David's writing regime played out much as it had in Greece, only without the sunshine and shingle. In the morning he rose at about five and went downstairs to his workroom. Around eight, he came back to the bedroom, woke me up and made love to me without a word. Afterwards he gently told me I was keeping him from his work and went back to his room.

I rose soon after and took a hot bath in the pine-panelled chalet-style bathroom, to draw out my lover's fluids and shake off the emanation – perhaps it was just pervasive Cornish damp – which I still felt in the house. As I was getting dressed something impelled me to look in Jane's side of the long bedroom wardrobe. I can only say in my defence that I had never before and have never since so much as opened a bathroom cabinet in anyone's home, but on that sole occasion I felt something close to a compulsion to look through Jane's clothes. It seemed a necessary deviation for survival at the time. Like the bear who went over the mountain, I had to see what I could see. But there was nothing *to* see; just the other side of the wardrobe. Nothing that told me anything worth knowing or gratified my deviant impulse.

Then one garment caught my eye. It was the dreadful striped top David bought with his trunks in Plomari. Did Jane see it among his clothes when he came home and take a liking to it? Did he say he'd brought it back for her? Or was claiming it for herself a way of establishing a connection to the latest of his long foreign trips that she hadn't been allowed to accompany him on? And when she wore it, seeking that connection, did it remind David of our secret 'honeymoon'? Was that why he'd brought it back? I closed the wardrobe on my questions, wishing sincerely I hadn't looked. I finished dressing and went downstairs.

*   *   *

My only strategy for coping with David's kaleidoscopic moods was to stay in some sort of quiet balance myself. But it wasn't easy to do. He could spring a trap from any direction.

He'd asked me to compile a list of quotations from *The Good Soldier* that might be useful for his new book. I'd brought the list and gave it to him, receiving what seemed genuine thanks. I'd also brought *1984* with me, to finish cutting, and sat with it by a window overlooking the terrace while he remained cloistered in his workroom. At about eleven he made one of his silent entrances when I was in the middle of a word count. After a morning's writing he always looked strangely insubstantial, almost transparent, as if he'd beamed down from some other planetary surface and stepped too quickly off the teleporter pad, before his atoms had properly gathered themselves.

'Hullo,' he said dully, interrupting my count. 'What're you reading?'

I raised the book amicably so he could see the cover.

'Hah. Haven't you read that before?'

You see? Not *Are you reading that again, my love?* or *Has Graham got you taking work away with you?* which he might easily have guessed from the pen in my other hand. Only the familiar tone of mild rebuke.

I kept my reply pleasantly neutral, saying it was a rush job for the studio. The reader had asked to record as soon as possible, because he was going skiing in December.

'Who's the reader?'

'Derek Jacobi.'

'Hah!' he said again, this time with greater animation. 'Well, you know why that is, don't you? He came to a party at my house and I lent him my chalet in Wengen for two weeks then, that's why. Fancy a snoot?'

While we sat with our drinks, he announced we'd be going over to see some more of his friends, Derek Tangye and his wife Jeannie, for lunch. They lived about a mile away at Minack, we'd walk over. Again, I recognised the name. Tangye was author of such lending library stalwarts as *A Donkey in the Meadow* and *A Gull on the Roof*, a series known collectively as the 'Minack Chronicles', the sort of pastoral reminiscences my mother liked to read.

It was another blowy cloudy day, the pale grey sky and dark grey sea stretching for unbroken miles all round. David suggested I wear the windproof jacket again, and though I could never stand that type of garment – 'country lifestyle' and all that – I was grateful for its protection as we stomped along the clifftop path in the headstrong wind. After twenty minutes we neared a tumbledown cottage, which I first took to be a donkey shelter until David turned in at what might once have been a functioning gate.

'*This* is their place?'

The Tregiffian cottages had been transformed into a gentleman's abode. Sancreed was a restored Georgian rectory. I'd expected Minack to be something similar, but instead, I was looking at what must have been the inspiration for Connie Sachs' tin-roofed shack in *Smiley's People*.

'This is their place,' David confirmed. 'Don't eat any more than you have to and drink absolutely as much as you can.'

He'd brought along a brace of heavyweight premier cru reds, one in each pocket of his waxed jacket. I'd assumed this was simply his bringing our welcome with us, but now I saw it as an ominous sign.

Ahoy!

A rumpled figure, a good stretch older than David and far more worn, hailed us like a dry-docked sea captain from the ramshackle front porch. Tangye – for it was he – was wearing a faded blue fisherman's smock over somewhat less disreputable rust-brown cords that were rather baggy on him (and which I instantly suspected were David's cast-offs), with a gaily spotted neckerchief knotted at his throat. He clamped David's hand then turned to me.

And this is the lovely Sue!

He would have embraced me freely, I could see. There was a rheumy glimmer in his eyes and his mouth was moistly open, ready for an introductory, not to say exploratory, kiss. His battered Boxing Blue nose had a burst of purple grog-veins on its end. I quickly offered my hand before he could close in.

Here's Jeannie!

Everything Tangye had said so far was an exclamation, at the pitch of Captain Bligh ordering ratings in a Force Nine gale. Somehow I was already certain it was going to be the tenor of the whole visit. Jeannie, who became visible when he stepped aside, was a tiny bird of a woman with a permanently smiling trilby mouth and pink dumpling cheeks. In contrast to Tangye's raddled fly-blown appearance, she possessed a girlish glow, her unlined fresh complexion and her eager bright eyes quite belying the fact that she was well into her sixties and married to Tangye for north-wards of forty years. Within moments of looking at her, it came to me that this was the agelessness of the certifiably insane.

'Come in, won't you?' she said.

As we crossed the threshold, David gave me a quick *told you* dig in the ribs, which he had no right to do since he'd done no such thing.

'Jeannie's been cooking!' Tangye cried, at a slightly lower volume inside, and took my coat. 'Marvellous! What'll you drink?'

Milk of magnesia, I wanted to say as the smell from the oven hit me, *a large one*. The kitchen was a narrow galley to one side of the cramped main room and mad little Jeannie began to show me proudly around. It was simply disgusting. There wasn't a surface without a stack of dishes on it and not one dish in any of the stacks that wasn't caked with leftover food, from how far back I dared not consider. The place couldn't have been cleared for weeks, not cleaned for far longer, and as I edged along behind our hostess the soles of my shoes were sticking to the floor. David caught my eye and passed something to me over the counter; a shot glass with greasy smudges down the side, filled with clear liquid.

'Vodka,' he told me softly as Tangye bellowed *Down the hatch!* from across the room. David had brought that bottle with him too, 75cl of Stoly in an inside pocket. He and Tangye downed theirs in one gulp, like Cossacks, and for the first time in my life I did the same. David produced a corkscrew he'd also brought along – *what, no glasses?* – and started to open the wine. With my instincts flying, I realised why. If he hadn't opened both bottles immediately, Tangye would have squirrelled the good stuff away and served up some evil plonk of his own, most likely a home-brew. God, they were appalling, these two. It was all simply appalling. And on one level in particular – there was another – it was also infuriating. People who lived like this didn't do so out of genuine hardship. People who are genuinely hard-strapped will most often take every care to look after their surroundings so that their true circumstances don't show. Cornwall being the neglected backwater it was in those days, they could have lived like princes on as little as five thousand a year, so it was glaringly clear to me that the Tangyes lived this way because they were both as mean as mouse-shit with money and too bat-crap crazy to think anyone noticed.

My other level of infuriation, for the record, was with how David was treating it all as though it were a minor lapse in house-keeping, rather than a gruesome pathology. Did he think he was helping these people by ignoring how they lived? He could have donated an annual five grand to their upkeep out of his back pocket. Did he believe, by bringing me over and knowing I would follow his lead and act as if everything were normal, that he was protecting their finer sensibilities? They didn't *have* any finer sensi-bilities – and he certainly wasn't protecting *mine*! I knew from my mother's reading that Tangye had written upwards of a dozen books and when we were walking over David told me that Jeannie had written several herself. But as I looked around at the squalor this pair lived in I could only wonder how many copies they would have to sell between them before either one prioritised the purchase of a bottle of bleach. Why hadn't David invited them over to his place, for God's sake? What on earth made him decide to bring me *here*? Was it another test, to see how I'd react? Wasn't it enough for him to see me 'swallow on my disappointment' – did he have to see me swallow lunch with this God-awful pair as well?

Jeannie reached down into a kitchen cupboard and held up the latest thing they'd discovered in culinary convenience; a vacuum pack of salmon.

'Look at this,' she said, still smiling inanely. 'We get all our meat and fish this way now.'

'Marvellous firm!!' Tangye exclaimed, with the glee of a Crusader spearing a Saracen. He refilled our shot glasses till the vodka spilled over the sides. 'Send you anything you like in the post – meat, fish, poultry, game – all in vacuum packs. Marvellous!'

Their enthusiasm was due to the fact that the kitchen had no refrigerator. *Of course it didn't.* Their rancid shack wasn't connected to the power grid, because you have to *pay* for electricity. But what neither of them seemed to have noticed – since, as I may have mentioned, *they were both completely insane* – was that the seal on the vacuum pack wasn't sound and the plastic wrapping had inflated to the dimensions of a rugby ball. Ptomaine poisoning by post – *marvellous!*

'Would you like their address?' Jeannie asked me.

Like the condemned at their last meal, David and I took our places at the table with deliberate cheer. David shared local chit-chat with Tangye while from the disgusting kitchen Jeannie brought out the disgusting food she was preparing to kill us with. She covered the entire surface of the rickety dining table with her offerings: potatoes with a greyish gleam, spinach (or something green and steaming) and two great pies, one for each course, with crusts on them like village kerbstones. The savoury one, when she cut into it, had a filling that smelled like hot dog food and which I would have eaten rather more easily if I'd known for sure it *was* dog food. Each mouthful wanted to rise again as I swallowed it, but to prove to David that I could be what he wanted me to be – whatever *the fuck* that was in this loathsome scenario – I managed to eat every last fetid lump our demented little hostess piled on my plate. The second pie, our dessert, with the luxury of tinned cream on the side, contained berries. Locally gathered, Jeannie announced blithely. They could have been brambles, they could have been deadly nightshade, she didn't say. But she did add that they were cutting down on sugar – *of course they were,* these raving misers – meaning I could feel the skin on the roof of my mouth begin to blister at first bite. But by that stage of the ordeal nothing mattered any more. David was bound to have antacid tablets at his place and if he didn't then I would go straight to the bathroom once we were back and – also for the first time in my life – stick my fingers down my throat.

Tangye was another old spook, it transpired, with MI5 during the war. *Of course he was.* Could there possibly have been another reason for David wanting to keep the company of this ghastly old fart and his no-sharp-objects asylum escapee of a wife? Was Miller too? As ever, I didn't ask and by then couldn't have cared. I just assumed that anyone David knew with any degree of familiarity could be placed somewhere on the spook spectrum, even if they were mad as hatters and ten times as dreadful – *zum Beispiel, unser Host.*

When David and Jeannie took the dishes to the kitchen, disgusting old Derek felt me up under the table.

'Come over any time David's too busy to entertain you properly, won't you?' he told me in a phlegmy growl with his hand firmly on my knee.

'My mother loves your books,' was all I could think to say.

134

(By the way, I didn't ever ask David how he came to know Miller, demonstrating conclusively that I would have made the world's worst investigative reporter. But on the other hand, David didn't ever tell me and I suspect he would have deflected my question if I'd asked. I first learned the truth of their original connection from Adam Sisman's exceptional book, *John le Carré: The Biography* (Bloomsbury, 2015), where he writes, 'One of David's agents, John Miller, would become a lifelong friend.')

That foul experience actually brought us closer together and for a while dispelled David's weekend-long moodiness and distance. We headed back at marching pace, laughing away the worst of it as we walked off mad Jeannie's appalling garbage of a meal. (I found a convenient clearing in the bracken to pee, since I would have preferred risking the need for a catheter to using the facilities *chez* Tangye. David evidently took the same view, availing himself of a nearby gorse bush.) The minute we were in we promptly downed more neat vodka as a digestive aid and managed to have a happy, funny, sexy evening together. This was the way it could always have been between us, if David would only have let it happen that way, if he could have found it in himself to save the misery for the part of his life that engendered it and just enjoy the good stuff, the bonus, with me. That was what he claimed he wanted, what he always seemed to start off aiming to achieve. But there was something lurking deep within him that would emerge to take a stab at our good times, something that wasn't ever content until it had spread the old contagion to the fresh wound.

At the end of the day we fell asleep in the middle of the huge unyielding bed, lying together like spoons. But even so, David's ghosts still stalked him through the night.

When George Greenfield and his girlfriend Gigi arrived on Tuesday afternoon, I quite unexpectedly found myself close to tears with relief. It was like the moment in those 1950s science-fiction films when the hero's girlfriend discovers that not all of the townsfolk have been turned into pod-people. For the first time since arriving I felt I was among friends, though, as with all the others, I hadn't met either of them before. George brought a welcome camaraderie with him and an elegant city ease. He greeted me cordially, as though we were already established colleagues. He was older and shorter than David, but lean and trim, with dark twinkly eyes and a tight but broad smile under a thin moustache. I'd been feeling caught up in something decidedly *Rebecca*-ish the whole weekend – the young *ingénue* deeply in love with the brooding older man, on a first visit to his daunting Cornish pile where everyone was in on the big secret except me.

But with George's arrival all that vanished and my sense of the real world returned. I hardly realised how far it had receded until then. Now I *knew* there was something odd and encoded about the lunch with Miller and his boyfriend – I hadn't imagined it. Even the barking Tangyes had been part of the pre-arranged show. George proved it to me with his easy genuine affability. So did Gigi, who was just wonderful. She was vibrant and glamorous and witty, and I instantly felt we could become great pals – as indeed we later did. (She asked not to be identified here, so I've named her after George's initials.) But as David had arranged things, one good evening was all I got. I could have taken the sleeper back on Wednesday night and still made it to the studio on Thursday. But David made no offer to change the arrangements. I was to leave first thing on Wednesday morning, as planned.

The renewed confidence I was starting to feel needed more shoring up than it could get in a few congenial *normal* hours. *Had* I been moody, as David charged? I didn't know, there was no way to tell. David certainly had been – and far worse for most of the time. His reality was always the dominant one, though he only seemed to see the depth of his own dark eddies when the backwash spilled on to me. No previous lover – no one in my life until then – had ever accused me of being like that before. If I was guilty as charged, then it was only the natural response to my current lover knocking the living *levitas* out of me for three days straight.

All the long way back to London I stared out of the train window, feeling lost and confused and somehow worn away.

David's next letter was dated 5 November and was a suitable powder-keg for the occasion. He began ominously by saying he wished he could write a happier letter, then dived headlong into a description of all the tensions and problems and bad things the weekend had left him with. He felt a failure, he said, and concluded that I must too. (Perhaps so, but at least I knew I'd tried for success. And anyway – *failure*? It was just a weekend in the damned country, not UN peace talks.) Then he declared that we must not fall victim to our own rhetoric. (*Our* rhetoric?) Said he couldn't shake off the bad memories despite a happy last night. (I was only surprised he didn't write happy last *supper*, his letter was such a self-awareness- and irony-free zone.) He claimed to be going ahead with the flat nonetheless, but finished by saying that he didn't like being pushed around. (*He* didn't like it?) I was to write back *poste restante* Hampstead, he insisted, citing our first official dead letter-box, though still without any trace of irony. He said he wouldn't call me again until I did.

Christ Almighty. All that *Sturm-und-Drang* just because I asked him 'what happened?' over half-term.

Thank God I didn't ask him 'what happens next?'

I had entered into this relationship thinking of David as an enigma; a man whose hidden heart and complex mind would be an enormous challenge to interpret but an even greater reward to ultimately understand. Now, after the visit to Cornwall, I had modified my view. I still didn't doubt the reward, but the complexity and the challenge were both far greater than I'd imagined.

I had first assumed that secrecy – with its corollary, encryption – was simply David's *modus operandi*, his standard method of approaching the world, left over from his training and career as a spy. I hadn't taken the issue too seriously, seeing it as a professional habit of mind, nothing more.

But that was a hopeless misinterpretation. What I'd taken for David's *m.o.* was his essential self. Secrecy was a survival instinct deep within him and encryption was the mechanism by which it was maintained. I'd seen it in relentless operation that weekend. Just when I thought I understood some part of him, the mechanism would re-encrypt with a fresh turn of his inner cogs and I'd be confounded once more. As I began to grasp the next new element, the cogs would turn again. So now I began to see David not so much as an enigma, but rather as an Enigma machine, with uncountable combinations lying within him, just waiting for the gears of limitless permutation to engage. Only *I love you* seemed to escape the obscuration of code – and the sex which invariably followed, in limitless permutations of its own. If I wanted the relationship to continue – and I had never wanted anything more – there was one vital thing for me to do. I had to try and crack the code.

I took a couple of days to decompress, from the trip and from the letter, then wrote back. I have no idea now what I wrote; I had precious little idea even then. I just let my pen cover the page and posted it as soon as it was done. All I could do after that was wait.

David called me a couple of days later.

'Wow. You can't half write a letter, my girl, I'll say. That one doesn't go in the shredder, I can tell you. I love you, my Sue, I love you enormously. What are you doing tomorrow night?'

I was enormously relieved, of course, that it was all fine again. But was that all it took to get him right-side-up – a good letter? I didn't believe what I'd written could be entirely responsible for the turnaround any more than I felt entirely responsible for his despondency in the first place. If David could haunt himself without supernatural help – as I'd seen he could, perfectly well – then he could probably capsize and right his own emotional boat all on his own too.

We met 'for a quick Chinese' somewhere in Paddington, before he caught the train back down to Penzance. He was sweet and kind and loving during the meal and plainly desperate to be with me again. He said he could hardly stand to see me for a meal and not make love to me afterwards, but something had cropped up so this was the only time he had and he couldn't stand not to see me at all.

Something so often did crop up. His accountants, his lawyers, the movie, the script, the builders – even his babies, as he persisted in calling his grown-up sons, though never the one who was actually still a child. Any of these had a claim on his time and attention prior to mine and, since he'd already complained to me about their depredations into his life, I didn't feel I could say anything. I loved him for spending what free time he did have with me and trusted that the process he was going through would eventually free him substantially, partly for us but most importantly for him. His most abiding lament was that he was constantly being taken away from the new book. I always sympathised, but his schedule at times resembled the plate-spinning act that used to appear on old TV variety shows, where the guy kept spinning more and more plates on top of more and more poles and then had to race around madly trying to keep them all from crashing to the ground. I couldn't understand why David arranged his life in such a way, though Miller had already told me the key to it. I just hadn't caught on.

After some more calls, all of them loving and reassuring – *It's all good, Sue, all good* – and promises that he'd write me *lovely long letters*, which actually were lovely when they arrived, he returned briefly to London. (The frequency of his travelling was dizzying. In the three and a half months of our relationship, I'd been abroad with David twice, knew of three other European trips he made by himself and he'd been to Cornwall more times than I could count.) A further cancelled lunch became dinner, with a movie first, something David said he was keen to see – *Zelig*, Woody Allen's latest. He watched with great attention throughout, but afterwards said he didn't think much of it. The irony of his choosing that particular film – about a man who is a perpetual chameleon, slotting into moments in history without really being part of them – wasn't a line he pursued. He saw the thesis in the film, but not the irony of his choosing it. Some prod of intuition made me decide not to point this out.

After the cinema we went to Fakhreldine, the big Lebanese restaurant overlooking Green Park. As we dug into a gargantuan meze starter, David advised me that I really shouldn't raise anything to my mouth with my left hand.

'Why not?' I asked.

'Because it's the one you wipe your bum with.'

'But it isn't,' I replied, before realising he was speaking culturally.

I might have added, *Aa-ow, me bloomin' beads!* David had a pretty wide streak of Henry Higgins running through him, at least with me. But it was odd that he should care what a bunch of waiters in a Lebanese restaurant might think of my otherwise standard table manners. It wasn't as if we were in Beirut, and even if we had been, so what? I was sure none of them cared about anything we did as long as it didn't involve a food fight and he left a good tip.

After the restaurant we headed to Paddington station. David was going back to Cornwall *again*, in advance of a family weekend for his youngest son's birthday, but not until the first train next morning. He'd booked us in for the night at the Great Western Royal.

What was once an ornate stuccoed Victorian hotel was now a tired old Miss Havisham's wedding cake of a place. Our room looked as though it had last been decorated for the Coronation. But David seemed to like the dilapidated grandeur.

'Lady Docker has a suite here, I believe,' he announced, as if that were a recommendation. (Her name had been a byword for extravagance a couple of decades earlier, when she was a notorious spendthrift, most notably on a string of luxuriously personalised Daimlers. Her husband, Sir Bernard, was the Daimler chairman until he was ousted for charging his wife's excessive running costs to the firm.)

David surprised me by saying he wanted me to go down to Cornwall again at the end of the month. Well, well. Tangye and Miller must have filed favourable reports. George probably put in a good word for me too. Or maybe the time he'd spent back in the bosom of his family since then had made my lover re-evaluate whatever problems he thought he had with me.

I agreed to go – on one non-negotiable condition.

'No Tangyes this time,' I said flatly.

'No Tangyes this time,' he confirmed. 'So you needn't bring a stomach pump.'

Meanwhile, Graham and I were in the studio with Derek Jacobi and *1984*. Jacobi was an instant sweetheart and a first-rate reader. He apologised for making us rush the recording because of his skiing trip, but said he was going to Wengen just before Christmas. Graham said what a coincidence, he was going skiing in Wengen just after the New Year. It took them about four seconds to realise what I already knew, that they'd both be borrowing David's chalet.

'He's a lovely bloke, isn't he?' Graham said, adding rather artfully, 'My co-producer and I have both rather taken to him.'

Jacobi readily agreed. 'Delightful,' he said. 'Simply delightful.'

I went along with the Cornwell love-fest, chiefly because they weren't wrong. David *was* lovely, he *was* delightful. He was just, well ... *and the rest*. They had seen only one aspect of the man; I'd already seen so many more. Neither of them was sleeping with him, of course, which accounted for most of the difference, though I dare say Jacobi wouldn't have minded having his name in the hat.

David called that night from Cornwall to ask how the recording had gone. He was once more *tout seul* and rang after having supper at Miller's, saying he'd left the first pages of the new book with him. He sounded fine but broke off after a few minutes to take a call on another line. When he rang back, his voice had changed.

'Book's no good, Our Sue. Miller says so. He just rang. Told me all about Job.'

(I can't quite remember when David started that variant for my name. It was one example of a sort of mock-Cockney lingo he would sometimes lapse into and would brand it 'Belgravia-Cockney' in his books. There was a lot of this going around the smarter areas of London at the time, with Chas & Dave riding high in the charts and the BBC about to start a new soap opera called *EastEnders*. But I think David may have been using it since his army days, although his usage was never quite as convincing to my ear as Graham's, whose expressions were drawn from real Londoners like Frenchie and the other engineers in the studios. But anyway, 'Our Sue' stuck as an endearment for me.)

He didn't seem to want to say anything further about his book – or about Job, for that matter – but asked if I'd watched Alan Bennett's film, *An Englishman Abroad*, based on actress Coral Browne's unlikely association with defector Guy Burgess, which had aired that night. He'd missed it, being out at Sancreed, and this was before the general advent of video recorders. He asked if it was good and I said it was terrific. The waspish actress played her even more caustic younger self and the once-beautiful Alan Bates had gone full-throttle as the degenerate and impossibly fruity Burgess. The two had met in 1958, when Browne was touring Russia with the Shakespeare Memorial Theatre Company and Burgess stumbled drunkenly into her dressing room in Moscow after the first night of *Hamlet* and vomited prodigiously into her sink. I relayed the scene to David, expecting him to laugh, but he still sounded wan and distant at the other end of the line. His mind was on Miller's critique and, though he'd asked, what I was saying didn't help. The subject of Burgess was too close to Philby and, as I didn't yet know, Philby was too close to the central matter of the new novel. And Miller had just trashed his first attempt.

It seemed to me – perhaps in my prejudice, but I don't think entirely – that Burgess's life in the USSR was something like David's life in Cornwall, the bleak and inhospitable location where he took himself to evade capture and confinement in the Hampstead slammer, with only a couple of fellow ex-spooks who'd also defected from civilisation for company. But even in his self-imposed exile, David couldn't escape a domestic situation which – I hesitate to say Kremlin-like – seemed to monitor his every move.

Cornwall was more than a little lovelier the second time around. Not that I was ever going to warm to the locale, but David was lovely again himself, all right inside his head as he would so often put it. This time I took the overnight sleeper, the train that Smiley takes to see Ann before setting off on his final quest for Karla. David was waiting for me at the station, but on the wrong platform, and it took him a while to pound his way over to the right side of the track. (Sometimes the metaphors write themselves …)

He made me a little breakfast when we got in and then we hastened to bed. The book was going well now, he told me, which was probably as much the root of the easy atmosphere as anything. He was over a false start, he said, meaning the book but quite possibly meaning our relationship as well.

'There's only deeper with us, my darling – it's the only way.'

As before, David wrote in the mornings while I read, but this time when he came to find me for lunch it was with an easy, contented expression on his face, asking *Fancy a snoot?* with a sweet smile, or *Would a girl like a quick fuck? Or even a slow one?* We talked and talked the whole time I was there, then had a lot more sex and then talked some more. We walked and walked too. David was a huge walker and told me that when he was down there with Jane he would get her to drive him ten or fifteen miles out from the house and then leave him to walk back. He offered this detail as something constructive, as I suppose it was, for him. But it struck me as being just one more thing his wife couldn't join him in. There were already his foreign research trips – from which, of course, I was currently benefitting – but there was also what he'd described as his daily routine at Hampstead. He wrote all through the morning, then passed his hand-written pages to Jane to type while he went off for whatever lunch and afternoon refreshments he'd arranged for himself, which were also currently to my benefit much of the time. I'd already concluded they had no sex life and, although David gave parties at the house and seemed to know a lot of people, he'd told me Jane didn't really like socialising. All in all, at this point I couldn't quite see what the marriage was *for*.

We went over to Sancreed again for lunch with Miller and Truscott and this time were joined by Miller's elderly but very sprightly mother, Reni. It was a nice, cheery, easy occasion. Real, instead of show.

There was evidence of building work at Tregiffian now. David showed me floor plans and talked about new wings. His aim was to have the house divide easily between all his sons and their families in the years to come. This wasn't really his place, he said, although only last month he'd expressly insisted it was. This place, he said, was for his sons. His place was really the chalet in Wengen.

Poop-poop!

'Do you ski?' he asked.

I confessed I did not.

'Really? Ah, well – you're no use to me if you don't ski. We could go there all the time if you did.'

He gave me another red box from S. J. Phillips. My Christmas present; a gold pendant, set with a delicate coral and lapis carving of Venus rising from the sea.

'It was something to do with a girl on a beach,' he said sweetly.

Next morning a tiny piece of history repeated itself when a wren needed rescuing in the kitchen. I did my wrangling act again and it co-operated like an old hand. Perhaps it was even the same bird and had flown down specially to deposit some more micro listening devices. Or perhaps it was simply that the living metaphor of imprisonment and escape accompanied David wherever he went.

At the end of my visit we took the train back to London together. As we sat across the little table from each other in first class, David announced that he had an idea for me. I heard this with a certain trepidation, with no clue to what he had in mind.

So, he asked after a careful pause, why didn't I help him with some research for the book?

Oh. In a million years I wouldn't have guessed that.

'I need you to find out about my dad,' he told me. 'There's a mass of stuff about his life that I don't know. Official stuff. The phoney businesses he started, the court cases when he was up on fraud charges, the slammers he was in when he got sent down. He agented for parliamentary candidates during the war. You got leave from the services to do it, you see. It was a good wheeze – I don't think he ever finished basic training. He had race horses, too, and knew radio and showbiz sorts. He entertained the Australian cricket team when they were on tour. Think about it and let me know. It might be fun and the pay will be excellent, though one of the terms of your contract will be that you are required to engage in frequent bouts of intensely inventive sex with your employer. And, of course, more seriously, it means I would give you a credit in my book. That could be quite a good qualification, if a girl decided she wanted to do more literary research afterwards.'

I said yes, it did sound fun (though privately I wasn't so sure) and I would think about it and let him know. David seemed pleased with my answer and looked contentedly out of the window as the West Country slipped away.

David's sister Charlotte lived somewhere south of the river and David picked me up from my flat in a cab. It was a long, slow journey in the evening traffic and on the way he informed me that Lady Docker had been found dead in her suite at the Great Western. Recalling how neglected the hotel had seemed, I wondered whether she might already have been dead when we stayed there. Then he told me that he'd visited his mother a couple of days earlier and asked her about her sex life with his father.

'She told you?' I asked, though whether I was more incredulous that David had asked her or she had answered him, I couldn't have said.

'Oh, yes.' David shifted to the county matron voice he always used for his mother. '"It was pure Krafft-Ebing, dear. Pure Krafft-Ebing."'

For once, my failure to ask a follow-up question was quite intentional.

For myself, I was in high good spirits; Cornwall had been wonderful, Cornwell had been wonderful. I anticipated an enjoyable evening ahead with David's sister, who had already expressed her approval of our relationship. But it didn't go like that. After an initial hello, Charlotte completely blanked me out. She had eyes only for David, wanted to talk only to David, make him listen to her problems and her family stuff. Seating me awkwardly at the head of the table, she sat down directly across from him, leaned forward on her elbows and talked intently to him for the rest of the night. It seemed like a deliberate snub at first, but I began to think she didn't know she was doing it. Had we been in a restaurant – and this was possibly why we weren't – unwitting diners would have picked Charlotte, not me, for the new girlfriend at our table. And yet, for all that, she didn't crack a smile once through the whole evening.

At one point Charlotte's infant daughter took herself out of bed and came downstairs. The girl's father, Charlotte's partner, actor Kenneth Cranham, hadn't joined us that night, most likely by deliberate design. The presence of her actual lover might have cramped Charlotte's unwholesome focus on her brother, who in any case had been less than complimentary about Cranham in the cab coming over. When she spotted the small figure at the foot of the stairs she quickly scolded her, saying sharply that it was long past her bedtime and she had no business getting up. David greeted the little girl with an odd fixed smile, a little like the Queen Mother accepting a posy.

'Hello, Nancy Grace,' he said. 'How are you?'

Nancy Grace didn't appear to recognise her uncle. Charlotte scooped her up and carried her back upstairs.

After the evening was over – whatever that evening *was* – we headed to Heathrow to spend the night at an airport hotel. David was leaving for Zurich again in the morning. More business with Rainer. In the cab he said scornfully, 'Charlotte has no idea how to present a face to children.'

I gave his remark no thought. I was just glad to be out of yet another Cornwell house full of deeply weird vibes.

He called from Switzerland the next evening to say he'd spoken to Charlotte and she'd told him how very much she liked me.

'She says you're lovely and that you have a gentle heart.'

That couldn't be right. I suspected he was making it up. But I was wrong.

With David's insistence on Moscow Rules, I'd told only a very few people about our relationship and those few I'd sworn to secrecy. One of them was a girlfriend I'd met when I was working as a researcher at Thames Television. She shared a flat with an actress whom I'd met briefly once or twice and unbeknownst to me, but arguably Exhibit B in the case for David's insistence on the perpetual need for cover, was a great chum of Charlotte's. Shortly after that supper, my friend rang me with a story. The flatmate had just taken a long call from Charlotte about her famous brother's new girlfriend and was astonished when she heard her give my name. She eagerly repeated everything to my friend – all of it really good – only to be put out to discover that she already knew all about it and hadn't said a word.

'I was sworn to secrecy,' my friend told her flatmate in her defence.

So David hadn't made it up. His sister actually did think well of me. Yet I'd spent a whole evening in her company feeling like I wasn't even in the room.

Next time he called from Zurich there had been an IRA bombing in London and he was concerned in case I'd been anywhere in the vicinity. I told him I hadn't and didn't know anyone who had.

'Well, I want you to keep safe, Our Sue, so just you stay away from all that.'

I wasn't sure how to implement his advice, but was touched that he'd instantly worried for my safety when he heard the item on the news.

A new spy series called *Chessgame*, based on novels by English author Anthony Price, had just started its run on ITV. (Along with the Bennett film, this was part of the ongoing vogue for espionage drama in the wake of the huge popular success of the BBC's two big Smiley series.) I hadn't watched it, but one review in particular had made me chuckle and I passed it along.

'They're saying it's like Smiley with sex,' I told David.

'Well,' he replied simply, 'that's what you've got.'

I also relayed the story about Charlotte, thinking he'd appreciate it as a funny little tale and be glad to hear that a friend of mine could be trusted with our secret. (As they all could. If I'd put them all in a room together and plied them with drink they still wouldn't have breathed a word even to each other.) But David's reaction was suddenly very clipped. He told me to wait by the phone and rang off. Ten minutes later he rang back, saying he'd called Charlotte 'to have words'.

'So *that's* all settled,' he said with a snort. I pictured him dusting himself off after the fray. 'Don't let anyone think I'm *cross* …'

He hadn't liked Charlotte spreading the good news. He must have sworn her to secrecy too.

Then it was nearly Christmas and school holidays. That meant radio silence till the New Year, David told me, using that exact phrase.

'But don't worry, my darling. Our love is singing.'

Just before the start of the holidays he called one last time.

'I've got a flat! I'll show it to you when I'm back – Happy Christmas! It's going to be a wonderful New Year – I promise!'

1984

St John's Wood

Mistress and wife can well supply his need,
A miss for pleasure, and a wife for breed.

John Gay

A man who has two women loses his soul.
But a man who has two houses loses his head.

Proverb (epigraph in *A Perfect Spy*)

The new flat wasn't quite finished by the start of the New Year, but David couldn't wait to show it to me anyway. He told me to meet him at the exit to the tube station at St John's Wood. I was to be there at four o'clock.

It was a cold gloomy day, not meant for hanging around outside, but as I came up the escalator to the street, digging my gloves out of my pockets and turning up my coat collar against the icy north London wind, David was waiting for me. There I was *at last*, he said, though it was only a couple of minutes past the hour. He'd been waiting for me *for ages*, why wasn't I here *hours ago*? He wasn't scolding me, I realised. He'd been waiting ahead of time because it was so important to him. There was exhilaration in his expression. He seemed oblivious to the whipping cold.

'So hurry up and come with me – I want you to see my new pad.'

This was why he'd directed me to come by tube, not a cab. He wanted to *take* me to his new place himself, not have me arrive at the door. We raced along hand in hand, David in high gear, and turned into a side road off the High Street, turning again into a small courtyard. Like so much of London at the time, it was 'under development'. It might once have been an old mews or a merchant's yard, but now it was new and spiffy and residential, almost college quad-looking. David unlocked an outer door to a stairwell, releasing the smell of fresh paint and plaster, and geed me up three flights to the apartment on the top floor.

'Here—!' he said, excitedly turning his latchkey and flinging the door wide. 'This is it—!'

Inside was even colder than outside. Our breath was fogging ahead of us as we went in. The flat was small and neat but an unfinished shell, sans heat, sans light, sans everything except painted walls and new carpet throughout. There was a narrow hall, with a bathroom to the right, a bedroom to the left, and five paces ahead lay the main area, an all-in-one living room and kitchen. The ceiling was high and sloping; dormer windows set into the front overlooked the street and skylights at the back gave a rooftop view over the courtyard. The whole place had plainly been an attic not so long before. Now, post-developers, it was David's new bolthole.

'You're the only one I'm ever going to let in here,' he declared and kissed me to set the seal on it. Within minutes we were lying on the factory-fresh wool twist, doing what we did best – better than anybody ever, even fully clothed in the tomb-like cold, overcoats and all – sending up steam that was visible in the hazy yellow light from the street-lamp outside.

'It's hard to imagine without you,' he told me as he locked up when we left.

A lunch date we made for a couple of days later became tea at my place instead. I said I was taking myself off to the States for ten days to see some friends and David made an only half-joking joke that he was sure it was to see my other lover, that *much older* fellow with *nothing like* his staying power. You're so good at guessing, I said, though he wasn't even close. He said he awarded me *a lot of Brownie points* for taking myself away like that, by which I understood he was tired of people waiting for him to tell them when to jump. (Not that he didn't like it when they deferred to him and asked how high ...) I gave him my best friend Barbara's phone number in New York as a contact. He stayed until very late, probably later than he'd intended now he knew I was going away.

Graham rang me the next day with some new titles for me to abridge. By the time I was back from the States he would have just left for two weeks in Wengen and he wanted me to have them done for his return. So I should probably make a start on the plane. He wished me a happy trip, then added as a cheery afterthought that he'd been driving along the King's Road the previous night and *saw a bloke coming out of your place at midnight.*

We were going to have to tell him, I realised; it wasn't right that he still didn't know.

I flew TWA to Boston Logan to meet up with Roger, a pal from Oxford who had moved Stateside. We hit the nearest supermarket and liquor store, piled the brown paper grocery sacks along with our stuff into the trunk of a rental and headed up to New Hampshire, where one of Roger's friends had lent him his ski lodge in the White Mountains. Mindful of David's only partially lighthearted remark that I was 'no use' to him if I couldn't ski, I'd decided it was time to learn.

Next morning I surrendered all dignity and joined a total beginners' class made up entirely of seven- and eight-year-olds. By lunch I was able to descend the barely discernible gradient on the green baby slope in a wide plough at about two miles an hour. By the end of the week Roger took me down the easiest of the grown-up slopes, so that I could say I'd done my very first blue run.

We celebrated as we'd always celebrated the end of exams, with – what else? – quantities of champagne. We were only half of our old Oxford foursome – Roger and his then girlfriend, me and my lovely Canadian – and instead of getting rowdy in Christ Church Meadows we were sitting modestly in swimsuits in the hot tub at the lodge, but it was a sweet moment nonetheless. As we chinked glasses Rog declared, 'The *gurrrl* dun *guuuhhd*,' in an excruciating John Wayne impersonation he had saved for the occasion. Then, reverting to best English, he added, 'This has to beat getting an alpha-plus in Anglo-Saxon, wouldn't you say?'

Not that I ever had, but he was so right.

I took the shuttle down to New York to spend the last two days of my stay with Barbara. We'd met on my first trip to North America in the summer before I went up to Oxford. Barbara was the Harvard room-mate of an American girl I'd become friends with at school and she'd insisted I come to stay with her in her NYC summer sublet – at the exalted address of 45 Fifth Avenue – so that she could show me the city. It was the beginning both of our beautiful lifelong friendship and, with Barbara as my guide, of my unshakeable love affair with New York. Barbara was a staff writer at *Time* magazine and lived with her (first) husband, a reporter on the *New York Post*, in an apartment on Horatio Street in Greenwich Village. As we hugged on my arrival, the first thing I saw over her shoulder was a vase of purple orchids on her dining table.

'They're from David,' she told me. 'They came yesterday. He called as well, a couple of days ago.'

'Did he ask where I was?'

'He did.'

'What did you say?'

Barbara shrugged. 'I told him you were out.'

'What did he say to that?'

'He wanted to know where.'

'Did you manage to put him off the scent?'

'Yeah. Kind of.'

'What did you tell him?'

Barbara shrugged again. 'I said you were at Bloomingdale's.'

Barbara's husband joined us for supper. He was a big le Carré fan, so we let him in on the secret.

'Wow,' he said, taking it in. 'Well, I know one thing. You must be a very special lady. And you're very lucky – 'cos he's the best.'

When I said that David had asked me to help him with the research for his new book – I was circumspect about the details – he gave me a further 'Wow' and continued to listen avidly as I passed on what I knew about the *Drummer Girl* movie. Basking in the vicarious admiration, I went on to say that David had also told me he thought I would make a good continuity girl in films. But that instantly triggered the city-desk reporter's bullshit sensor.

'I thought you had a *master's* degree from *Oxford*,' he said scornfully.

I was suitably chastened by his remark. It was only what I should have said to David at the time.

Back home after the overnight flight I heard the phone ringing as soon as I opened my front door. David was calling from Hampstead, starting with an urgent apology.

'I didn't mean to call you from here, but I couldn't wait. I never want to call you from here again.'

Did I have a good trip? Did I get the orchids? Had I finally done the decent thing and given up my other far inferior lover? Had I decided to do the Ronnie work? Would I let him fuck me soon and then again immediately afterwards?

Yes to all the above, I said, and heard him sigh with contentment.

I was to keep my passport handy then, he said, because we were going to Zurich the day after next. He'd have the spook travel agents send the plane tickets round by courier, with some of the folding stuff just because, and by the time we returned the flat would be ready.

'Then,' he declared, 'our new year can really begin.'

Soon after the tickets and money arrived there was another courier at my door. David had sent a couple of his sleeping pills to help me over my trans-Atlantic jetlag.

We stayed at the Dolder Grand, another one of David's magnificent *Schloss* hotels, set high on the Adlisberg and commanding a sweeping view down to the city and the lake beyond. As soon as we were in our room, I made him a present of my ski pass from the White Mountains, gift-wrapped in coloured tissue paper and ribbon.

'Oh, my *darling* – that's so wonderful, so absolutely wonderful,' he said, holding the little laminated card in his hands as though it had been a fragment of the rood. 'I adore you for doing that – my darling girl – I really do.'

Of all the people I have ever known – of all the people *you* have ever known, I guarantee – only David could make you feel so good about paying him his tribute. Only David could spoon-feed you with such tender and glowing appreciation that it made you want to please him all the more, just to have him spoon-feed you all over again.

And yet, even though he was being so lovely and was evidently so truly and deeply touched by what I'd done, some weasel suspicion at the back of my mind was already laying odds that he would never utter the word 'ski' in my presence again.

David was his best Swiss self for the whole trip, Zurich suiting him like the more stylish clothes he was wearing, the more attractive way he brushed his hair, the way his whole appearance seemed to flesh out in that country. For me, though the city was cold and stark and wintry, it spoke to my profoundly urban soul. There was a crisp elegance to the light, a pewtery sheen to the surface of the river, a reassuring historical solidity to the buildings that was a bulwark to the cold. If David had decided on the spot to leave Hampstead for this place, I would have moved there with him in a heartbeat.

He took me to meet Rainer at Mohrbooks on Klosbachstrasse. As we passed through the bustling corridors of the old building, Rainer appeared from his office, looking like a wise court adviser from a previous epoch; tall and spare, beautifully *soigné*, he was elegance and urbanity personified. He took my hand as David introduced me and bowed over it with the first and so far only '*gnädige Frau*' I have ever received. He had a particular smile for David – Miller had it too – that said they went way back and he knew it all. Several of the more senior female staff joined us – Swiss 'mothers', I couldn't help thinking, but on the second floor there, not the fifth – to say a cooing hello to David and to cast a smiling but 'we have to remember this for later' eye over me. One of them had a little dog with her which, at a rather wordy command in German from Rainer, promptly rolled over onto her back with her legs in the air, drawing oddly girlish giggles from the assembled staff. David translated for me.

'Rainer said, *Show them what the little ladies in the red-light district do—*'

The magic wand of money had been waved over the flat by the next time I was there, on a day that was positively beaming with unseasonal sunshine. (That darned pathetic fallacy.) In the intervening few weeks since our chilly but heated session on the carpet, the place had been plumbed in, wired up and fully furnished. The bathroom and kitchen were appointed in rather sail-boat scale, as the dimensions were tight, and the bedroom proved big enough to hold a double bed if it was wedged against one wall. In the main room a slouchy sofa and two armchairs were arranged around a coffee table under the skylight, while the space at the dormer window was entirely taken up by a large table for David to work at. (So large it had to be sawn in half to get it up the stairs and reconstituted *in situ.*) A whole team of fitters must have been tasked with perfecting this miniature Camp David and the last member of it was leaving as I arrived for lunch. He appeared to have been working on the front door.

The man promptly packed up his power drill and left, but David kept the door open once he'd gone, smiling proudly. I was supposed to notice something, I realised; the tilt of his chin tipped me off, but it didn't help me guess what he was so pleased with. A thousand guesses wouldn't have got me close.

'Bulletproof!' David declared happily and rapped his knuckles on the door, generating a hard metallic ring. 'Solid steel facing, a quarter-inch thick.'

There was a spyhole too – naturally – and when he shut us inside, the door closed with a heavy jailhouse clunk, which seemed to please him tremendously.

'By the way,' he said, undoing my blouse in the process of taking my coat, 'I didn't mention it, but you are going to spend the whole of the day and night here with me, aren't you? I bought a spare toothbrush.'

There was champagne along with caviar and other goodies chilling in the little fridge in the little kitchen, but it all had to wait while we christened the new area rug. After that we made a picnic on the rug and after that we needed to launch the bed. Then I lay with my head on the crook of David's arm while for the very first time he read me the pages that he'd written there that morning. He read to me in a softer tone than in the studio – Frenchie would have wanted to adjust his level – but with no less power to transport. I closed my eyes and let him take me on a magic carpet ride to Vienna, to spy on the shambles of the Pyms' diplomatic residence, whence his new hero Magnus had vanished overnight.

Afterwards, David began to tell me more of the story he was creating.

'So it starts with my guy disappearing. They fear the worst, of course. He's a diplomat – read spook – so they think he's defected. But he's really gone back to his roots to write his life down in a letter to his son. Rick, his old man, has died and he's just buried him. Now, suddenly, he feels free. The rules don't apply any more. He wants to tell it all, set down his life, now that he can. The life he had to lead because of Rick – what Rick made him into. It's a sort of atonement, but it's also his ticket out. So there's the story of his past as a baby spook and I want to wrap it round the story of his adult spook life and what they're doing to try and find him – what they turn up in the search.'

As with all our conversations, although I learned so much there was still so much more to know. But I didn't probe further. I knew David would read me the pages as they emerged, most likely as we were now, lying together in bed. It was thrilling – astounding, in fact – to be so close to the man and to his process as he created what he was determined should be his finest book yet. I asked whether he had a title. In Greece he'd said his initial idea had been *Agent Running in the Field* until Rainer pointed out that the word-play wouldn't work in the foreign editions.

'Yes,' David answered contentedly. 'Now I do. It's called *A Perfect Spy*. It's going to be wonderful, I think. Yes, I really think so. I'm finally writing the book I want to be buried with.'

This seemed to me to be a strange expression of satisfaction. But of course I knew nothing of how it must feel to have created a liter-ary legacy – beginning when he wasn't much older than I was then – such that your pen name became a byword for the real-world version of what was in your fiction. Graham Greene was the senior example of the ex-spook turned world-renowned novelist and 'Greeneland' was often used to describe the instantly identifiable doubt-ridden internal landscape of that writer's narrative. But no one ever said of a scenario in real life that it was 'just like a Graham Greene novel', as they so frequently did with le Carré. After *Tinker*

Tailor, David's own spook argot had entered the general vocabulary and you couldn't count the variants of his *The Spy Who Came in from the Cold* title that turned up in everything from Hollywood scripts to newspaper headlines. (For the first article ever written about this book, in fact – The Spy Who Came into the Bedroom; *Sunday Times*, 5 June 2022 – and there was a genius tabloid take on another of David's titles in 2016, when Taylor Swift was photographed in a surreptitious clinch with *The Night Manager* leading man Tom Hiddleston: TINKER TAYLOR SNOGS A SPY!) It all spoke to David's power to conjure such tangible authenticity in his writing. (Sisman, by the way, gives an entirely different origin story for the novel's title in his biography – which is not to say, given the nature of our subject, that either of us is wrong.)

I asked which of his books he considered the best to date, meaning the one which would have accompanied him into his casket up till then, and he seemed pleased that I'd joined him on this patch of his own psychological terrain. But, as was so often the case, he didn't quite answer the question.

'Well, we know which one is generally held to be the *worst*, don't we? That would be *The Navy and Sentimental*, wouldn't it?'

I chuckled at his own little twist in the title, something he often did with names. Waterstone's, the bookseller, was invariably Wasserstein; his publishers were Odders and Sodders.

'Have you read it?' he asked.

'No,' I confessed. I'd only reached *A Small Town in Germany* in my 'required reading'. 'Do you want me to?'

'You might like it if you did. It's a pretty little book. You know what it's about, don't you?'

A *ménage à trois*, I seemed to think, but I wanted David to tell me his own way.

'It was about my time with James Kennaway and his wife, Susan. He was this big Scottish brawler, a drinker, but a fine writer. *Tunes of Glory* was his big book. He wrote the screenplay, too; Guinness was in the film. After a while of knowing him, I realised he was trying to feed me his wife, just to watch the drama unfold …'

I watched his face as he revisited this landmark episode from his past. I could see he was giving me just the top notes while the full score played privately in his mind. As he lay on his back staring up at the bedroom ceiling, his amber-flecked eyes were seeing scenes projected there, his pupils wide black pools of memory despite the bright winter sun that was streaming into the bedroom. (This was the second time I observed his unlikely control over his autonomic nervous system, the first being the episode with the ice cube.)

'Susan wrote a memoir a few years ago,' he told me. '*The Kennaway Papers*. You might be interested in reading that too.'

No, I thought immediately; I didn't want to read an account of one of David's past affairs at this stage of ours. I did read it, of course, and Kennaway's own novel about their sparky threesome, which was his last publication before he died in a car crash and prophetically titled *Some Gorgeous Accident*. It was also the first of their three accounts to be published, though David didn't mention it.

My guess then – that David was revisiting moments from his love affair – was both right and wrong at the same time. He *was* recalling the love affair, but it was only once I'd read *The Naïve and Sentimental Lover* that I realised which of the Kennaways had left the deeper impression on his heart. David's self-hero Cassidy is a successful but unfulfilled manufacturer of advanced brake systems for prams (wonderfully Freudian, since David would leave his wife and three small children a couple of years after the affair). Cassidy encounters the uncompromising iconoclastic writer Shamus and his beautiful wife Helen as squatters in a dilapidated country 'pile' which Cassidy has designs to buy. The names of all three main characters are freighted with meaning. Shamus – the pulp-fiction moniker for a private detective – leads the hero on a riotous journey of self-discovery, helping him sleuth out the secrets of his desires. The name goes to 'sham' too; is he a true artist or just a convincing con-man, the book seems to ask. The mythically named Helen is the wife temporarily stolen from the mighty Agamemnon-Shamus by the young Cassidy-Paris and becomes the *casus belli* between them, when a snowy Swiss rooftop doubles for the gleaming towers of Ilium. Cassidy himself seems to be named for the single purpose of attaching the prefix of his Wild West namesake – Butch. Shamus makes the connection suggestively, calling Cassidy 'lover' and drunkenly claiming them to be 'a pair of pooves' in their new friendship. But there is the hero's first name, too – Aldo. Did David want us to hear 'All-dough' for the rich businessman? Or just 'all dough', no hyphen, because Cassidy is still unbaked, soft in the middle, and in need of the leavening belief that Shamus – not to mention the mysterious Flaherty – will provide?

There are always so many possible interpretations with everything David wrote and even now, I still find myself trying to catch them all. Later in their Quixotic adventures – with Cassidy hopping along as the faithful Sancho Panza beside Shamus's delusional Don – the new friends register in a Parisian hotel under the names of two actual spook 'pooves', Burgess and Maclean. Despite the absolute straightness of both characters, it *is* a love affair. Cassidy loves Shamus with a kind of febrile schoolboy passion, as an idolised older chap in a senior year who models all the dash and daring and iron-clad certainties that he himself has yet to embrace. Next to this, his relationship with Helen barely registers. It was as though David had embarked on the affair with Susan as a proxy for her husband; not in any suppressed homosexual way, despite the jokes, but in order to please his idolised 'lover', James, who simply dared him to do it. It became my view that, when Kennaway died, David subsumed certain aspects of his freer, bolder friend, who had shown him how to live on a different level, how to loosen the shackles of a system run by the Gerrards Crossers of the world.

While David never attempted his late friend's level of womanising – at least no more than briefly after his divorce – it was really only after *l'affaire Kennaway* that he began to allow himself 'other Susans' (in Sisman's cute phrase). In his biography *James and Jim*, Trevor Royle claims Kennaway had a 'violent hatred of reviews and critics'. David adopted this attitude himself. Kennaway claimed a German soul, a Recording Angel and called his children his 'babies', no matter their age. David made these, and many other Jim-isms, his own. And finally, just as Kennaway had always done, he learned to put his writing first and foremost, above all other considerations, no matter the damage and disappointment this caused to others. It was as if there had been a psychological estate sale after the Scottish writer's death – subliminally suggested by the old house in the opening scene of *The Navy and Sentimental* – and David bought up the heritage pieces. Kennaway seems prescient of this, too, in *Some Gorgeous Accident*, calling his own character Link; a man who connects his David character, the faithful and socially obedient Richard David Fiddes (so – *Dick*), to his undiscovered freer self. Kennaway's Fiddes is a doctor in a maternity hospital, what's more, delivering babies for what, in David's book, will be the accessorised prams of Cassidy's business success. Their shared woman is called simply Susie.

Did David adopt these aspects of Kennaway's character deliberately, consciously? Or was it rather an organic assimilation for survival, the way a foetus will sometimes absorb the material of its less viable twin *in utero*? Something of the unconscious rebirthing process is indicated when Cassidy first arrives at the ancient pile, along a dark narrow lane – in the 'businessman's womb' of his Bentley! – mistakenly believing it to be Shamus's ancestral home and wanting to make its history his own, which, at the close of his expansive adventures with Shamus, he actually does. Again, I wonder how conscious David was of his own imagery. I only wish I'd seen all this at the time and had been able to ask him.

If Ronnie's criminality had frightened David into becoming a dutiful servant of the system, albeit the clandestine section of it, then Kennaway's own lawless example showed him how he could escape the whole thing, break all the rules and still stay legit – as an artist, who only ever had to be true to himself. *The Navy and Sentimental* was a tribute to the man who not only loaned him his wife for a few months, but threw in a fresh lease on life for his 'lover' as part of the deal.

I came to see that the success of *Tinker Tailor* was also due, indirectly, to Kennaway's influence. David must have realised that he had followed Kennaway's literary example too closely in *The Naïve and Sentimental Lover*. His embrace of the Scotsman's impressionistic, at times phantasmagorical, style, while producing 'a pretty little book', had fallen largely flat with readers and critics alike. In the face of his first public thrashing, he reined himself in, harnessed the best of his own native powers and finally wrote a book that fulfilled and even exceeded the literary promise of *The Spy Who Came in from the Cold*.

'Jim always claimed he wouldn't live past forty,' David continued as we lay there. 'Six months after his fortieth he was driving home and had a head-on collision with another vehicle. They found him dead at the wheel.'

'Was it suicide?'

'They thought so, of course. But the post-mortem showed he'd had a massive heart attack. He was dead before impact. But I just wasn't supposed to change tack like that.' He'd gone back to his own book of the affair. 'The critics had a field day. I think my readers felt a little lost, too, at the sudden shift in direction.'

I asked if that was feedback from fan mail and book signings.

'I don't do signings,' he said flatly.

'Why not? Your readers love you, don't they?'

'They do. In great numbers. Sodders are always trying to get me to do them. Press the flesh. Talk.'

'So why don't you?'

'It's just not me.'

Like a knighthood. Or the Nobel.

'They write to me, though, my readers. And I reply if I can.'

'Do you get a lot of letters?'

'Mmm. Quite a lot. Sackfuls sometimes.'

That tone of *Weltschmerz* I hadn't heard for a while had crept back into his voice. The demands of others weighing on him.

'Do you like getting the letters,' I asked, 'or would you rather do without?'

'Well, some of them can lift your heart, it's true.' He launched into his Essex housewife voice, a prim nasal pitch with estuary vowels. *Dear Mr le Carré, I just had to write and tell you that I consider you to be one of the finest authors of the twentieth century ...*

'That must be gratifying,' I said. But it wasn't his voice for unqualified praise; something dismissive was coming.

'Oh, yes,' he conceded. 'Until they go on to say,' reverting to the voice, *and I put you right up there with that other great English writer, Frederick Forswyth.*

'I take your point,' I said, chuckling at the deft insult and another little twist in a name. 'Do you know him?'

'Who, Forswyth? No. Can't say I've had that pleasure.'

After that, David declared we needed to get some air and so we went for an 'explore' of the new neighbourhood while it was still daylight.

'Everything your Jewish mother's heart could desire,' he commented, as we passed the delis, bakeries, *chocolatiers*, florists, jewellers and beauty salons that lined St John's Wood High Street. There was a French restaurant called Au Bois and a Chinese one called The Fortuna, both within crawling distance of the flat.

'I think we'll make the Chinese our new local,' David said.

And so, that evening – after we'd returned to the flat to anoint the new and, I trusted, newly Scotchgarded sofa, then bathed and dressed – we did.

'It's really The Nova Fortuna,' he told me as we went inside. 'For us, anyway.'

Considering the neighbourhood, it turned out to be a pleasantly unassuming place, quietly busy, with nice lighting and lots of plants. As we sat with our menus, David said how wonderful it was to be free, to have finally escaped.

'No one knows us here,' he said with a sigh of real relief. 'It feels like sanctuary at last.'

I was happy, of course – happy that he was happy and that *we* were, too, which wasn't always the same thing. But I was sorry as well, that this wonderful man could only see freedom in the qualified terms of escaping without detection. The schoolboy revelling in sneaking out of the boarding school dorm at night, as long as he knew he could make it back before register in the morning. I hoped in time – after more times like these – that he'd be able to come to a different understanding. That he'd see being free as simply that – an essential state of *being*.

But he ought to have known he was tempting Fortuna herself with that last statement about no one knowing us. Like a fast sketch Jeremy might have written for *Laugh-In*, our New Fortune turned into the Fickle Finger of Fate before we'd had time to give our orders. David had been doing his usual room-scanning over the top of his menu when he suddenly gave a whispered exclamation.

'*Christ— it's Freddie!*'

I looked up and, sure enough, there was Frederick Forsyth. (It was a couple of years before they made *Beetlejuice*, so David wasn't to know, but I think he'd said his name too many times at the flat.) He and his wife Carrie had just walked in and were being warmly greeted by the smiling Chinese maître d'.

'And he's just clocked me,' David added, setting down his menu. 'This should be interesting—'

(Before I label this Exhibit C in the case for cover, I feel I should point out that if David hadn't been sitting so that he could scan the entrance, Freddie would probably never have noticed him. There was a self-perpetuating component to his paranoia.)

'*Good Lord!!*' boomed the unmistakable phoney-colonel voice across the restaurant, as the author of *The Day of the Jackal* (and the rest) made a beeline for our table. 'David, old man – we meet at *last!*'

A general stir rose up in the restaurant. Forswyth – as he shall forever be known – was making such a big thing of the encounter that other diners were turning to stare. The previously imperturbable proprietor clearly had no idea who David was, but, because he knew who Freddie was and Freddie obviously knew who David was, he was getting himself into a flap. He had his entire staff hovering around in case the flag should go up for a table for four, which would have taken some serious manoeuvring since their table for two was on the other side of the dining room from ours and there wasn't another bigger one that was free.

Somewhere in the midst of it all I wasn't quite introduced, but it didn't appear to matter. Freddie was all for David and Carrie was all for me, saying that she was *so* pleased to meet me and *whatever* brought us *here* to *their* local?

Eventually they moved to their own table and things settled down. David picked up his menu again – we still hadn't ordered – and whispered to me around one corner.

'What's the betting they ask us over to their table for coffee and then back to their *Schloss* for brandy and liqueurs afterwards?'

Chez Forswyth was a Spanish-style villa in one of the lusher St John's Wood avenues and Freddie and Carrie were very proud of it. They hadn't had the house for very long and were thrilled to ribbons to be entertaining the Great Man within its white stuccoed walls. They seemed pretty thrilled to be entertaining me, too, which didn't make sense at first, but after a few minutes the reason became clear.

'Brandy, David?' Freddie asked at the drinks trolley.

'Thanks,' he said.

'What about you, Jane?'

'Just a small one,' I replied.

Freddie declared he wanted to pump David on his views regarding the state of the world's secret services, though from the way their conversation progressed it was apparent that what he actually wanted was to expatiate on his own views now that he had the acknowledged master of the field cornered in his living room. David paid out his subtle give-them-what-they-eat line, tossing in the occasional 'oh, yes' and 'well, quite' to chum the water and keep Forswyth thrashing around. From the passionate flush on Freddie's face and the intense animation in his manner, it was clear this was the best audience – in almost the Papal sense – that he'd ever had.

Carrie, meanwhile, wanted me to tell her *everything about your lovely house in Cornwall*. It was all I could do to stop myself from inviting them down.

We stayed about three-quarters of an hour. David had it nicely timed; long enough to be sociable, but not so long as to induce the belief that he wanted to become pals. Before we left, Freddie presented him with a spiffy edition of his latest tome, which he signed specially. It was then I noticed that the only books in evidence anywhere in the house were those written by its owner. On our way out, the happy couple gave us a tour of their wintry garden, making sure that we noticed the kidney-shaped outdoor pool.

Next morning as we were leaving the flat, David told me how pleased he was that I'd decided to do the research on his father.

'It'll be wonderful having you on the inside of the book with me,' he said.

Things had been going so well since the second Cornish visit – there had even been a third good one over the New Year – that I was beginning to agree. He seemed to have found the right arrangement of things in his head. A new and better balance of all the warring parts.

'I want you to have these too,' he said, and handed me a set of keys.

I wasn't expecting that – the handing-over of access to the new place – and his lack of ceremony as he did it was very telling. I understood instantly that it wasn't the practical gesture that was of consequence. He was making a symbolic gesture to show how much he trusted me; how much he trusted me not to betray his trust. And it was as if he might be beginning to see the logic of meeting in the middle instead of planning a great escape, with each of us just keeping mostly to our own corners while enjoying the good times in some clear space between.

As he walked me down the High Street for a cab, David pulled us into one of the shops – Georgie's, a *chocolatier*-cum-florist – saying that a girl needed some provisions to take home with her. When we came out I was carrying a vast bunch of freesias and a large beribboned box of fresh-cream truffles.

'I've been thinking,' he said, as we walked along again. 'Would a girl like a little cottage in Cornwall so as to be handy for her lover? And maybe a starter-kit car to get her there? A *deux chevaux*, perhaps, and driving lessons to go with it? Think about it, my darling – I'll call you.'

He hailed a cab, kissed me deeply as it drew up, put me and my goodies inside and prepaid the driver excessively for the journey ahead.

Going home, with my flowers in my arms and my truffles on my knee and the keys to the new flat in my pocket, I did think about it. But not for long. David was always generous with his money, as I hope I've shown. I loved him for it and for thinking about me in that way. But frankly, sometimes he didn't have a single wire earthing him to the ground. I was all for meeting in the fresh territory of St John's Wood. But adding another bolthole in Cornwall was an unnecessary complication. That he'd be able to slip away to see me when he was down there would have been fine – *when* he was down there. But in the few months we'd been conducting our affair I'd already seen how erratic David's comings and goings were. I should forever have been trailing up and down the motorway in his tracks, arriving at one end only to find his plans had changed and he was heading off to the other. He would probably have turned it into my fault too, however sweetly he might have phrased the rebuke, if I wasn't in the right place at the right time. It wasn't as though I liked the area or relished the idea of getting to know the natives in St Buryan, who had made such excellent extras in *Straw Dogs* … How long did he think it would be before the beady-eyed locals caught on and realised where their famous neighbour had stashed his bit on the side? How long before someone told someone who told his wife?

Oh, and – Christ Almighty – just imagine if I were ever stuck down there by myself and Tangye got wind of it!

Thinking it through further, as the cab carried me home, I also began to be a tiny bit peeved that David could picture me in a Citroën *deux chevaux*. I was no longer a student, when that type of car might have been acceptable. All I'd had at Oxford was my old sit-up-and-beg pushbike, with a wicker basket in front and no gears. Having one of those motorised sardine-cans then might have been pretty neat. But a 2CV now? Really? How did that fit into the fantasy of his dream girl on the beach? Smiley's Ann wouldn't have been seen dead in one.

By the time I got home I knew I was going to decline David's generous but nonetheless looney-tunes offer. I only wished I could have been enough of a tart to ask for a Chelsea flat and a Golf GTI instead.

Audience of One

'This is our place, my darling,' David told me on virtually every occasion we were at the flat. I wasn't going to commit the folly of believing there was any true substance to the claim; I'd already seen how mutable the definition of 'his place' was and doubted 'our place' was a declaration of any firmer conviction. But I liked to hear him say it, all the same. I saw it as a sign he was still taking steps towards a freer, easier and less encumbered existence than the one in which he was currently, by his own phrase, 'banged up'. Whether he managed to achieve it by staying married or getting divorced didn't matter to me, I just wanted him to find a way. Not that the problem was a quadratic equation or three-dimensional chess, but the straightforward approach seemed to escape him, even though he'd availed himself of the solution once before.

Nevertheless, the encounters at 'our place' began to develop a sort of regularised irregularity. We would meet often, but almost never without one or two dates being cancelled or re-arranged before we got one that stuck. Could I make it for a late lunch tomorrow? he would call to ask, after saying the day before that he couldn't see me again for the rest of the week. Next morning there'd be a courier at my door bearing a big bouquet from Georgie's with a tender handwritten note cancelling. Then I'd get a phone call the same evening, telling me how wonderful I was and how about an overnight the day after that? Sometimes, with no notice at all, flowers would arrive first thing with a card that read, *Fancy caviar and a fuck at 12.30?*

This erratic on-off-on scheduling caused me a kind of semi-permanent background anxiety as I grew to anticipate it. *Would* I be seeing him on the next date he'd given me? Would it *hurt* as much as last time if, at the very last minute, I didn't? Would I still believe him the next time and could I stand the disappointment *again*? This teetering on the edge of things was counterweighted by the wonderfully restorative order of events whenever we did meet. One thing fed energy into the other. David made every bottle of perfectly chilled Krug and every tin of caviar seem like a first, for him as much as for me. Our on-the-rug picnics were a smorgasbord of deli delights. Then there were the surprise trinkets – invariably period pieces, though not always from Phillips – and so many other gifts besides, each ascribed a special significance and each presented with a sort of worshipful awe that I should keep offering myself to him as much as I did and permit him to love me as much as he did and let him spoil me absolutely as much as he wanted. And over everything was the ever-flowing wellspring of intoxicating, head-turning blandishments and praise, followed by the limitless desire driving the overwhelming sex. I loved and adored David completely and utterly, ached for him whenever he was away. Yet somehow he was always able to find ways to make me love and adore him even more when I was with him, to build me up again after he had previously let me down.

If you remove the element of sex (perhaps, in certain cases, even if you don't), this may also have been how an agent, a Joe, was run. Normalising the otherwise irregular meetings of the covert relationship. Ensuring the continued acceptance of uncertain terms and clandestine conditions by offering treats and praise and the promise of great future reward, creating dependency along the way, instilling the belief that such means were the only way to the glorious ends. In short, by turning the hazardous secret meetings into encounters of irresistible seduction. It became my lingering suspicion that David was running me. Even when I wasn't physically with him, I could still feel his control.

With the book fully underway, there was always also his reading me his latest pages after sex – or, more often than not, between bouts. Lying in bed or on the rug, my head on the crook of his arm, I would listen to his voice as he made me his audience of one – and the seduction would be complete. I knew there were only two other people in the world – his best friend Miller and his wife – who were given access to these early pages, who had the extraordinary privilege of knowing what the next le Carré novel was about. But David read the pages he wrote here to me first, before anybody, with the pale blue ink of his handwriting barely dry on the paper. His own satisfaction after he finished reading was much the same as after sex. He would lie back, replete and spent, his arms flung out, his ankles elegantly crossed. Only David could relax so contentedly in a pose of crucifixion.

Giving me the keys to the flat as a gesture of trust didn't mean he left it at that. He started testing me, fine-tuning the level of trust. If I arrived while he'd stepped out to get something from the High Street, as sometimes happened, he would have left his papers turned face-down on his table and arranged in such a way – only seemingly at random – so that he would know instantly if I'd turned them over to look at them. I wonder now whether he left the flat deliberately on those occasions, in order to expose me to the temptation. He would have Pym do the same thing in the novel, to catch his wife out when they're staying in their little brown house in Plomari (which of course was ours). But it wasn't any temptation since I knew David would read me whatever he wrote. (He'd already shown me the next most interesting items he kept in the flat: his collection of current passports, two dark blue British ones and three or four others in different colours, all in his own name.) But he couldn't seem to resist setting the trap, as if checking to see what bits of his own tradecraft I'd acquired in the course of our association. Perhaps too, since I had the keys and he was so often away, he hunted for traces of my 'other, far inferior lover' there, the one who nagged at his suspicions while existing purely in his imagination. That guy was always 'far older' in David's only half-joking remarks. I think the spectre of a younger competitor was too real for him to articulate. *I'd know if you ever took anyone else while you're with me,* he'd assured me in a smiling, sweet-spoken warning over a restaurant table on our last Swiss trip.

Being the secret mistress of the world's foremost espionage novelist and former spy may naturally have coloured my vision in all this. Perhaps my imagination outran the facts. Perhaps, back at my own flat, I was only imagining the strange new buzz on my telephone line whenever I picked up the receiver. But if it wasn't my imagination then it was something more serious than another test from David. It would be Special Branch with a Home Office warrant authorising a wire-tap.

We talked about a lot of stuff at the flat, nearly all David stuff, naturally, which meant Ronnie stuff too. He gave me pointers about where to look as I embarked on the research, though sometimes they were just random moments from his father's life, whatever rackety episode was uppermost in his mind as he reincarnated the relentless conman who had so dominated his life – even ten years after his death from a heart attack while watching a cricket match on television – as the central rogue in his autobiographical novel.

I'd already brought him a selection of father–son memoirs, titles he hadn't read and said were helpful. The Gosse was chief among them, of course, and the Ackerley. An American one, *The Duke of Deception*, also went down well and he even liked Susan Cheever's father-daughter *Home Before Dark*. Now I set out to find everything I could about Ronnie and brought each new discovery to the flat. There were the court proceedings and convictions, the bogus companies and the bankruptcies. There were the wartime by-elections where Ronnie agented for candidates, his 'wheeze', as David called it, to get out of the army – William Douglas Home, the playwright and brother of the former PM, was one of them – and there was the 1950 general election where Ronnie had stood as a candidate himself in Yarmouth. There were the neverwozzers whose every race entry was helpfully recorded at the Jockey Club, along with Ronnie's racing colours and occasional prize money. There were the bulging files neatly stacked and available for photocopying in the cuttings libraries at the *Mirror* and *Evening Standard* and *Express*, and there were the chilly neglected vaults of local newspapers in Bournemouth and Yarmouth and Poole, with no photocopiers and hardly even chairs, where I had to pore over fusty old bound broadsheets to find glimpses of Ronnie's name and make endless longhand copy.

I wrote letters to anyone who might have tales to tell. Two cricketers from the Australian touring team that Ronnie had entertained at the house, Donald Bradman and Keith Miller, were among my respondents. Bradman – the Don – replied in a courteous letter that he remembered the garden party, while Miller, to whom Ronnie had lent money, left a hasty message on my answering machine to say that he had nothing to tell me. Gordon Richards, the Queen Mother's favourite jockey, who'd advised Ronnie on the purchase of a questionable nag, didn't reply at all. There were mentions of Ronnie in various old celebrity memoirs. One was by Douglas Home, who invited me to talk to him at his London flat. 'Honest as the day', was how Ronnie had seemed to him and he said his agenting efforts were wholly responsible for how well he'd done in his losing campaign against a fellow Old Etonian army officer. 'I shouldn't have got ten votes without him,' he told me cheerily at the recollection. 'As it was, it was nearer ten thousand.' Joe Davis, the snooker champion, had written about Ronnie's legendary ski-season parties in the Swiss Alps and the Cornwell Cup he donated for curling. Ronnie's old school in Dorset regretfully informed me that, between a fire and relocation to new premises, all their records for the years of his attendance had been lost. It crossed my mind that Ronnie had started the fire himself. Finally, there were the records of his birth, his marriages – to Olive, Jean and Joy – his divorces and his death. The only details that completely evaded me were of his service record during the war. Ronnie's 'wheeze', of by-election agenting to get out of basic training, had served him well. The Army Records Office said they were unable to find any listing for an R. T. A. Cornwell in their files. David was thrilled with every item I brought him. Howard Carter could not have taken more delight in the treasures of the pharaoh's tomb. Ronnie was coming to life again before his eyes, his life story playing out like a movie in his son's head. But considering how much damage and mayhem he'd caused, the Ronnie movie didn't appear to be a serious drama, rather a mash-up of old British comedies and crime capers. Ronnie might have been the hapless Will Hay, falling foul of the law but intending no harm; or Alec Guinness in *The Card*, a clever deceiver climbing the social scale on the gullibility of others. (David called the town Gulsworth where Rick stands for election.) Once Ronnie was established in top-notch Mayfair, he seemed to become an amalgam of well-spoken schemers like Jack Hawkins and Nigel Patrick in *The League of Gentlemen*. And when he was banged up to do his time, with his adoring 'lovelies' and devoted old mother waiting for him on the outside, he morphed into Peter Sellers' irrepressible Dodger Lane, driving Lionel Jeffries' Prison Officer Crout into teeth-gnashing comic fury. David's face would light up as he read the material, sometimes even laughing out loud. In the Ronnie movie it didn't seem to matter how many pratfalls the supporting cast had to take, though in real life they frequently sustained lasting financial injury; Ronnie was his son's indefatigable leading man, who always managed to carry on regardless to the next reel. I knew there were other episodes that played in David's mind, he'd told me of some of them – dark haunting scenes from his childhood, of abuse and depravity and torment from the truly appalling man who was his father. But for his present need to turn that monster into Rick Pym, the terrible but lovable rogue of his new book, David had to summon up all the smiles and laughs he could.

Soon after bringing him these files, sometimes only the next day, I'd hear the old details revivified on the new pages as David applied the subtle alchemy of his craft to the historical evidence. It had taken him his whole lifetime to reach the point where he could use it to safely transform Ronnie into Rick.

Raymond Chandler once wrote of wife-murdering physician Hawley Crippen that even after reading all about the case he somehow couldn't help liking the guy. It seemed to be that way with Ronnie. But for all that his powerful bully-boy charm had a half-life glow that still radiated through the tales, he was a terrible man nonetheless.

As the material began to mount up, files and files of it, David surprised me with another suggestion: *Why didn't I go the whole hog and write his father's biography?* He said he would ensure I had free access to everyone who could help me get the full picture of Ronnie. He said he believed I could do it and that he thought it would be a really good idea. It sounded at first like a big leap, but I gradually began to wonder whether I might be up to it. Ronnie was already an inescapable presence, not just in the research but also in the singular experience of being so close to David as he spun his new fiction around him. I would have David himself, of course – not to say le Carré – to guide me through the process, the sort of one-to-one support a first-time writer could only dream of. It was a unique, once-in-a-lifetime opportunity and I agreed to give it some serious consideration. I came up with a title, *Hitch Your Wagon to This Star: The Riotous Life & Ruinous Times of Ronald Cornwell* – sometimes the life was ruinous and the times riotous, I could never quite decide – and set about drawing up an outline, to try and nail all the angles. The main one that gave me pause was how to acquire so much of the lives of both Cornwells, *père et fils*, in my head – with the *fils* also in my heart – and not obliterate my own existence in the process. But I was going to try and nail that angle too.

*   *   *

David must genuinely have felt what he claimed about the flat, that it was a sanctuary, because he began to talk more freely than ever when we were there. The current book required him to revisit his childhood, though the memories were so seared into him that I began to think it had never been very far from his thoughts. But he'd made his hero an only child and couldn't include some of the most poignant tales he told me. How his brother Tony, who was only two years older, had tried to look after him when they were both motherless little boys. How Tony had actually told him that he would be his mother, to try and make things better. How they were first sent away together to pre-prep boarding school, but Tony soon had to go to another school for older boys, some small distance away. How they would write to each other and arrange to meet at a place halfway between.

'We'd each cycle there,' David said to me, 'just to meet up in a field to hug each other and cry …'

He also spoke about his past loves. I'd wondered before if there was anyone else he'd opened up to on this subject. I hoped there had been, most likely someone in the inner circle he'd introduced me to. But since he was lying naked with me in his own private safe house, I think David may yet have been most open with me, there. It was in one of these moments that he asked me if it was safe to love me, because he'd never before let anyone '*this far in*'. It was undeniable in so many ways, but it still didn't mean he ever gave me the full story, about anyone or anything.

With the publication of the paperback edition of *The Little Drummer Girl* and the first anniversary of the Beirut embassy bombing both approaching, he spoke again about Janet Stevens. George Roy Hill was talking about dedicating the film to her, which David found exasperating, not least when Jane got wind of it.

'George Roy hadn't considered the larger problem, you see. Jane assumed there had to be a reason beyond the book. *Were you her lover?* she asked me.'

'What did you say?'

'I denied her utterly, of course.'

But he couldn't deny the relationship to himself. He told me again how he'd gone to the States for her funeral, how wretched it had been. What wasn't clear to me was how he'd presented himself there at the time. I couldn't think he'd told her family the truth of their relationship. It would most likely have distressed them more if he had, and it wasn't in his nature to do so anyway. He must have passed himself off as someone who'd known Janet as a friend, a colleague in the field, one among several who were lost in the bombing. But even though I knew he had genuinely mourned her, it seemed to me rather indulgent of him, even a little selfish, to have attended the funeral dishonestly – as it were, under a false flag. Once again, it didn't seem the moment to ask for clarification and it was almost another quarter century before I discovered the true reason behind his needing to be there and what really made the months afterwards such a 'rough summer' for him.

In 2007, after reading a news item marking the twenty-fifth anniversary of the Sabra and Shatila massacre, I googled Janet Stevens. I hadn't thought of her name since last seeing David a few years previously and wondered idly whether anything had emerged to link her story to him. It appeared that something had, just one small detail.

The first result to come up was an open letter from an American academic and civil rights lawyer named Franklin Lamb. It was posted on the Palestinian Chronicle website and was written as if to Janet herself. Lamb recalled her life, work and death and – so it seemed to me – was using the letter to set the record straight. A fellow Palestinian rights activist, he had apparently been on his way to join Janet in Beirut when the explosion occurred. They had last spoken when he'd called her the night before and were looking forward to seeing each other. They were very evidently a couple; other articles gave Lamb as her husband, though he didn't explicitly say. But he did say that Janet was pregnant when she died, with a son. Lamb named him Clyde Chester Lamb III.

David must have known these details. How could he not? But he didn't tell me. And it wasn't like him to miss the chance to talk about the poignancy of things, to say what a wonderful mother she would have been, how her family suffered two losses in one, compounding their grief at the funeral. Yet he didn't say a word – and his silence on the subject was the dog that didn't bark in the night. David knew, I think, or sincerely believed, that it wasn't Lamb's son who had died with her. That was why he'd attended the funeral. He was being a good soldier under his false flag.

It seemed that Lamb had been on his way to see Janet in Beirut while David was waiting for her in Larnaca. Exactly how Janet had been running her two lovers for those last few months of her life was lost to the explosion. Neither man saw her alive again – though Lamb had to identify her body in the hospital morgue – but they would meet each other at her funeral, when she was buried with her unborn son. It was a storyline that John le Carré himself might have devised and yet another fractal episode in David's life. It illustrated in the most terrible way how all the layers of secrecy and duplicity were the only way for him to maintain all the moving parts within himself, the self that from his earliest years and ever afterwards had to be divided between competing loyalties and hidden loves.

That small connecting detail: Lamb wrote at the end of his letter that he'd recently spoken with some Palestinian refugees who had known Janet. He said they remembered her dearly and still called her 'our little drummer girl'. I'd always understood that David's title was chosen before he went back to Lebanon at the end of '82, before he met Janet, but Lamb made it sound as if the soubriquet had originated in the camps, among the refugees who knew and loved her. Whichever was the case, the novel had no particular currency by that time, so I was left to wonder why Lamb had revived the title, with its implicit association, for the whole world of online readers and possibly David himself to see. Was it to finally claim back the twice-promised girl from her famous lover? Or was it a nod of acknowledgement to him and to his secret relationship with Janet, as she herself might have wished to make?

Life imitating Art – Art imitating Life. With David, there was simply no other reality.

He also told me about Yvette Pierpaoli. She was a French aid worker he met in Phnom Penh in 1974, when he was undertaking research for *The Honourable Schoolboy* (and while Jane, whom he'd recently married, was in England with their infant son.) David told me what the sex had been like with Yvette, though I hadn't indicated I wanted to know. His account came with a French accent.

'Eet was vey queek wiz 'ehr, n'est ce pas? Just go, do, oui? *Va, va, va – ooof!!*'

He couldn't have realised it, but for emphasis he made the same '*Boom*' gesture with his hands that he'd used when he first told me about Janet being killed in the embassy bombing.

He told me how he admired Yvette for her ceaseless work with refugees, children for the most part, in conflict zones around the world.

'She needs to be needed, you see.'

She was still a good friend now, he said, adding the surprising detail – surprising to me, at least; David seemed to see it as quite natural – that she often visited him and Jane and particularly liked to go down to Tregiffian. I thought instantly of our last night on the island, when he'd suggested we call it a day and just stay friends. I'd stood my ground and refused, but it must have been what he'd done successfully with Yvette; 'turned her', to apply the spook term.

'Does Jane know?' I asked. 'About you and Yvette?'

'No, naturally,' he replied, as though it were a perfectly brainless question, which I suppose it was. I already knew the First Rule of

Spy Club: *DENY EVERYTHING*. By this point in our relationship I'd already asked him what he would do if Jane ever found out about us and he'd replied with exactly the same formula he'd used when she actually had challenged him about Janet: 'I'd deny you – I'd deny you utterly.' But he added pleasantly, 'I might introduce you to Yvette next time she's over.'

I nodded vaguely, wondering how he'd react if I declined the introduction. Much as it seemed to have given my ex-spook lover great satisfaction to relate intimate details of his prior secret love life as we lay there in his new safe house, I wasn't sure how he thought I benefitted from the intelligence briefing. But aside from his two wives – of whom he never spoke in such terms – Janet, Yvette before her and Susan Kennaway before either of them, had been the most important past loves of his life. I was the current one and David had already told me I was the last.

I'd imagined we would have wide-ranging conversations about other writers, about literature and writing in general, as we'd begun to do in Greece, but David never really ventured beyond a few general observations. I understood that he didn't read other fiction while he was writing, but he didn't seem to want to say much on the topic at all. When I asked his views on contemporary authors, he responded with a mildly despairing shrug.

'There's just nobody out there. That's why this book has to be my best, you see. I've only my own act to beat.'

I felt I had to single out Greene, the senior ex-spook novelist who was still writing and who also had a multi-layered love life. Surely David had views on him?

'Well, one reads him, of course,' he said. 'But the thing one finds is that no single work really deserves the praise heaped upon the canon. But he speaks of the chip of ice in every writer's heart. He got that right.'

He evidently didn't want to discuss the Greene mistresses, the Greene affairs, or even the Greene novel that was about one of them. But then he hadn't wanted to discuss *Zelig* either. He didn't seem to see – or didn't want to see – reflections of himself and his concerns in other men's work. He hadn't even mentioned Kennaway's novel about their own conjoined affair.

But I wasn't ready to give up. With living writers regretfully but nevertheless summarily dismissed, I asked which ones he admired from history. His reply was only a little less measured, though when the select few names emerged – Ford, Conrad, Mann, Schiller – it was my turn to exit the subject. Mann to me was only the Visconti film of *Death in Venice* and a vague memory of reading an English translation. For Schiller, though I could have offered the *University Challenge* clever-clogs answer of 'chief figure in the *Sturm-und-Drang* movement of German Lit.', his works too were completely unknown to me. If only we could have talked about his *Über naive und sentimentalische Dichtung*. If only I'd known to ask. I had read Conrad of course, extensively for Moderations, but unfortunately still loathed him (*the horror, the horror*) and my only Ford was *The Good Soldier*. It was a novel I'd come to love and David had called it the book of his life, but now that he was writing his own, I knew he didn't want to be drawn on what he saw of himself in the earlier work. In any case, exactly *how* close Ford's character Edward Ashburnham was to David I had yet to fully understand.

'And of course, there's Johann Wolfgang von,' he added. 'Have you read any of him?'

Only translated extracts from *Faust*, I answered – at this point feeling I barely deserved my second – for essays on Marlowe.

'You should try him again,' David advised. 'Even in translation there's a lot to be had. You might like his *Elective Affinities*.'

Hearing the tone of high seriousness when he said the name, I took Goethe to be his literary Supreme Being. Something of the same tone generally coloured his voice when he spoke about anything German. Earlier that day, in response to a news item, he'd proclaimed how loathsome the East German regime was, how it couldn't last and how the reunification of Germany was inevitable. How right he was, though it didn't seem that he could be at the time. Maintaining the tone, David next declared that he believed he had a German soul. I didn't know then that he had this idea directly from Kennaway – indirectly from Mann – and would give it to Pym later in the book. But I was coming to notice in the general way how he would say these notions aloud and then work them into the new novel. He also freely recycled some of his earlier usages. I don't mean the bigger themes that were the mainstay of all his work, but little things, short phrases, passing ideas, often paradoxical ones, that must have mattered to him enough to give them another airing. The notion of spies doing the dirty work while the masses sleep peacefully, which occurs in *The Spy Who Came in from the Cold* (and which had come down, variously expressed, through Kipling, Churchill and Orwell), was something he reworked for *A Perfect Spy*. He once remarked that George Greenfield had a smile like an iron bar and I subsequently found the exact simile describing Haldane in *The Looking Glass War*. He didn't re-work that into the new book, but I think he was trying it out to see if he could. He'd done this recycling in earlier books, too. Connie Sachs' 'God bless all who sail in you' greeting to George Smiley when he unexpectedly visits her at her Oxford flat in *Tinker Tailor* is an echo of a toast Shamus and Cassidy make in *The Naïve and Sentimental Lover*. The indistinct cry Cassidy later hears Shamus utter in his sleep – Cassidy can't decide whether it's *No!* or *Go!* – recurs in *A Perfect Spy*, after already being reused in *The Little Drummer Girl*. At the end of his long confessional letter to his son, Pym makes the claim that he is the bridge Tom has to walk over to escape from Rick. David recycled that line in an interview decades later about his own sons and Ronnie. I could give hundreds more examples, but it would only be to say again that David's life and art really were all one to him. I could never clearly identify where one ended and the other began, though it might have brought me less heartache if I hadn't kept trying so hard to do just that.

'Did you do any languages at school, my love?' he asked me next.

'Latin and Greek.'

'No Moderns?'

'Only French. I gave it up the moment they let me.'

'So no German?'

'It was either German or Greek. I really wanted to do Greek.'

'Ah, well—' He paused and I half-guessed what was coming. 'You're no use to me if you don't speak German.'

He wrote a one-act, one-man play for Guinness that year and read that to me at the flat too. Titled *Before you go out into the world*, it was Smiley addressing the graduation class of new young spooks at Sarratt. Guinness later went off the idea, having initially sounded keen, so it was never performed. But listening then, with my eyes closed, it was as if Guinness were performing it anyway. David's capture of the actor's lugubrious timbre was quite uncanny.

There's a grainy video – now on YouTube – where the elderly Kim Philby can be seen addressing an audience of Stasi officers in East Germany in 1981. He's wearing heavy-rimmed thick-lensed glasses and looks really rather Smiley-ish. Seeing it recently made me wonder whether David saw it too, prior to writing the play, and if the sight of his ageing nemesis lecturing to a room full of younger operatives provoked him into reclaiming the role of wise elder from the traitor, to return it to his own elderly spycatcher. Philby, almost as much as Ronnie, was never very far from his creative thinking, never closer than at that time. I only wish I could have made the connection then myself. But much as I knew how autobiographical David's new novel was, I still didn't realise that only half of the book was written to exorcise the ghost of his father. I didn't yet understand how the other half was an attempt to excise the contamination of Philby.

The never-performed play would also be recycled and become the framing device for his portmanteau book of short stories, *The Secret Pilgrim*. David actually pinched one of the stories in it from me, something I'd told him from my time at Asprey, when the wives of various London-based sheikhs would come in with their well-muscled, well-armed bodyguards and just take – actually shoplift – whatever they fancied, hiding their loot under their burkas, while the staff had to hastily but discreetly keep count of all the items for later billing.

When Graham came back from skiing in Wengen it seemed the right time to tell him about us. David invited him to lunch and we broke the news at La Capannina.

'That explains something,' Graham said when he heard, grinning at me.

'What's that then, Gooders?' I asked.

'Why you've been turning up at the studios in the morning all bright-eyed and bandy-legged.'

Well, I did give him the feed-line. I think he may have sussed us all along.

'I'm happy for you both,' he said and I knew he meant it. 'Sounds like a good match, too,' he added, after a moment of looking at each of us, and I knew he meant that too.

It was a sublimely lovely lunch and I could only marvel at the fact that I was sitting there in Soho's finest staff canteen with these two wonderful men whom I loved dearly and who in their different ways both loved me back and seemed to have become such great chums with each other. I waxed lyrical about it in the taxi going up to St John's Wood afterwards, with the mellow buzz of the lunch still in my head. In smooth reply, almost as though he couldn't help himself, David shifted his voice into donnish-observation mode.

'Yes, of course,' he concurred with a faint smile. 'But the thing about Graham, one always feels, is that there's somehow less to him than the sum of his parts.'

It was the lofty oh-so-reasonable tone, as much as the gratuitous comment itself, which made me fly at him. How could he speak so dismissively of Graham, when he knew how I felt about him? Who the hell did he think he was anyway? Which part of the fucking universe did he think he ruled to make such a high and mighty pronouncement on anyone, let alone *my* great friend? Did he want to hear *my* pronouncements on his po-faced gagging-for-his-cock sister? Or on those revolting lunatic misers he'd made me sit down and eat with in Cornwall? Did he want me to start adding up the sum of *those* parts?

The cab was in the middle of traffic so he had to sit there and hear it. I knew I was going too far, but he'd crossed the line about Graham – and done it so casually, as if it had been nothing more than the obvious next thing to say. It was intolerable.

After I'd said my piece, the force of which astonished even me, we sat in palpable silence the rest of the way up to the flat. When he got out, I quite expected him to tell me to take the cab back to Chelsea and never darken his bulletproof door again, but he paid the driver so I got out too.

It was remarkable really, but he seemed to take it. He didn't apologise – I'd come to understand he never did, under any circumstances, to anyone – but I knew he'd taken it, all the same. David lived in a world – had actually created a world around himself – where his opinions, no matter how absurd or ill-founded, were simply accepted. Save for George and Miller, and certainly Rainer, who I'm sure each chose their words carefully, there was no push-back – only a full-time paid-up Greek chorus chanting, *Of course, David, of course.* I think it likely that no one in his life had ever gone full fishwife on him until then.

We spent the rest of the afternoon in bed, with no further reference to the episode, and had a surprisingly good time.

My birthday fell a couple of weeks later. It wasn't a significant one, just a middling twenty-something, but David was intent on making a great fuss about it. He'd cleared the whole day, he told me a couple of days in advance, so put on a really posh frock and come round to the flat. And get there early. Then we can have a party.

I followed his instructions and when he opened the door his arousal was so great it was all he could do to let me in without ripping my clothes off. We made love urgently and fully clothed on his big writing table. He'd already cleared it, so I didn't get the dramatic sweeping-everything-aside gesture first, but I considered it a literary milestone nonetheless. I must have worn the right dress. When we'd put ourselves back together again he gave me a gold wristwatch, with a note tucked into the box. *For time present and time past and time forever – Happy Birthday my darling, darling girl.*

The intercom buzzer sounded and David gave a conspiratorial giggle as he went to answer it.

'Come on up!' he said into the speaker.

'Who's that?' I asked.

'You'll see – I promised you a party! We'll have drinks here first and then I thought we'd all go off to the Connaught for a birthday bash.'

He threw open the door and, as I peered eagerly over his shoulder, I saw George and Gigi coming up the stairs. George was carrying a brace of Dom Perignon and Gigi a chic little present wrapped with a bow. It was so lovely to see them again; we instantly hugged and talked and laughed like four great friends. It all made for a wonderful, perfect day, full of the special excitement, the extraordinary sense of occasion, the sheer bubbling *joie de vivre* that it was David's unique talent to be able to conjure up. And when he did, when he made the magic happen, it was impossible to remember that things had ever been any other way, or to imagine that things could ever be any other way again. There were simply too many rabbits coming out of the hat.

We said goodbye to George and Gigi – after a lunch of legendary proportion and expense – and headed back to the flat. We only stopped making love when David had to leave for Paddington to catch the midnight sleeper to Penzance. I took the taxi with him and saw him onto the train. He said he'd be at Tregiffian alone and would miss me madly, but he needed to throw himself into his work.

Then, just as the flat seemed to have become a safe haven for him, a point of constancy and creativity and love and trust, David suddenly defected. He rang from Tregiffian early one morning a couple of days later.

He couldn't go on, he told me. He couldn't work at the flat any more. It was too close to Hampstead, too accessible. He knew he could always see me there and he wanted to see me too much. There were too many good times. He needed to stay away. He didn't think he could go on, he said finally, and rang off.

The fright response from the awful adrenalin jolt this shot through me was so disabling that I stood rooted to the spot, holding the dead telephone receiver to my ear for several pointless moments afterwards. Then, without giving it a moment's coherent thought, I grabbed my bag and coat and raced to Paddington. I caught the next train to Penzance after first telephoning a girlfriend from the station – in those pre-mobile-phone days – and giving her David's number to call once I was on my way, to tell him when I'd arrive. There was no point in calling him myself. I knew I had to see him to stand a chance of bringing him back in from the cold. The long hateful journey was like waiting for a bad diagnosis.

He was at the station, looking pained but tolerant, and drove us back to the house, where we got into hacking jackets and walked and walked and talked and talked. It was an amplified, extra-band-width version of our conversation after the storm in Plomari, with David saying it was impossible for him to continue, for the reasons he'd already given me, and with me saying his reasons made no sense and I wouldn't let him – each of us trying every permutation in our considerable joint-and-several command of the English language to make our case. I remember that the wind prevented my tears from falling by driving them sideways across my cheeks. I *hated* that damned cliff. In one of the milder moments, when the wind stopped howling, or when I did, I likened him to Tigger – a less damning character than the equally inconstant but self-pitying Toad of Toad Hall (*Poop-poop!*), whom at times he more closely resembled. Tigger enthusiastically declaring what he liked best, then defecting from it as if it were suddenly the worst. When we got back inside, he took the waxed coat from me delicately, as if I'd had the bad diagnosis after all, telling me, 'I can't disagree with anything you say.'

I doubted there were too many people who'd ever had quite that kind of acknowledgement from him after an argument, but it was small consolation. He finally stopped my tears with the most glorious fuck either of us had ever had in our joint-and-several lives.

Next day we drove back to London, stopping for lunch at a pub on the way. The journey was quiet and a little polite, but at least it wasn't the train. We agreed – i.e. David insisted, I acquiesced – to maintain 'radio silence' for three weeks until, appropriately enough, 1 April, All Fools' Day. By then he'd have hacked something out, he said, because he didn't want to lose me. He'd be in London, but not at the flat. It would be all right if I wrote to him. *Poste restante* Hampstead.

Friday 9th March [my diary entry reads] – Sent D a Tigger card with a note.

Tuesday 13th March – D called, got my card. Loved it. Loves me. 'I'll call you every day.' (No more radio silence?) Then sent me a vast bunch of flowers and called twice more.

Wednesday 14th March – D rang. Said he just had lunch w. Charlotte, who has a new man. She still thinks I'm wonderful. Told him so. 'You <u>got</u> to get out, David,' she told him too, meaning his marriage.

Thursday 15th March – 9.45am at St John's Wood for the day.

Friday 16th March – More flowers.

Tuesday 20th March – 12.30 at St John's Wood. Lunch, then D read me all his latest pages. 'I've so been wanting to do this. I so want to read it to you.'

Wednesday 21st March – D rang to say meet him by the Round Pond in Kensington Gdns. Fed the ducks. Said he'd just had lunch with Jean & asked her to come & meet me in the park but she declined.

Thursday 22nd March – D rang. Would I like to go with him to Vienna on Sunday for a few days, then on to Munich?

I've let these entries stand to try and convey how frangible, how transmutable and almost entirely quotidian David's personality was. When the disparate parts of him coalesced he could fill your heart with his song – but then he would suddenly take flight at nothing, whirl in the air and vanish, like a startled flock of birds. And just when you thought the best of him was gone forever, you'd hear him singing in the trees again. Beyond sharing a capacity for ever-shifting certainty with Tigger and Toad, there was another childhood character he resembled: the Little Prince, who kept moving his chair so that he wouldn't miss the sinking sunset on his own little planet, when, if he'd only sat down in one clear spot and faced the other way, the rising dawn would have come to him time and time again.

Further Adventures in the German-Speaking World

He wanted to be looked upon as a sort of Lohengrin.
Ford Madox Ford, *The Good Soldier*

So, at the start of what would have been week three of the reissued and almost immediately abandoned 'radio silence' directive, we went to Vienna. It was where the Pyms were based in the new book and, David told me, where he'd once before thought of setting a novel, the story of resurgent fascism that he ultimately moved to Bonn for his fifth novel, *A Small Town in Germany*.

'I was advised that Vienna was a fruitful location for the phenomenon at the time,' he said. 'Some might tell you it still is.'

We stayed at a boutique hotel a little out of the way. The Sacher, he told me when we later took coffee and *Torte* there, was a little too famous for cover. David had lived in the city with Ann for a spell in the early sixties, but had first known it when it was divided into sectors between the Allies immediately after the war. I'd never been before. Having forgotten anything I may have learned about the Hapsburgs in school, my main association was with *The Third Man*. Echoes of the film were everywhere in the cobbled streets and squares, aided by an old accordion player sitting on a stool in Stephansplatz, his cap on the ground in front of him as he squeezed out a passable version of the Anton Karas theme. As we set out on the first morning, I assumed we were heading to the diplomatic quarter to case a suitable official residence for the Pyms, with David jotting down promising details of the architecture, but we went directly to the Viennese equivalent of Bond Street.

'I think a girl needs to inspect some serious shops, don't you?' he announced. 'Since we're here, it's got to be leather.'

We spent the entire morning in various select establishments, where I happily tried on any number of garments and David happily waited and watched and offered thoughts on what suited me best – finally settling on a beautifully fitted suede coat, as soft and smooth as butter, and a sleek and sturdy weekend bag.

David was pleased with my choices and especially approved of the bag. 'You'll have that for the rest of your life,' he told me. 'It's the real thing here.'

(In the end, the bag lasted nearly thirty years. But since I used it almost every day, not just at weekends, his estimation wasn't too far off the mark.)

It was only when we chose a restaurant for lunch and David was in the men's room that I had the chance to open the store carriers and look at the receipts that had been discreetly folded over and slipped between the layers of tissue paper. After doing the calculation from schillings to sterling, I realised he had just spent something like £3,000 on me, with an understated elegance about his manner as he did so, as if it were as natural as our taking a cab or checking into a hotel or any other relatively unremarkable expenditure. I so hope that he knew how well he carried his wealth, how utterly faultless and fluent and light of touch he was with his generosity.

He took me on a cultural tour the next day and was a most eloquent guide. (I wonder now whether he had any remembrance of this when he made Ted Mundy assume the same occupation in *Absolute Friends* a few years later.) We went inside the cathedral, with its soaring Gothic architecture, to marvel – as every visitor must – at the glories that were achieved before the advent of power tools. But as we approached the aisle David did a very strange thing. He dipped his fingers in the shallow font of holy water. Then he genuflected while crossing himself. He performed the act so smoothly that anyone watching would have taken him for a born-and-raised Catholic. Yet he was a man of no religion; in fact, I was fairly sure he had no belief in any deity at all. Were we at Fakhreldine again, only with David's concern now being for the sensibilities of the priests instead of the Lebanese waiters? It was the most extraordinary thing.

On our way out, I glanced through a rack of educational pamphlets while David found some large notes in his wallet for the donation box. On a list of famous *Kapellmeister* I smiled to see that one of them had been called Johann Joseph Fux.

Munich was for an award presentation. David underplayed the event, not going into any detail about what exactly he was being awarded or why or by whom. Naturally, I wasn't to accompany him to the ceremony, but I liked seeing him get into his best bib and tucker in the hotel room and took photos of him before he put on his pants and when he was tying his black tie. I took myself down to the hotel bar after he'd left, to have a drink and a light meal by myself. Two young fellows started to chat me up as soon as I sat down and insisted on buying me a drink. Between their halting English and my guesswork German we managed a happy chatty hour or so. But their easy company brought me a sad pang of understanding, too, of how relationships between the sexes didn't need to be beset by such seemingly insuperable problems as being with David entailed.

After bidding my two new friends *gute Nacht*, I returned to the room and switched on the television set – to find that David was on every channel. One station had live coverage of the award ceremony, three more were showing le Carré documentaries of varying vintages and yet another ran a long segment about the event on the main evening news. He wasn't carrying a statuette or the keys to the city when he came in, so I still wasn't clear what he'd been awarded and he still didn't seem inclined to tell me. Whatever it was it must have been pretty significant, at least to the Germans, but David didn't seem especially concerned to have received it. When I told him how extensive his television coverage had been, he only replied, 'Yes, I know. The Krauts love me.'

*　　　*　　　*

After seeing once again how the German-speaking world brought David's best self out of him, I enrolled on a four-week *intensiv Sprachkurs* at the Goethe-Institut in South Kensington. Our *Lehrerin* was a German woman with a delightfully wry sense of humour. The first thing she told us was her name, explaining that she was married to a New Zealander, so that it was Frau *Cole* as in Old King, not Frau *Kohl* as in cabbage or the wife of the German chancellor. The second thing she told us was that we should forget any German accent we'd ever heard in films or TV shows, especially those set in the last war. Illustrating the kind of accent she meant, she explained, *Zis iz because, here et zee Goethe-Institut, vee have better vayz of making you talk*.

Herr Flick would have been proud. I liked her straight away.

I made a new girlfriend on the course, Sascha, and every morning we claimed our preferred seats in the classroom *an der Wand, in die Ecke*, as we were soon able to say. The course was planned with Teutonic efficiency and soon the basic elements of the language started to become a joined-up understanding in our heads. Frau Cole's witty touches made it a really fun course.

'I can tell you did English,' Sascha said to me at one point. She was a recent History graduate herself. 'You ask about subjunctives.'

When I told David about the course at the flat – only after I'd got a good half of it under my belt – he was thrilled. He was always a big talker during sex, which was already erotic enough, but that day he switched to German and suddenly everything was off even his previous charts.

Over lunch afterwards, he wanted to hear more about it. Did I find the accent easy? Was I enjoying the grammar? Did I have a good tutor?

Yes to all, I said, telling him how our tutor, Frau Cole, had told me I had a very good accent.

But Herr Professor Higgins immediately stepped in with a correction.

'*Ach, nein! Nicht Frau Coal – sondern Frau Kohl.*'

'*Ja doch!*' I had the immeasurable pleasure of being able to answer back from the minuscule amount of German vocab at my disposal. '*Sie heißt Cole – C-O-L-E. Wirklich. Ihr Mann ist Neuseeländer!*'

The Great German Soul didn't care for a correction himself, it seemed, so couldn't leave it at that, though he might have seemed a somewhat bigger soul if he had.

'Oaaoh,' he said, assuming my tutor must therefore have been English and employing the mealy mouthed Essex accent that was his go-to voice for a put-down. 'You mean *Frow Cole.*'

Later on there was a photography exhibition at the Goethe and I asked David if he'd care to see it with me. Against my expectation he said he would and so we went along. By then we'd been all over London together and no one who hadn't met him before – save for Freddie – had so much as raised an eyebrow in his direction. In those days, it was the name that carried all the recognition, not the face behind it. But all that changed the second we walked into the Institut. It was quite, *quite* astonishing. The sudden arrival of royalty – I could say of *deity* – wouldn't have produced such a moment. The usually *über-höflich* staff all stopped whatever they were doing to stand and stare. They began to gather at a discreet distance as we moved towards the exhibition, watching us as we took ourselves through it. Somebody must have got word to the director of the place, because he suddenly appeared and presented himself, addressing David in German in what even I could tell was a tone of worshipful awe. I think he may even have bowed. Other staff members had scurried away, only to scurry back with their copies of his books for him to sign – which, even more amazingly, *they evidently had to hand.* I introduced Frau Cole, who looked at me fondly, as though I'd achieved the highest application of the foundation course she'd taken me through. We spent no more than forty minutes there, but I was left with the clear impression that it was an event each of those present would tell their grandchildren about in years to come. The director asked David if he would do them the honour of signing their *Gästebuch* before we left, which of course he did. I didn't doubt they would have it framed.

'The Krauts love me,' David said again, quite as straightforwardly as before, as he hailed a taxi to take us up to St John's Wood.

It wasn't long before he returned to Munich, without me this time, for a meeting with film director Wim Wenders – whose *Alice in the Cities* I'd always liked – to discuss a project. Wenders wanted him to play the German sea captain, Dollmann, in a TV film of Erskine Childers' 1903 espionage novel, *The Riddle of the Sands*. David clearly liked the idea of acting – I'd already seen his Strasberg technique in spontaneous action at Athens airport – and his success with his own audiobooks may have encouraged him to indulge Wenders' suggestion. He declined the part, however, though not after reflecting that it was yet another flaky idea from the *Meryl-Streep-Is-too-Icebergy* movie-production handbook, but only, as he told me when he returned, because he didn't have the time.

Return to the Land of the Pod-People

David wanted me to go down to Tregiffian again for a few days. I'd privately forsworn the place, but since we appeared to be in a period where no decision of his stuck for longer than it took for a letter of repeal to reach me in the post, or the time one of mine could withstand a seductive phone call to change my mind, I agreed to go. It was the middle of May and technically spring – though someone should have told the weather – so perhaps for once the end of the country wouldn't feel quite so much like the end of the world. David must have registered how much I disliked the long train journey and this time suggested I fly down.

He was waiting for me at Newquay airport and seemed really pleased that I'd made the effort. For the rest of that day, that evening and overnight, things were perfectly fine between us. Really good, in fact. There was even a blue sky over the ocean the following morning, which stayed there throughout the whole weekend, demonstrating once and for all how aptly the pathetic *fallacy* was named.

We were talking easily over mid-morning coffee when the phone rang. The phone was to hand and David answered it where we were sitting. I soon gathered it was Jane, ringing about some matter of concern in Hampstead. His voice acquired a tone of pained endurance and they seemed stuck in for a long exchange. I didn't like the thought of hearing what was going on between them and so I took myself out of earshot into the sitting room, getting comfortable on the big red sofa in front of the fire that was still burning to keep the background chill at bay.

The call ended after a few minutes and David came through to where I was sitting. I suppose I was anticipating a few words of appreciation for not hanging around to fag-end on their conversation, prior to picking up our own conversation where we'd left off. Or we might have started to make love on the sofa, as we had on every occasion I'd been at the house before. But instead of moving in like a lover, David suddenly sprang on to me like an assailant. He thrust me against the cushions, pinning me down with his whole body, his forearm pressing hard and rigid just underneath my throat.

'You did that *deliberately*, didn't you?' he hissed in icy fury, his face close and savage, his eyes piercing.

I had no idea what he thought I'd done or what he thought he was doing. He had me so I couldn't move. I couldn't respond for shock.

'She *heard* you!' he continued through bared teeth. 'She heard your *footsteps* across the floor. "You've got someone *with* you," she said. "I can hear her *heels* on the *flagstones*—"' His breathing came fast and shallow as he snarled out his wife's accusation. 'You *knew* she'd *hear* you if you walked away—!'

I genuinely hadn't given the possibility a thought. I'd been sure I was quiet. But in the insanity of the moment I was too stunned – and fearful – to be sure of anything. *Had* my heels made a noise? Or was it simply that after a generous decade of David's infidelity and denials Jane had developed bat-like sonar to detect frequency changes at her husband's end of a telephone line? That seemed to make as much sense as anything right then, because nothing made any sense at all. I was out of my depth. I had no comprehension of the world he and his wife lived in. It wasn't just the damn awful house and the damn awful cliff; their whole damn awful existence was an alien planet to me.

I still hadn't answered him and in a quick expert shift of his body David inched his forearm up to my throat. I could feel him willing me to say something that would make things worse, to give him licence to escalate to his next trained move.

I could only tell him the truth.

'I was just trying to give you some privacy,' was all I managed to say.

He continued to rake his eyes over mine. I hadn't realised how their colouring was so feral, almost wolven it seemed to me then, with bright streaks of amber and hazel and green and grey narrowing to the deadly black pin-points of his pupils.

'Your credibility hangs by a *thread*,' he said at last, and let me go.

I can't explain how we got through the rest of that day and the night that followed, or why I didn't call for a taxi to take me to the airport or station or all the way back to London by road. I suppose I could even have called the police. I don't know now why I stayed on and I absolutely didn't know then. If there is any explanation then it's another iteration of what I've written before, that David's hold over any situation was so absolute that it was as if he could bend reality, and one's own reactions within the distortion, to his will.

Not that it would have mattered if things hadn't gone to such hell that morning, because they were going to go to hell anyway the following day.

By the time I dressed and came down next morning, David was in his workroom. Or so I thought. I poured myself a mug of coffee in the kitchen and took it back upstairs – I don't know why I did that, either; that vast hard bed was hardly a refuge – only to find David coming out of the bedroom carrying my belongings, including my spongebag and the bath towel I'd just used. He must have waited upstairs somewhere till I was downstairs myself, or perhaps there was a second staircase I hadn't yet seen. He didn't explain what he was doing. He had no words for me. I followed him mutely, assuming he'd called a taxi for me after all, though why he'd taken the towel just then was puzzling, not to say demeaning. But when he went into the guest bedroom I realised he wasn't removing my belongings, only transferring them. He ruffled the bedclothes as he dumped my things on the bed, then laid out my toiletries in the adjacent bathroom as though I'd used them there, complete with the damp towel tossed casually over the edge of the bath.

Then I remembered what he'd told me when I first arrived, when he was still my lover and not a wild-eyed ninja. (Not that he hadn't converted to being my lover again as recently as last night.) Someone was coming to lunch. His accountant, or money adviser, or some such; a man called Hale Crosse. This was for his benefit. David was setting the scene for his own method acting before the cameras started to roll.

Just why he'd arranged for this man to come down while I was there remained a mystery. It might have been simply for cover, to discourage his wife from joining him. Or I suppose he may have wanted us both there together to brush up his Strasberg technique. Or just as possibly, it seemed to me then, since we were already so far down the rabbit-hole, it was so we could all play croquet with flamingos in the garden after lunch.

I remember nothing about Hale Crosse except that he had a voice a little like the actor Richard Bebb, though even that may be an *ex post facto* addition to back-fill the blank in my mind. David introduced me as his researcher, in an offhand way that translated to 'minion'. I took my cue, removed a book at random from a shelf and sat with it outside – under what should have been the cheering blue spring sky, but was quite as depressing to me then as the previous winter grey – leaving David to talk to his man in the kitchen as he prepared lunch. I trusted that he would see I was doing all I could to play along, though I knew he would give me no sign that he too was playing a part. I could easily have burst his play-acting bubble altogether and told his money man what was really going on between us in the most graphic terms, just to be done with the whole lunatic charade. David could hardly have pounced on me again in company. But I think he knew I wasn't up to it. He'd beaten me down, psychologically if not physically too, so wasn't taking much of a risk.

After a little while, David came outside and crouched down over a patch of the garden by the kitchen. I walked over and saw he was cutting sprigs of mint.

'Hello there,' I said. 'Need a hand with anything?'

But he still had no communication for me. He didn't even look up, just tossed out a cool 'No, thanks.'

'Are we having lamb?' I asked, still trying to make contact.

'No. This is for the new potatoes.'

'Oh dear,' I said, momentarily forgetting my reduced role in the movie that was playing; the Saturday twelve noon first show. 'I don't like mint in new potatoes.'

He offered no reply and went back inside, leaving me standing there abjectly. The kitchen window was open and I caught what he said to Hale Crosse, as I was probably meant to.

'Huh! Sue *Dawson* doesn't like *mint* in her *new* potatoes.'

His intonation was masterful, the exact pitch to carry the scene. Perhaps Wenders had known what he was after.

Leaving by train next morning, I came to two conclusions. The first was that David didn't like being at Land's End much more than I did. It was a surprise revelation, but I was pretty sure it was correct. I've read acres of interviews with him over the years, as well as almost everything he ever wrote as a personal account, and though journalists refer to it as *his beloved Cornwall*, I've yet to find one truly fond sentiment for the place from David himself. From everything I witnessed, it brought out the very worst in him, which I somehow think he knew. I believe he tolerated it as a kind of *ultima Thule*; the farthest he could be from Hampstead, which he seemed to hate most of all, without leaving England. (He died with an Eire passport, claimed through his descent from Ronnie's Irish mother, Bessie, and obtained as a reaction to Brexit. I rather think now that if Brexit had happened twenty years earlier he would have used it to leverage a permanent move and found himself another *Schloss* facing the Atlantic there. Not because he had any love for Ireland either, but because of his constant drive to escape from whichever slammer he'd last built for himself and find a new location to build the next one. The only country which did have a *locus* in his heart, I believe, was Switzerland, and I dare say 'the Swissers' would have happily had him. But it wouldn't have suited David to move there. Firstly, it would have associated him with the Roger Moore-type UK tax exiles, which he couldn't have endured, but, far more importantly, having his domestic set-up transplanted there would have invaded the life-long personal secrecy the place preserved for him.)

My second conclusion was that I was never going to set foot on that damn cliff of his ever again.

Wimbledon and Beyond

Why can't people have what they want? The things were all there to content everybody; yet everybody has the wrong thing!

Ford Madox Ford, *The Good Soldier*

It was hands down the most depressing summer of my life. Not that I didn't see David; in fact, I saw him quite often. He would call me to St John's Wood or visit me on the King's Road. There were still the restaurants and a movie or two – *Silkwood* was one of them, which I think made him regret not agreeing to Meryl when they were casting for Charlie – and more flowers and gifts and expressions of love and praise. And there was still the endlessly astonishing and inexhaustible sex. All that, *per se*, was as fine as ever. But now there was all that went with it – the constant threnody about the book, how everything and everyone was taking him away from it, including the time he spent with me. There were unceasing complaints about his wife, his family and whomever else he felt encumbered by, which appeared to be everybody. When he was back in Cornwall there were also his letters, which would either freely and sometimes nastily blame me, or 'us', for what he believed he was enduring, or prove encouraging and loving, if he decided once again that I was his last great hope. There was no way to tell which sort they were until I opened them, unless he'd added a smiley or frownie face on the outside of the envelope, which he didn't always do and, anyway, sometimes they were both.

David was in a howling state, that was certain, and had arrogated the right to put me in a state too, as though I were some sort of safety valve for him, a means of EQ-ing all the discordant levels in his head. You would have thought he had survived prolonged torture in some heartless regime ... Well, there was Ronnie originally, I suppose, who had done something of the sort to his son's psyche. Yet it was also a more general malaise which afflicted him, as much for what he was as who. I'd finished Susan Kennaway's book by then and read other accounts of literary love stories – Sheilah Graham on her time with Scott Fitzgerald, Pamela Hansford Johnson on Dylan Thomas, Anaïs Nin on Henry Miller, Martha Gellhorn and Mary Welsh Hemingway on Ernest (and years later, Joyce Maynard on Salinger, Carole Mallory on Mailer and Emma Tennant on Ted Hughes). A common pathogen was evident. The same high pitch of often thuggish self-indulgence in whatever form it took – drink, sex, emotional turmoil, violence, manipulation, on and on, in any combination – was what each writer believed necessary, if not vital, to release his creativity. It was the self-indulgence that Kennaway had demonstrated and the self-indulgence David subsequently allowed himself, in his own particular combination, after the Scottish writer's death. (Though I would still have to say, in fairness, that after reading all these other women's accounts, David wasn't even close to being the worst.)

It boiled down to the basic premise of great artists suffering for their art. Art – as Shamus puts it in *The Naïve and Sentimental Lover*, probably in a phrase of Kennaway's, via Petrarch – being a kind of lovely agony. The only problem I ever had with that concept was the co-factor that their women – the writers' molls – had to suffer for it too.

Next time Graham called round for a Famous Grouse he told me I was getting thin. He gave me a long straight look and declared I needed a day out. The next day we were sitting under a grey sky in Centre Court, Wimbledon, on debenture seats courtesy of Audrey's late father, watching an early round men's singles match as dull as the weather.

'Great match for radio, isn't it?' Graham remarked with a sniff, as the pair of baseline players relentlessly pounded the ball back and forth like metronomes. 'It's the cure for insomnia if the Beeb ever release it on tape.'

With the tennis providing little diversion, we started to talk. Graham said he could see I wasn't a happy bunny at the moment and that I hadn't been one for a while. I could only agree, telling him it was David's here again/gone again, come here/leave me alone, I can't do it/I can only do it with you behaviour that had me down. Saying this to Graham – who was so constant, so stalwart, always so very much the full sum of all his parts – I suddenly felt ashamed for letting myself be reduced to this condition. I was always bright and quick and funny and capable before David, at least before the worst of how he could be. Now I was the kind of woman I despised, the kind who moped around complaining how her man had done her wrong.

'Well, them's the rules of the game, honey,' Graham replied. 'You're a rich man's mistress now.'

Christ – I wished! I countered instantly, saying that was all I wanted from the start. Just the good times together, like George and Gigi, and the rest of our lives in our own corners. It was David who couldn't stick by the rules. He was the one who insisted he had to get out of his marriage, insisted I had to help him do it, be there for him, be inside the book with him, then be banished when he didn't like having me so close. There were all the broken dates, all the doubled-down promises that followed to patch things up, then those were broken too, with the implication it was somehow all my fault for believing anything he said. Now he was insisting on 'radio silence' – again – right through the rest of the summer, while he worked on the book and 'hacked out' a way to get himself out, the never-to-be-resolved plan that was nobody's idea but his own.

'Nah,' Graham said dismissively after patiently hearing me out. 'He's got you snowed. The bloke's terminally married. He's never gonna leave his wife, so don't believe him if he swears different on his mother's grave. Anyway, why should he get out? He's got you in a nice convenient box, all hot and lovely and waiting to pop out and entertain him whenever he lifts your lid. He's got the wife in another one, doing whatever she does for him – don't ask me what – keeping house, typing his deathless prose, making sure his socks match, like he's still living at home with his ma or else she's the nanny a bloke like him never had. So what've you got to offer that he isn't getting now? You spread your legs whenever he's got the urge, listen to his moans about how much he suffers to earn a fortune, and he never has to take any earache from you because he's got 'er indoors to run back to if you try and dish him any. Bet *she* never gives him earache, or she'd've been traded in for a quieter model a long time ago.'

The match reached set point in the second set and still wasn't worth watching. Graham had put it all horribly well, but I still tried to make my case.

'Then why does he keep saying he wants to get out? Why all the bloody aggro? I don't care if he stays married or not.'

'You're not listening, honey. You just said it yourself. If the man *persists* in going around with his arse in a sling about the way his life is, you can bet the farm it's because he *likes* it that way – either for some miserable reason best known to himself or so that he can moan about it and get special consideration from lovely sympathetic girls like you. If he really wanted out of his marriage, he's got all the money and lawyers in the western hemisphere to throw at it to make it go away. If he didn't like it, he would've left her for whoever he was screwing before you, or the one before that. Don't tell me there weren't others, though probably none with an Oxbridge degree and your legs. It's obvious it's the *tension* he likes – creative or otherwise – the ducking and diving between all the moving parts. That's what races his motor.'

Graham saw how his words were hitting home and planted a big kiss on my forehead.

'Sorry, sweetheart. He's just got you believing a rather literary version of the old my-wife-doesn't-understand-me line, that's all. You fell for it because you fell for him and he's got your number. It's shitty, I know, but that's the way the guy is.'

'I thought you liked him,' I objected pathetically.

'I do, honey – I think he's great. But then, I ain't sleeping with him, am I?'

The next afternoon I had an unexpected visitor for tea. My great friend and ex-beau Jeremy Lloyd, as slim and elegant and idiotically handsome as ever, paid me a call at my flat. We quite often saw each other, but hadn't for a while. I hadn't really seen anyone for a while. David had me too wrapped up in coping with whatever it was he was doing, or going to do, or not going to do next.

I made a pot of tea, found some biscuits and we were soon laughing away like old times. Graham had probably told him how miserable I was and they'd decided he should call round to cheer me up. It would be like them to do that.

As he left, Jeremy gave me a long, rather sexy hug.

'We have to do this more often, darling,' he declared. 'I'd forgotten how funny you are.'

Darling JL. Before he called round, I'd forgotten too.

A couple of days later, I decided to make an unannounced visit myself – to St John's Wood, to see if David was at the flat. He'd said he wouldn't be, but I had the strongest feeling that he was. He always unplugged the phone when he was working there – and whenever we were there together – so I knew there was no point in calling him first and, anyway, I didn't want to give him the chance to say no. Revived by the combined efforts of Graham and Jeremy to buoy my spirits, I'd come to a decision about doing the Ronnie biog and wanted to tell David in person before the nebulous end to the current radio silence. For some reason, I'd thought it would help.

I let myself into the stairwell, but knocked first before I opened the bulletproof door. He was there; surprised to see me, but neither smiling nor frowning at my arrival. It was awkward between us – I hadn't quite timed it so that he'd finished his morning's work, though if I had he would probably have already left – so we stopped attempting conversation and went to bed. Afterwards, I told him that after a lot of careful thought I'd decided to do the biography of his father as he'd suggested. Now that I'd finished all the research he needed for his novel, I felt it was a good time to take the material forward into a full project of its own. I was sure that with his—

But David cut me off. He said he didn't think my doing the Ronnie book was a good idea anymore. It could be difficult, there'd be problems. He no longer wanted me to do it.

I think something close to hysteria hit me then. Was there any rug he would place me on without pulling it out from under me? Was there another way I could possibly stand on my head for him – or balance on any other body part for that matter – that would be enough? Was he *ever* going to stay true to his own words on *anything*?

After I'd levelled these fresh accusations at him – I may have screamed some of them – David looked as if I'd scalped him alive. It was his particular talent to drive you to the very edge and then appear shocked when you finally flung yourself into the abyss. But I suddenly didn't care what his reaction was. I couldn't have said another word or listened to one more from him. I dressed and left.

David sent me a letter in reply. It was quasi-apologetic but fully self-justifying; understanding but unaccommodating; he said he believed in our love but doubted his own faith; he claimed I wanted a structure from him (when I didn't), said he had no excuse for his 'zigzagging' and then proceeded to make several excuses and zigzag some more. He put everything down to his not having taken on a relationship like ours before, never any at all while writing a book, though he added that it was the book I'd breathed life into him to write. He ended by declaring another arbitrary deadline for his decision – now it was 1 October – though I'd already lost all track of what it was he was aiming to decide. If he still knew himself, he didn't elaborate. Meanwhile, he intended to go 'hellbent' with the book and would stay at Tregiffian.

Suddenly, 1 October didn't seem at all too long to be away from him. Right then I'd had – as he wrote – far more words from him than I could eat.

After Wimbledon and sending Jeremy round, Graham thought of another antidote for my condition; some recordings for me to do in New York. I packed my new Viennese weekend bag – I'd be hitting the stores between studio sessions, so didn't need more – and flew out. I spent the next two and a half wonderfully David-free weeks recording at Celebration Studios, enjoying the city with Barbara and staying in a little basement apartment on West 12th in the Village, a direct equivalent of my own studio on the King's Road, cat-sitting for a journalist friend of hers who was away.

I hadn't told David I was going. It shouldn't have mattered, if he'd meant what he said about this latest radio silence, but he'd called Graham when he couldn't raise me at my flat and rang me as soon as I was home. He told me he would be in London in a few days and wanted to see me very much. Would I be able to meet him at St John's Wood and stay overnight? He'd be so pleased if I said I would …

And so it went. After barely a month of summer *en famille* in Cornwellshire, David had re-certified the St John's Wood flat as a sanctuary and wanted to see me there all the time. He managed to make things lovely again – so lovely that I once turned up at the flat wearing nothing but my Burberry raincoat and high heels, to make it as lovely back for him.

'And you really came all the way on the tube like that?' David repeated in awe after I'd told him, as if it were the most wondrous erotic notion ever.

He visited at my flat too. But he let me know that, while radio silence was suspended, his 'decision date' of early October still stood. Meanwhile, the show was back on the road.

We went to Dawlish, the rather twee coastal town in Devon that David said he needed to get the feel of for the book. He met me off the train at Exeter St David's and we drove the rest of the way, finding a room in one of the less *jejune* B&Bs. We fell straight on to the bed for an Olympian session, the intensity of which surprised even David, then went out for 'a small wet', as he called it, using Ronnie lingo almost compulsively now. It was mid-afternoon and the pubs were about to shut so we went to the local Co-op and bought a bottle of Smirnoff, a carton of made-from-concentrate orange juice and a pack of paper cups. Suitably *declassé* for the area, we walked down to the front and sat on a bench under the wooden arcade, knocking back the British-made voddie like a pair of derelicts sharing meths. When the evening opening-hour came around, we had an early pub supper of scampi and chips and went back to the B&B for further acrobatics.

'If you ever take another lover, you'd better not let me find out about it,' David told me as we finally turned out the light. 'I'd know, anyway.'

He slept peacefully, his ghosts for once slaked, and woke me at dawn for round three. When we checked out – we may have been the only guests – I was puzzled to see the proprietor look sheepish and red-faced behind the front desk. David saw it too.

'Do you know what, my darling?' he said as we walked to the car. 'I reckon that fellow had a spyhole in the wall and was watching us. That's why he couldn't look me in the eye when I paid the bill. I think he rather felt he should be paying *us*.'

Apparently we'd just spent the night at the Bates Motel, Dawlish.

On the drive to Teignmouth station, where I was to catch the train back to London, David said how amazed he was by the amount of seminal fluid he produced with me.

'It's just so different with you, my darling. Everything about the sex is so different, so much freer and truer. Everything in me is so much more willing. When you get a rotten little duty fuck, you surrender very little …'

I'd never thought about it till then, but now my latest worry was that he was still availing himself of these when he wasn't with me. I asked him later why he still shared a bed with his wife, hoping he might take the hint. He sounded puzzled by my question and his answer – because I misunderstood it, because he made it deliberately oblique – only made my worry worse.

'Then there really would be no point to the marriage …'

When the projected 'decision date' arrived there was – axiomatically, at this stage – no decision. I didn't even have to ask when I got to the flat; David was primed and ready with his rationalisations. How could he possibly be held to a date? He couldn't run his life by anything so arbitrary. What did I expect from him?

I reminded him, perhaps not so gently, that it was his date, not mine, and that if I was expecting anything at all, it was only what he'd told me to expect, whatever that may have been when he'd last articulated it, since I was no longer clear on the matter.

Faced with the internal illogic of his own contrivance, he started to sidle around the subject, saying a move now was impossible, but that once the book was in, he definitely meant to move out, just for weekdays to begin with – maybe Oxford, maybe Berlin. That would be doable, wouldn't it?

That he could contemplate adding yet another point on the compass for himself – after Hampstead, Cornwall, Wengen, Zurich, LA for the movies, and anywhere else for everything else – showed how unmoored he was in his present frame of mind. I couldn't let myself be lured down a new rabbit-hole, so I said that I just wanted to see him, however he managed it, but couldn't cope with the unnecessary *Sturm-und-Drang* he attached to the process.

But he didn't like to hear that either. It was too straightforward. I don't think the German phrase troubled him; it was 'unnecessary' that jarred his sensibilities. He'd detected a small rise in my voice – nothing approaching my more full-throated level – but it was enough to hang his self-righteous hat on. He said he didn't need anyone upsetting his equilibrium at this stage of the book; 'anyone', as I understood it in the present context, meaning just *me*, not the whole besetting regiment of *them*, and 'equilibrium' being the turmoil I now knew he created around himself so that he could charge his own system from the swirling emotional chaos, like the dynamo on a bicycle wheel.

I surprised both of us by taking him at his word and leaving. I still had Graham's voice in my ears saying *it's the tension he likes* and knew I couldn't keep draining my own batteries to generate it for him. When I got home I parcelled up all the jewellery he'd given me and sent it by courier to the flat.

David's birthday was coming up. I sent a card to the flat a few days early, so that he'd get it somewhere in the vicinity of the occasion. I didn't know when or if he'd be there and, the way things had been going, didn't expect to see him for a celebration lunch this time round. But it seemed churlish not to send anything. It wasn't actually a birthday card, just a neutral one with a drawing of a dog in a garden. I couldn't think of anything to say that would make any difference to the state of play currently between us, so I sello-taped the slip of paper that was printed with *This card has been left blank for your own message* to the inside and signed my name below. It seemed to say it all.

For all the baffling inconsistencies and contradictions of his behaviour and the murderous drama he generated, on some never-to-be-expressed level I realised it all made a dreadful kind of sense. The central essence of the man was that he had once been a terribly hurt and fearful little boy who never had his tears kissed better. His mother walked out when he was five – or six, or seven, it varied with the telling – and he was left with Ronnie, who was living proof that the Very Bad Man of the scariest-worst childhood tales really existed. As an adult David had spent his life searching for a love that wouldn't let him down, as each of his parents had done in their different terrible ways. But when he did find love he couldn't let himself trust to it, in case it let him down again. So he tried to banish it, break it, make it leave, anything to deprive it of the chance to let him down first, even if – as in our case – it never would. He had to make it hurt first, before he was hurt again. I believe shrinks call this 'anxious attachment'. It's not something you just get over.

He surprised me by calling the next day.

'Hello, my darling. Thank you for your lovely card. How are you? It's lovely, did I tell you? I'm all right between my ears now. I wanted to tell you that. We could make it twelve o'clock at the flat the day before my birthday, couldn't we?'

And because it was impossible to hold out on David when he was looking for love, and asking for it so sweetly, I said we could. An enormous bouquet from Georgie's arrived at my flat by motor-bike despatch rider later that afternoon.

When I arrived at the flat at 11.45, David wasn't there. But he'd laid out a caviar picnic for two on the rug and put a present that I assumed was for me, another red jeweller's box, on one of the plates. I'd brought a present for him and wanted to hide it first, so I'd timed it well – or perhaps he had. He might have been somewhere in the street watching me arrive, waiting for me to go up first – how to ever know? I put a little gift tag on the other plate, then hid the present, which was large and flat, in the only place that would take it – under the bed.

Then I heard him pound up the stairs in threes, his huge feet slamming the treads. He burst in carrying chocolates and more flowers from Georgie's.

'I knew you were here,' he said, inhaling deeply, as though he hadn't breathed fresh air for weeks. 'I could smell that delicious light scent you wear the moment I was in the stairwell. Oh, do come here, I want my skin on you—'

David was so, so lovely when he was like this, all right between his ears and trusting to love – if only in the moment – and giving so much more back than he took.

When we finally disengaged from that initial long embrace, he wanted me to open my present. He'd bought me an art nouveau bracelet, silver with a leaf detail and set with amethysts and aquamarines for berries. He wrapped it round my wrist and closed the fastening, his big fingers delicate as lace.

'Please don't throw it back at me,' he said softly, holding my wrist as if to seal the piece there forever. 'It's my love and I do love you so. And do take all the other stuff with you when you go this time, because that's my love too and I don't give it to everybody.'

Then he picked up the gift tag from his own plate. It was attached to nothing, but he studied it solemnly.

'It's more than I deserve,' he said at last.

When I told him that his present was hidden his face lit up.

'On your person, I hope!'

'Wrong dimensions!' I answered. 'Find it—'

The hunt took five seconds. Under the bed was the first place he looked.

'Oh, it's a picture!' he exclaimed, tearing at the wrapping round the frame. 'It's not of a girl on the beach, is it?'

It was, of course. I'd had a poster-sized blow-up made of his favourite naked holiday shot of me.

'Oh, look. Just look—'

The bed took us directly, with the picture of me now hanging on the wall over our heads.

For the rest of the year, David was extraordinarily attentive. We saw ourselves all the time, frequently spending nights together at the flat. He couldn't keep me far enough away over the summer; now it was as if he couldn't keep me sufficiently close or ever get his fill. He was so concerned not to lose me, he said, though now there seemed no possibility that he ever would. Everything was easy between us again, fresh and flowing. No more radio silence. David said it was a new beginning, a new way forward.

'Wait until the spring,' he said. 'That's all. I'll have done the book and then we can sort ourselves out. It's not long, is it?'

He went on to say that I'd opened a door for him and, if I was clever, it might be that he could go through it.

'So shut up,' he said. 'I love you.'

He bought a new item for the flat – a cheval glass – and put it in the bedroom, strategically positioned by the bed. It was just what we needed to be even more narcissistic in our lovemaking – and for me finally to become his looking-glass whore.

In the middle of November, Graham, David and I were back at John Wood to record *The Spy Who Came in from the Cold*. There was a lovely mellow feel to the session, right from the start. We were all on form and no one had anything to prove. Lunch at the staff canteen was a nice easy schmooze.

'He's mad,' Graham declared as we lined up for the afternoon session. David was already in the sound booth and couldn't hear. 'You're obviously good for him and great together. Any village idiot can see it. I want you to know, honey – I've changed my mind on the subject. He bloody well *should* leave his wife.'

*   *   *

At the end of the month David gave me an early Christmas present at the flat. He wanted to offer me a prepared speech first. He'd evidently made notes.

'Darling, my darling—' he began, standing in the centre of the little living room as I sat on the sofa, his audience of one in the front row. 'When I loved you, I showed you how I loved you. When I desired you so much that my whole body wanted to live inside you and around you forever, I showed you that too. When I despaired, I made you share my misery with me and punished you for sharing. When I wanted to retreat to the confines of an empty relationship, I pushed you away so that I could do so, and expected you to be there when I wanted to bounce back ...'

There was more in the same beautifully paradoxical vein. It was lovely and sad by turn, always poignant either way, but, as I listened, I realised that David was always coming full circle in his thinking, arriving where he started and – to invert the Eliot – *not* knowing the place for the first time. Not even recognising the recursion. He knew himself so well. But it didn't seem to matter, because he just couldn't progress *from* himself at all. It was round and round in circles all the time.

That was what the books were always about, I'd read them all by then; saying everything so beautifully but getting nowhere, his heroes always baffled by their own perceptions of paradox, turning and turning – to invert the Yeats now – in the *narrowing* gyre, making the ineluctable recursion to their starting condition. Leamas never does come in from the cold, though it was David's most famous title ever. Given the chance to climb back over the Wall, he deliberately drops back down to his death on the Iron Curtain side. In the next book, Turner – the perfect name – keeps revisiting tired old-war techniques that fail time and again in the new conflict, refusing to learn. Cassidy banishes all remembrance of the liberating bohemian love he experienced with Shamus and

Helen in order to return to the confines of his conventional bourgeois home. Even when Smiley achieves the crowning success of his career, he can barely bring himself to acknowledge it as a final concrete fact.

Circular images reinforce this inescapable mechanism of rinse and repeat; the Circus, Moscow Centre, the nursery round embedded in the *Tinker Tailor* title and Smiley making his rounds of the suspects. Guillam, David's younger-self character, actually says about George at one point that the paradox might kill him, but in le Carré *knowing* the problem doesn't mean *doing* anything about it. The centre holds because the paradox pins it there. That poor Pym was doomed to repeat this recursive pattern – fleeing *the Ring* in Vienna, but only returning to the sad little corner of England where he originally started, with not an inch of progress made – was as frustrating as any of it. This was David's great *autobiographical* novel, and yet still no birds sang. There was to be no progress, no epiphany, no resolution at the end save for death; in Pym's case, David's case in fictive form, taking Kim Philby, his internalised double, with him when he blows his brains out looking at himself in the bathroom mirror. If David's 'going south, tell them north' rule applied to how he chose his pen name, then I had come to think that le Carré – the square – was really cover for le Cercle.

But when David was so lovely and so loving like this, I could only love him back, without thought of the circle returning. Love him because of everything he was and in spite of everything else. The gift he'd bought me was circular, too – did he see the irony? – an antique eternity ring, of platinum set with diamonds.

'From your eternal lover,' he said, as he took my hand and gently eased up my ring finger to receive it. 'For the eternity of pain I've caused you and the eternal future that we may or may not have.'

The metaphor continued. When he slipped the ring on my finger, it didn't quite fit.

David wanted one last getaway for us before resigning himself to the family holiday in Wengen. In the middle of December we went back to Zurich for four nights, staying at our usual hotel, the Dolder Grand.

Zurich Nochmal - Und Schließlich

We arrived at the hilltop hotel in the last of the afternoon light and for once didn't go straight to bed when we went up to our room – not from any faltering desire, but because the view of the city in the gathering winter evening as the lights began to sparkle below was so crisp and dark and enticing that it drew us out into itself. Of all the travelling I did with David, somehow Zurich always felt like 'our place'. We dumped our bags, found gloves and mufflers and grabbed a waiting cab. We got out at the Altstadt and walked along the winding lanes together in the inky frozen night, David's arm snaking through mine as he clutched me to his side.

We soon found a *Bierkeller* and went in, through heavy felt blankets drawn on brass rails across the inside of the door against the cold. The log fire that was blazing in a great sooty hearth gave off enough heat to warm a stadium. The patrons sat at small tables, their hats and heavy coats hanging on racks between. A conversational burr of local dialect filled the room, with occasional bursts of low congenial laughter breaking through, and there was hazy lambent light all round. We sat at a little corner table, holding hands, watching and listening and just soaking it all up. Before long we both had tears in our eyes. We'd reached a new level that was beyond lovely, beyond love, beyond anything we'd experienced together before; some plane of being that was even beyond perfect.

Back at the hotel that night we shared the most tender and truest lovemaking either of us had known in our lives.

Next morning I woke early – very early for me, on the cusp of first light. David was lying beside me on his back, completely still, and I knew instantly that something wasn't right. There was a rigidity to how he lay, I could feel a strange tension across the mattress. It must have been what had woken me. In the semi-darkness I could see that his eyes were open and staring blankly at the ceiling. For one terrible moment I thought he was dead. I reached out and laid my hand on his chest and, to my relief, felt the warmth of his skin and his heart beating underneath. But he gave no response to my touch. He didn't move. He didn't even blink. In a flash of dreadful intuition I knew that he had lain like that for hours, unmoving in the dark. I couldn't begin to guess what was so wrong, but something had to be – badly, badly wrong. I didn't have to ask him what it was, because as soon as he knew that I was awake and had seen that he was too, he told me, as though he'd waited all that time just to speak.

He was still unmoving, still staring at the ceiling. His voice was flat and empty, a terrible void.

'You have to go back,' he said. 'I can't be this happy.'

I didn't – go back – but I only know this because my diary entry gives the date of my return to London, alone, three days later. We must have done things together in that time, walked around together, had meals and drinks together. We must have had sex. But I have no recollection. I've written the same words before, so it must have been how I coped in those never-anticipated moments when he said something I had no means of processing, that left me too shocked or numbed to retain what followed immediately afterwards. I only know that for the first time in my life I experienced a state of absolute despair.

1985

But Still

For pervasive unreason has its own logical processes.
Joseph Conrad, Author's Note, *The Secret Agent*

As soon as he returned to London in the new year, David told me that Yvette was coming over and he wanted us to meet. I think he may have summoned her specially, for an attempt at damage control. I was resistant to meeting her. It felt like the last thing I needed at that time, but David presented it as a special request, something he wanted me to do for him, as though there were something to be achieved by it, so I agreed. He must have thought that the woman he'd successfully 'turned' from lover into platonic friend – I always suspected against her wishes – could persuade me that what had happened in Zurich really wasn't so bad and that she'd survived worse from him in Phnom Penh. Or perhaps he didn't have even that improbable rationale. Perhaps he knew he was flailing and was just trying to come up with anything to explain or justify himself.

We met at Au Bois in St John's Wood. David took me there and introduced us – Yvette was already at the table – then left us to our lunch *à deux*. Seeing her, small and dark with huge brown eyes, I realised for the first time that all David's most significant loves before me had been dark and petite – Ann, Susan, Janet, Yvette herself. My dimensions, I suddenly saw, were closer to the fantasy eight-foot-tall blonde that Cassidy makes a joke about meeting to his dark petite wife.

Yvette asked me how I was and how it had been, but she didn't say it in a particularly inviting manner and I wasn't particularly forthcoming in return. She was David's agent on this mission and presumably had been briefed. She may have been as reluctant to meet as I was. She may even have wished that she was still his lover herself and not a platonic family friend at all. I told her some of what had been happening, when she pressed me, but withheld the worst. I wasn't remotely interested in asking how it had been for her. We weren't two girlfriends sharing our problems over salad and spritzers. We were – well, it felt to me then as though we were two characters in search of an author.

He was how he was, she told me finally with a quick resigned shrug, that Gallic purse of the lips. He would never change. I didn't recall asking her if she thought he would. I went back to my own flat afterwards, no happier and no more encouraged.

Yvette must have recognised the signs anyway. She was supposed to be staying in London for another few days, but that evening David rang to tell me she was suddenly going back to France.

'She told me she doesn't like the idea of seeing me at the moment,' he said. 'She doesn't want me to contact her for a while.'

Her reaction had clearly surprised him, but I couldn't tell if he was acknowledging its validity in response to his recidivism with me, or blaming me for enabling her to see it.

I had another birthday. Barbara, who is just three days older than me, came over for a visit. I introduced her to David – they'd previously only spoken on the phone when I was skiing last year – and he was very sweet to her. Barbara's younger sister, Julie, was also over and David was very sweet to her, too. He was just very sweet all the time now. Whenever he and I were together over the next few months, which was often, either at his flat or mine, he was loving and caring and solicitous and kind. He gave me more flowers and gifts. He gave me some manuscript pages from the novel. I'm not sure too many people got those. He was still the most wonderful lover. And he talked about himself more than ever, as if desperate for me to understand him – not recognising that the problem was I finally did. However hard he tried to present the best of himself, after Zurich he just couldn't revive the part of me he had shot out of the sky. Turning the happiest time ever into the absolute worst, simply because it *was* the happiest time ever, was a paradox too far. He'd hung a sword of Damocles over our being that happy again and I didn't think I'd survive it, if it ever fell.

We made it through to the summer. The book was finished and who knows what David may have had in mind for us next. I never found out.

I took no conscious decision to end things. I still loved him as much as ever, still wanted to go on loving him and knew he still loved me, perhaps even more than ever. But when we were at the flat one time, my body took the decision for me. I couldn't hack the sex. It had always been the most extraordinary union, right from the first night. Now it made me feel as if I were one of those unlucky addresses that keep getting burgled. Only there was nothing left to steal. That was when I knew I couldn't go on.

It was over. Or, as I remembered Graham saying with such wonderful unintended irony immediately before it all began – *fin d'histoire.*

Leaving David wasn't easy, coming up from the depths, forfeiting the chance of regaining the heights. Had I missed the best of him by not staying longer, to see if he really could sort himself out 'after the book', after all we'd been through together? Or had I only narrowly escaped with my faculties and my emotional resources intact? My survival instinct at the time – battered and disoriented though it was – persuaded me that if I'd stayed, I should only have proved how completely *The Good Soldier* was the book of David's life, by turning into the girl who loses her wits after falling in love with Edward and ends up almost catatonic, saying 'Shuttlecocks!' spasmodically. But I suppose I could have been wrong.

Either way, it took me a long time to recover. Therapy helped. I found a wonderful therapist, Elizabeth, who diagnosed me as being 'borderline clinically depressed'. Well – at least I could still use the personal pronoun. Long talks and guided hypnotherapy with her gradually restored me back to my better self.

I continued working with Graham and acquired audio publishing clients of my own. Audiobooks were bigger business than ever and when we weren't running back-to-back sessions in London one or other of us would be flying out to record on the continent or in the States. There were more le Carré titles to record and I still did the abridgements, but I didn't attend David's readings. Graham would tell me how they went – which was invariably fine – and pass on David's best wishes.

'He always asks me how you are. Tells me to tell you he'd be happy to take you to lunch. You know, honey, I think he carries a bit of a candle for you.'

I didn't take David up on his offer, though he made it every time. There was only one way it would turn out if I did and I had only just managed to recover from the last time. We were over, but at the same time we'd never really finished, only stopped. Like the first time we parted, in front of Eros, it was a not-continuing, rather than an end.

Gigi and I saw a lot of each other and became firm friends. Of all the people I could talk to about David, she and Graham were the only two who actually knew him themselves. Like Graham, she was always enormously supportive of my side of things.

'I really don't know how you managed it, darling,' she told me, meaning two years with David and only requiring therapy afterwards, not a straitjacket or a padded cell. 'All that *Sturm-und-Drang*.'

That did seem to be the phrase.

'I think you were very lucky to have the strength to get out when you did,' she added, 'before he used you up completely.'

She'd already told me how George described Jane as being 'hoovered up' since her marriage. George had known her before, of course, and had even arranged the introduction. Another of Gigi's admirers had also known Jane – BC, as it were – though just as a pal. He too described someone who had formerly been sparky and adventurous, who loved hitting the road for fast driving; a far cry from what appeared to be her AD – After David – self. Gigi had noted the pattern of progression and was glad I'd escaped.

'I think he gave the best of himself to you, all the same. I think you brought it out in him. It was just a pity he couldn't live up to it. But then, if he'd finally escaped with you, he wouldn't have been able to complain about it all the time, would he?!'

The three of us met up in New York one time, when George and Gigi were on a trip together and I was over there recording. George invited me to dine with them at the Royalton, where they were staying. I was downtown at Morgans.

George had just retired after a long and illustrious career, but the story he told over cocktails was that David had not been best pleased at his electing to leave before he was finished with his services. We shared a hard-won chuckle of mutual experience and further tales of our respective times with the Great Man. George confessed his pet name for David was 'the monster' and called me his comrade-in-arms. It was how he saw it: that we'd both survived close combat with the many-headed hydra.

We recalled the time we'd first met, on my maiden stay at Tregiffian.

'It was such a disappointment when you had to go so soon after we arrived,' Gigi said, speaking for them both. 'David arranged it that way, I suppose.'

'For no good reason, either,' I replied. 'I could have stayed on another day, but he decided I had to go back out into the cold.'

'Yes, of course,' George concurred sagely. 'Having the three of us there together, getting on so well, would have tipped the balance too far away from his control. He would have felt outnumbered, with both flanks exposed.'

'We told him how terrific we thought you were, after you'd gone,' Gigi went on. 'I'm sorry to say, he showed his true colours there too.'

My ears pricked up at this. It was a part of the story I hadn't heard before.

'How so?' I asked. 'What did he say?'

I caught a cautionary look passing to her from George.

'No, George, I think she has a right to know,' Gigi insisted, reading his expression. 'It was hateful then, but it can't hurt her now.'

George shrugged, conceding to her judgement on the matter. 'Well, if you think so, darling—'

'D'you know, it quite shocked me,' Gigi continued. 'It really did. We'd had that lovely supper together and next day, when you'd gone, George and I were extolling your virtues, saying how bright and funny we thought you were.'

Ah, my *levitas* undid me again, I thought to myself – but it wasn't that.

'Then George remarked that you'd obviously got a first-rate Oxbridge mind and David absolutely pounced on him. Do you know what he said, darling? I'm sure you'd never be able to guess—'

I bet I can, I thought, as my mind flashed back to my debriefing from David over our very first lunch. But I let Gigi finish her tale.

'He said, *Oh, come off it, George – she only got a 2:1!* It was so mean of him, so petty. *Can* you believe it?'

I said I could believe it, quite easily. And it was even pettier than she thought, because David knew very well that what I got was a second. You can only get a 2:1 – the equivalent – at Cambridge. George was a Cambridge man himself and had taken a first; in English, no less. So David hadn't just put me down in front of him, he'd deliberately switched terminology to make sure the point was driven home. I don't know why he couldn't simply concur with a simple *Yeah, she's great*, as another man in love might have. Pick a reason, any reason.

'You should consider writing a book about it,' George urged. 'One of your predecessors did, after all. Did you ever read *The Kennaway Papers*?'

I said I had. 'But wouldn't you say,' I asked George, 'that he was really only a little baby monster-in-the-making in those days? He comes off quite well in comparison to Kennaway. I'd be revealing much more about him than she did.'

'All the same,' George replied, not disagreeing, but quietly pressing, 'I think you should try.'

'Wouldn't he just throw his legal team at me?'

'He might. He wanted to injunct Susan Kennaway at first, but I talked him out of it. I would expect any successor of mine to do the same. You might think about it one day.'

With George's advice in my ears, I did start to write. Or rather, it was as Dennis Potter once put it in an interview, that you don't *start* to write, you simply find that you *are* writing. But knowing that George's advice was no longer in David's ears, I didn't attempt *The Dawson Papers*. Not at first. Instead, I tried turning the story into a novel, making the man a playwright. Then I tried a screenplay, making him a world-renowned espionage writer, but one who was German-born. But whichever way I wrote the story out, I knew I hadn't done it justice. I could never find an ending that really worked. In the exercise of trying to nail it down, however, I found that I actually did want to write. And then I had a really odd dream.

Ever since watching and falling in love with the BBC's monumental dramatisation of *The Forsyte Saga* when I was at school, I had adored the Galsworthy novels, re-reading them many times. Once, when I was staying in a country hotel in Ireland with another lover after David, I even made a start on a German edition of *Die Forsyte-Saga*, for want of finding anything more enticing on its reading-room shelves. Over the years I must have read the whole *roman-fleuve* more than a dozen times, and some individual books more often than that. So when I woke up one morning from a dream in which an entire page from the *Saga* appeared in front of me – not unlike the scroll that moves up the screen at the start of *Star Wars* – my initial thought was that I'd finally read it once too often.

The page of writing wouldn't leave me, so I wrote it down just as I remembered it from the dream and, out of idle curiosity, went looking to find it in the originals. But it wasn't there, though it seemed so authentic that I'd been certain it was. Which was when the penny dropped. Sequels to classic novels had been something of a vogue at that time, with the stories of *Gone with the Wind* and *Rebecca* both being successfully continued into new fiction. It was suddenly clear to me that I could write a sequel to the Forsyte books. I'd always thought that Galsworthy must have intended to produce more of the story himself, the mechanisms and themes were all in place, but had died before he could introduce another generation. I told Graham about my idea one night over supper and he was enthralled. He also threatened never to take me out for a meal again if I didn't do something about it, since it was, as he put it, *yet another of your great ideas.*

'*My* great ideas?'

'Yeah. See, you don't even hear yourself. You tell me at least a couple every time we sit down over a bottle together, then I never hear anything about them again. This one's the best so far.'

Not that I could recall any others, which was perhaps Graham's point, but I did have a particularly good feeling about this one.

'What should I do about it, then?' I asked him. I didn't particularly like the idea of just writing it 'on spec', but then I really didn't like the idea of not having another meal with Graham. 'What you need to do,' Graham decided, 'is write up an outline and send it straight to Uncle George. He'll know what to do with it.'

So that's what I did. George wrote straight back, calling my thirty-page proposal 'a very commercial project' – high praise from George – and suggesting a literary agent who might be interested. This happened to be Ed Victor, whom George had first taken on at Farquharson's years before, and who was now one of the top literary agents anywhere in the world. Ed saw me – I could never thank George enough for his referral – but told me straight up that he'd never liked Galsworthy, so wasn't going to take me on. He added, however, that he knew a man who did and probably would – his partner at the agency, Graham C. Greene. I saw him the following week. He was very enthusiastic about my proposal and did, in fact, take me on. A former publisher himself, he was the son of Hugh Carlton Greene, who had been Director-General at the Beeb when they made *The Forsyte Saga*, and the nephew and namesake of the 'senior spook-turned-novelist' of my discussions with David. Sometimes things just seem meant to happen.

Through my new agent's sterling offices, I received permission from the Galsworthy estate to proceed with my sequel and soon had a contract with a publisher.

'They paid you *how* much?!' my original Graham exclaimed when I told him the great news. 'And you haven't even written the bleeding thing yet! Well, *mazel tov*, honey. I always said you could do it.'

It was true. He always had.

It was getting towards the very end of 1991 and Graham was in the studio with David again, with one of the earlier titles, either *A Small Town in Germany* or *The Looking Glass War*, I don't recall which. He called me after the session, with the usual update.

'So how was the reading?' I asked.

'Word perfect, as per. Not that it oughtn't to be, it's not like he doesn't know the script. But I did think he was getting decidedly prissy on the esses this time. He sounded quite camp in places. Maybe he's gone the other way since he stopped nailing you.'

'Well,' I said. '*Après moi …*'

'Yeah, I dare say,' Graham remarked dryly. In all the years of knowing each other and working together, and even with me in my contact lenses, we'd still managed to keep it clean. 'But you know, honey – looking back – you got out at the right time.' It was only what Gigi had said, but Graham was about to add his own take. 'I mean, let's face it – you wouldn't want to be going down on him in his Bath chair in twenty years' time, would you?'

I heard a snorting chuckle at the other end of the line. Graham could never resist corpsing at his own gags.

'But he was very pleased for you when I told him about your book deal.'

'You didn't tell him how much, did you?'

'Of course I did. Why shouldn't I?'

Graham hadn't heard George and Gigi's tale from Cornwall, or the Great Man's reckoning of the sum of his own parts – I'd kept both stories from him. He didn't know what was likely to follow once he inadvertently offered that detail up for sacrifice.

'He actually said you'd done very well,' Graham went on. 'Though he did make a point to say you'd've got a *lot* bigger deal if you'd written the whole thing first.'

There it was. For whatever reason, David hadn't been able to be just plain nice about it; he had to offer the rebuke and send it back to me, soft-route via Graham.

I was suddenly cross with Graham for telling him and Graham was cross back with me for suggesting he'd betrayed a confidence, which in fairness he hadn't, and it led to our very first row. Even at this remove, David had managed to transfer some of the old poison. I began to see how he must never have liked my loving Graham so much, right from the start. *I thought you were his bird at first—*

After the Christmas holidays I knew I had to patch things up with Gooders. I loved him too dearly to let any third-party crap – especially from Cornwell with an e – drive a wedge between us. But he called me first, to say Happy New Year. He sounded all revved up about a multi-voice recording that he'd just booked for later in January. He'd forgotten all about the spat on the phone. That was so like him.

'We've got Baddeley and the gang coming back for the next *Winnie-the-Pooh*,' he told me cheerily. 'Four actors for the voice track at Woodsie's, then full sound effects and music mix for you to do afterwards at Silk Sound. It should be a blast. I'll call round at yours next week and give you all the gen. Get the Famous Grouse in. Love you, honey. *Byee—*'

Graham never did call round. The following week I had a horrible dream about him. I spotted him walking ahead of me in a crowded street – his silver hair was impossible to miss – and called out to him. I knew he'd heard me, but for some reason he didn't turn around and kept walking away. An overwhelming panic seized me then and I knew I had to *make* him hear me. I'd never had a dream come so alive before. I only knew one thing – *I had to make him stop*. I shouted and shouted till I was hoarse, but he just kept walking away from me until I lost sight of him in the crowd.

I woke immediately with a pounding head and sore throat. I must actually have been shouting out in my sleep. I concluded that our brief row on the phone had upset me more than I knew and decided that when he called round I'd have to explain more fully what had bugged me about what David said, to make sure he knew I didn't hold anything against him. I got up, put the kettle on for coffee and began my day.

An hour later my phone rang. It was a former colleague of Graham's, someone we both knew but who had no good reason to be calling me. As soon as I heard her voice I knew what she was going to say. The dream suddenly made the most terrible sense.

'Are you sitting down, Sue? I'm afraid I've got some bad news about Graham—'

He'd had a massive heart attack that morning. He had died an hour earlier, exactly when I'd woken up from my dream.

I'd never shed more tears before in my life than when I saw Graham's flower-laden casket carried past me down the aisle. The little country church in Wiltshire was packed for the service and even the churchyard seemed crowded as we all left afterwards. Everyone who'd ever known Graham – which seemed like half the world – had made a point of being there if they could. I saw Jeremy outside but he couldn't speak to me. A glance and a nod were the most he could manage as he hurriedly left with his friend John Chapman, the playwright. Jeremy had driven every fast car ever built, some of them at breakneck speed across Belgravia after a night at Annabel's with me holding tightly to my seat belt in the passenger seat. He'd once held the lap record for a saloon model at Brands Hatch. Yet he'd asked Chapman to take him to the funeral, because he was so distraught at Graham's death he couldn't trust himself behind the wheel. They'd been best friends for more than thirty years. I saw Frenchie in the churchyard too. He gave me the same smile as always and the look that said *I'm ahead of you,* which even then he was. I threw my arms round his neck and fell completely to pieces. Good old Frenchie, who hugged me hard and mopped me up and was dead himself all too soon afterwards.

David wasn't there, but sent me a letter, saying how, after Audrey, he felt Graham's loss most for me. When his next novel, *The Night Manager*, was published, he sent me a copy with a little note. I saw that he'd dedicated the book to Graham, which more than redeemed him for not attending the funeral.

When my own novel, *The Forsytes*, came out, I returned the favour and sent David a copy. He wrote back sweetly with his congratulations, calling it *the only first novel you will ever write*, though I somehow doubted it would find a place on any of his bookshelves. He had already given me a rare quote for the cover – *'What she doesn't know about the Forsytes nobody does'* – the compliment couched in a characteristic double negative, but a generous endorsement all the same. My book was also dedicated to Graham and it was my greatest regret that he wasn't around to see it published. He would have been so delighted. He was the one who had encouraged me to write the proposal and send it to George, which began my writing career. Before that he had taken me into the sound studios with him and given me my audiobook career. Before that his good offices got me into television as a programme researcher. Since the wintry Saturday lunchtime at San Frediano in Knightsbridge twelve years earlier, when Jeremy had introduced me to him on our third date – *You must meet my best friend, darling* – Graham had been my great friend too. In fact, he was the *sine qua non* of my adult life. He was also the first – and last – conduit between David and me. Now that he was gone, I fully expected never to have any further contact with the Great Man again.

A Perfect Spy

*— you have all, I dare say, heard of the animal spirits, as how they are
transfused from father to son*
Laurence Sterne, *The Life & Opinions of Tristram Shandy, Gentleman*

There is so much to say about *A Perfect Spy*, the book I witnessed
David write, up close and in real time. But saying anything about
one of his books is to say something else about every other one of
them and then something again about the man who wrote them
all. Art and Life were always indivisible with him and it can all
appear somewhat of a conundrum, as I think David wanted his
creative processes to seem, as I believe he was to himself much of
the time. But there are trails that can be followed into the magical
forest of his fables, ways of decoding at least some of the secrets of
his own *Märchenland*.

The essential premise of this novel is that Magnus Pym is a
perfect spy because, as a double agent, he serves both sides of the
Cold War loyally. This is, of course, an impossibility in the real
world. A double agent might well end up betraying both opposing
sides, but it defies logic that he could remain loyal to both. But in
the world of le Carré the paradox stands. Just as Leamas is the spy
who comes in from the cold by doing the exact opposite, so Pym is
a perfect spy by being a perfect traitor. Magnus is indeed perfect in
his chosen role: perfect in his deceptions as he rises to prominence
in his field, perfect in his urbanity, his charm, his native capacity
for the work, perfect in his clever-clever dance of all-round betrayal
masquerading as unimpeachable loyalty, and latterly even perfect
in maintaining his cover in the face of growing suspicion until the
very last moment when he disappears, just before the game is up.

The hero's career closely mirrors that of Britain's infamous
traitor, Kim Philby, the Third Man in the Burgess–Maclean affair

and a member of the notorious Cambridge spy ring. It's the book's central parallel. Mary Pym believes she has the perfect marriage, with a husband who is attentive, thoughtful, dazzling, a constant lover and companion – until he disappears at the start of the novel. Until the stormy night her own equally uxorious husband suddenly disappeared in Beirut, Eleanor Philby believed exactly the same thing. Wind and rain lash the modest fictional seafront on the night of Pym's arrival at his safe house hideaway, just as they did the grand international waterfront on the night of Philby's departure. Pym's spook career ends in Vienna, where Philby's began. Philby disappeared shortly after the death of his father and Pym disappears shortly after the death of his. Mary Pym herself is a former 'Martha', recruited to the British secret services in her youth. So was Eleanor Philby, in America. Pym's Soviet recruiter and handler, Axel, is a 'charismatic cripple' beloved by the hero, just as Dieter was before him in *Call for the Dead* and as Sasha would be in *Absolute Friends* – as was Gábor Péter, a Hungarian refugee with a hunchback and limp, a high-ranking member of the Communist Party in pre-war Vienna and the man generally credited with being Kim Philby's recruiter. Axel and Sasha, written in more permissive times than Dieter, can also satisfy an endless line of women in bed, despite their disablement. This was supposed to be Gábor Péter's forte, too.

But this is David's autobiographical novel, surely? This is the book about his monstrous father, about his harrowing early life with Ronnie, living through all the conning and double-dealing that led to his becoming a spy. Where does Philby come into the story?

Well, Ronnie was always there in the books, right from the start. Something of his ruthlessness first appears in Scarr, the crooked garage owner in *Call for the Dead*. The phoney grandeur of his business dealings shows through in Old Hugo in *The Naïve and Sentimental Lover*. Jerry Westerby's father in *The Honourable*

Schoolboy is yet another sketch of him and his financial ruin plays into Charlie's childhood background in *The Little Drummer Girl*. Patricide was a persistent fantasy of David's in his youth, but it seemed he could never truly lay his father's ghost to rest in these minor characters, even after Ronnie died. Perhaps bringing him fully to life, as he finally did in *A Perfect Spy*, was the only way to kill him off properly. I trust I've shown some of the alchemy whereby David turned the base metal of his father's life into narrative gold, how Ronnie's rackety dishonest escapades and the apprenticeship in deceit he afforded his son became the backstory to the novel and the genesis of Pym the boy and youth.

But for the top story of Pym the man, the all-betraying double agent, David naturally needed to look elsewhere, beyond his own life. But with all his capacity for invention, why appropriate Philby? It took me a while to see it, to follow the grains of rice into the forest, but Philby too was always there. *He haunted my entire career*, David has said of him. In writing *A Perfect Spy*, he was drawing on all his considerable powers as a storyteller – as the premier fabulist of the Cold War – to slay not just one double-dealing monster, but two.

Tinker Tailor Soldier Spy is generally recognised as David's first exposition of the Philby *débâcle*. George Smiley is brought out of retirement to flush out the long-term Soviet double agent – the mole – whose treachery has turned the Service inside-out. The book was written in the seventies, but has its sentiments in the fifties, where so many of David's own sensibilities always seemed caught. Inevitably so, since it was the decade where it all went down. Burgess and Maclean defected in 1951 and Philby was immediately suspected of tipping them off. He might have been exposed then and there, but Kim – Harold Adrian Russell Philby, born in the Punjab and so nicknamed after Kipling's child spy – was by then too valuable to lose. He was the acknowledged golden boy of the Service and had risen to the heights in the secret world. Institutional denial instantly set in and saved him. If he could be suspected of being a 'double' then perhaps he was really a 'triple', insiders told themselves, and was playing the most dangerous loyalty game of all. (Graham Greene, who had known Philby during the war, believed this to his dying day.) So much belief had been invested in him by his British colleagues and masters that if Philby really was the Third Man then, as David said at that long-ago lunch, *there was no Tooth Fairy, no Santa Claus and Dumbo never could fly.* There was a mock trial, ostensibly to get at the truth, but where all the rules of interrogation were allowed to slide and the interrogator who was most likely to crack him – William Skardon, who had successfully cracked nuclear spy Klaus Fuchs and who himself was probably a partial model for Smiley – wasn't allowed a shot. By mid-decade, Philby was exonerated.

The fifties was also the period of David's early career as a spy and this is where I believe the fusion begins that would lead to their separate legends becoming so inescapably entwined. The two men never met. At least, David always claimed they didn't and Philby never counter-claimed that they did; beyond that, I suppose we can never know. But it is my own belief that David was always seen by his 'fathers' in the Service as their potential next 'golden boy', the most likely candidate among the new post-war genera-tion of recruits to be their future 'Kim', never more so than in those troubling, doubt-ridden years when Philby's own stellar career had begun to wobble. Nothing much less than that can account for David's own drastic, almost visceral response to Phil-by's sudden defection in '63 and the way he sought for years afterwards to mask its importance. First, there is the *Christ, it's Kim!* tale he told to Graham and me, when he took the coded wire that winter's night in Bonn. He probably told it many times and no doubt always, as then, as though it were a special confidence imparted to just a very few. But what did it really show? Young

Cornwell of the FO, the modest spook diplomat with a rising career, by chance the peripheral witness to a crucial moment of British espionage history – the 'Fall', as he would later term it, with Miltonic gravity, in *Tinker Tailor* – but only as other equally modest duty officers would have been when the same message came through to other spook stations at our embassies and consulates around the world. Though imparted as a secret specially shared, how David told the tale of this glancing intersection between himself and the double agent by whose level of treachery all other double agents would be measured seems to me now, paradoxically, to be a distancing device. David's true reaction was far more dramatic. The impact of the revelation hit him hard.

By that time he had already written two novels, effective and well-crafted but modest stories, one involving the world of espionage and both involving Smiley. There was nothing ground-breaking or earth-shattering about either; both if anything were rather old-fashioned. He had also written a partial story, not yet enough for a whole novel, centring around a mock trial to save a double agent. This was the first trace of Philby in his writing and who knows how long it would have lain dormant among his papers had David kept both careers going. But then Philby disappeared and David's third novel, *The Spy Who Came in from the Cold*, was the massive worldwide bestseller that rocketed him to fame and fortune. The mock trial becomes the very culmination of the story, as Leamas realises how he has been used as a pawn by his masters in the devilish plot to save the killer Mundt, a high-placed East German operative whom they've successfully 'turned' into a double to serve the West. Appropriating the key phrase of its title from Fleming's last bestseller – *The Spy Who Loved Me* – the novel was as far away from Bond's world of girls and gadgets and glamour as could be imagined. Overnight, it seemed, David had changed the landscape of espionage fiction forever. But the writer made no acknowledgement of the 'Philby factor' in his success. In fact, he took every care to cover its traces.

David claimed that he wrote *The Spy* in as little as five weeks, in a *state of fugue* in his shock at seeing the Berlin Wall go up, and knew when it was finished *that it was very good … that it worked.* This account of the novel's writing is nonsense, of course. The first barbed wire and breeze blocks that became the Wall went up in the summer of 1961 which, if we are to believe his account, would have meant that David inexplicably kept his 'very good' manuscript for a year and a half before handing it to Victor Gollancz early in 1963 for publication that autumn. But he gave this explanation of the book's genesis with a straight face for years afterwards and no one questioned its authenticity. By then he was John le Carré and authenticity was his special domain. (By the time internet searches offered historical verification at the click of a mouse, both the Berlin Wall and the Cold War were long gone and David had stopped offering this account.)

So no, the desperate and desperately creative 'fugue state' which birthed the real le Carré must surely have overcome him when he realised whose name was on the coded wire in Bonn. Find a word of six letters – first letter, P. It was the moment of absolute betrayal, when David must have understood that he was 'blown'. And in the very next moment, he must have understood that he always had been. Years later, David's first wife Ann, speaking more candidly than she was perhaps cleared to in a BBC documentary, would reveal that his bosses in MI6 'thought they really had someone special in David …'. Now, at a stroke on that dark night in West Germany in 1963, it was all gone. His life had changed forever. Suddenly, he no longer had a future in the Service. Given the long scope of Philby's treachery, he may not even have had a past. Or am I being fanciful here? Have I bought into the le Carré mythos myself? Perhaps David's Service career really was quite modest and his first wife was simply speaking on cue when she said that '*they thought they really had someone special*' in him. The comparison between Philby and himself may only ever have been an internal fantasy of David's own. But whether it was real or imagined was immaterial to the process of Art-Life fusion by which he turned himself into le Carré. Either way, David never forgave this betrayal and ever afterwards spoke of Philby in terms of loathing and contempt, flatly refusing the offer of a meeting with the old traitor when he was in Moscow years later, shortly before Philby's death.

But – but. What exactly *was* Philby's betrayal as David saw it? Was part it, for him, the fact that Kim had lost his nerve and defected? That he had finally surrendered the Great Double-Double Game? Was that really what made him the fallen idol? I think it may have been. Philby's absolute Miltonic Fall seems to have left David with a quantum of baffled leftover love – not unlike the young boy in Greene's story of the same name – that he needed to pour into all the fallen idols he would create in his books. Dieter was Smiley's discovery first, his own Caliban, before he crossed to the dark side. Even then, to Peter Guillam – forever David's younger-self character – Dieter stands as a heroic and all-but-epic figure of romantic manhood, more Byronic because of his crippled legs than despite them. Axel is never anything but an agent of the darkness that was Stalin's Communism, but Magnus loves him deeply, more than he loves his own father, more than he loves any woman. And Bill Haydon, the most Byronic figure of them all, is beloved by all to the end and suspected by none until the very last minute, not even by Smiley, whose own wife had loved Bill too. When Bill is unmasked as the traitor, poor Peter Guillam is so heart-stricken he sits at his desk the following morning with his tears pouring down onto his blotter.

This was all Philby's doing, I believe, the most despised figure in David's life, but the most beloved idol also, I would argue, before his Fall, and the *sine qua non* of the very best of the le Carré canon. Art and Life for David were always cut from one cloth and Kim Philby, no less than Ronnie, was inextricably part of the weave. Ronnie, as Rick Pym, is already securely laid to rest before *A Perfect Spy* opens, to be revivified only in the safe confines of flashback. But David still had to rid himself of the other haunting presence of his life. As the novel closes, in a final act of exorcism, Pym calmly wraps a towel around his head and, looking at his reflection in a mirror, puts a gun to his temple and dispassionately pulls the trigger. After internalising Philby in his hero, awarding him the 'quasi-homophonic' name Pym and fusing his own past life with the traitor's in his great autobiographical novel, David finally watches himself kill the turbaned Punjabi-born Kim.

Third Time a Blessing

March 1999

Theatreland

I had never dreamed about Graham before having that terrible vision of him walking away from me. It seemed to have been some sort of telepathy occurring at the moment of his death, though I can't say I really know. If it was that, then it must have come from the strength of the emotional bond that was between us. When I'd dreamed a new page of *The Forsyte Saga*, there was a strong emotional connection there too. As for David, I'd never had any dreams of him; not while we were together and not after we parted. I wasn't aware of harbouring any conscious desire to see him again, and if I had an unconscious one – well, I didn't know anything about it. But there must still have been a bond, because fourteen years after we parted for what I'd believed was the final time, I had the most vivid sleeping vision yet.

The living image of David's face appeared to me one night as I was sleeping. It approached suddenly out of the darkness and hovered lover-close above mine, with an expression of gentle anticipation in the eyes.

I think we should see ourselves again, he said softly.

I woke up immediately, to find I was standing shakily in the middle of the room. I had leaped right out of bed with the shock.

I thought about nothing else for the rest of the day. The last contact I'd had with David was the letter he sent to congratulate me on the publication of my Galsworthy sequel almost five years earlier. Since then – and without Graham as our go-between – nothing. But now this.

A few days later my friend Peter called. Peter knew all about my association with the Great Man and my failed attempts to write the story down. A writer himself, he well understood the process of grappling with a reluctant narrative. What he didn't know about was my dream. I hadn't mentioned it to him or to anyone else.

'Are you going to the le Carré lecture?' he asked straight away.

'Who's lecturing on le Carré?' I asked back.

'He is.'

I automatically rejected the information. David had always said he didn't care to 'press the flesh'.

'Can't be,' I said. 'He never did that kind of thing.'

'Well, he does now.'

He'd just read a piece in *The Times* about The Word, the new London literary festival, something I probably wouldn't have seen for myself. The lecture was billed as a headline event, to be held at the Peacock Theatre. It made me think that if Graham had been alive to see the article, he would have rung me too, but just to chuckle irreverently over the well-worn line about ageing actors: *Once a tour de force, now forced to tour!*

'I think you should go,' Peter suggested. 'It might give you an ending for your book. It might even be fun. You can sit in the back row and heckle.'

He gave me the details and left it at that.

The odd coincidence of the call following so quickly after my dream stayed in my mind overnight and in the morning I rang the ticket office. Not because I particularly wanted to go to the lecture, but rather to confirm, as much to Peter as to myself, that I couldn't go anyway. I was certain the event would be sold out – and it was.

There you go, I thought. Que sera.

But it didn't quite set my mind at rest. I was in the West End the next day and decided to go just a little bit out of my way to call in at the theatre box office. (The Peacock, in Portugal Street, belongs to the London School of Economics.) I still had no intention of going to the lecture, but told myself I needed to double-check that it wasn't possible. Graham might have commented that I had myself snowed.

'I expect the le Carré lecture's still sold out?' I asked the young guy sitting behind the ticket window reading a textbook. He looked like a postgrad from the LSE.

'Completely,' he answered without consulting his screen. He must have already fielded the same enquiry multiple times.

There you go, I thought again. Que sera, sera. Cue Doris Day.

Then something prompted him to set aside his book and check.

'How many tickets did you want, though?' he asked. 'Because there's just been one return …'

I doubt I'd have heckled from the back row, but I didn't have the opportunity. The returned ticket was for Row 2. That would be close to the action in any theatre, but when I took my seat on the evening of the lecture I discovered there was no orchestra pit ahead of me, just the front row and then the stage. Had it been the venue for a Faces concert twenty-five years earlier, I should have been able to throw my knickers at Rod Stewart and probably not miss. Not that this situation was comparable (I didn't think), but I wasn't sure I wanted to see David quite that close up.

The auditorium was packed to the rafters, though with an oddly disparate crowd. There were the usual theatre-and-arts-going professionals – the Sunday supplement crowd – but also a lot of bright-eyed students from the university, many clutching notebooks and pens. And there was a surprisingly large contingent of less home-grown types; elderly men in heavy overcoats and elderly women in equally elderly furs. Émigrés, I realised; le Carré devotees who had come in from the cold of the Eastern Bloc and saw him as the literary Moses who had led them out. David had once told me how his fans from these countries would come up to him, with tears in their eyes, and produce dog-eared mimeograph copies of his novels that they'd passed around in the years when they were forbidden texts. I thought at the time that he was exaggerating for dramatic effect. Now I began to think he had played it down.

But it wasn't only they who had come to touch the hem. There was an air of communion across the whole auditorium, an almost evangelical emanation, filling the social and cultural spaces between the groups as thoroughly as smoke from an Odeon circle. I recognised it for what it was – the dangerous leaven of belief – and wasn't allowing myself to inhale. Fate may have delivered me the last seat in the house, but I was not of this congregation. I was determined to maintain my apostasy.

The house lights continued to stay up as we – the congregants and I – were kept waiting. That was the one thing that was familiar to me in this strange setting, the Great Man making us wait. The lone lectern standing centre stage made me recall seeing the one in his workroom at Tregiffian. The huge video screen behind it made me recall seeing Fleetwood Mac at the Empire Pool, Wembley. Somewhat belatedly, I began to realise that even when they finally cut the house lights I would still be visible in the overspill from the lights on the stage. Not only would I be seeing David close up – if he happened to look down and a little way across he might well also see *me*. I felt uncomfortably exposed. My only hope of cover, very literally, was from an evil-smelling man-mountain occupying the seat in front of me, the rolls of fat on the back of his neck sweating like gelignite, who was another reason I'd been trying not to inhale. What was I doing there? I wasn't a student or a Cold War émigré. I never read the Sunday supplements and I hadn't even read a le Carré for years. I was no longer a believer. I didn't belong in this place. I wondered whether I should just get up and leave.

Before I could come to a decision, a church-like hush fell over the auditorium as the house lights suddenly dimmed.

But even then – exactly as the first time, after that long wait at the studios – the moment of arrival still managed to take me unawares. I'd expected some sort of introduction; not a drum roll necessarily, but at least a few words from one of the festival organisers. But with no fanfare at all, the writer simply appeared stage left and headed towards the lectern.

There were two of him as he walked out; the real one on the stage and the much larger double on the screen. (The metaphors, it appeared, were still writing themselves.) The two versions walked warily in step, soft-footed, as if between the cover of the wings and the sanctuary of the lectern lay a no-man's land that might be mined. The two pairs of eyes swiftly scanned the audience; perhaps, as ever, the exits too. Three paces out and a measured smile to the middle stalls brought thunderous applause. Three more paces and a nod of acknowledgement to the dress circle raised further tumultuous clapping and cheers. Then the last few steps, almost to the lectern, and time for a close reconnaissance of the front rows—

On the screen, the eyes of the enlarged public face, aware of their many watchers, appeared momentarily distracted by something off-camera. But the real eyes – the private ones, visibly worn and older than when I last looked into them – had received a shock. Just perceptibly – against all training and lifelong practice – they gave the tiniest start.

David had seen me.

And when I *saw* him see me, something inside me lurched towards him in response. Only a second earlier it was an impossible notion, not to say an altogether preposterous one, but now – more than anyone present – I *belonged*. My long-lapsed belief had been miraculously reborn in that startled half-second look. Once again, even in an auditorium of a thousand people, I was David's audience of one.

As he took his place at the lectern, with applause continuing all around, I could barely process the enormity of the moment and the sudden certainty of what it meant. It was going to happen again. Every last wonderful, dreadful part of it was going to happen all over again.

Familiar Territory

For every man there comes at last a time of life when the woman who sets her seal upon his imagination has set her seal for good. He will travel over no more horizons ... he will retire from those scenes.

Ford Madox Ford, *The Good Soldier*

I returned home that night in a state of – well, I had no idea. Shock? Disbelief? Exhilaration? Whatever it was, I was reeling from it. An extraordinary feeling of familiarity had flooded my senses as David walked out onto the stage. I *know* this man, I was thinking as I watched him; the way he carries himself when he walks, the way he tilts his head when he speaks, his every point of articulation when he makes the slightest gesture. And the voice. It was such an intense and immediate *knowing*.

I saw him at the book signing after the lecture. *Of course I did.* After that startling dream and Peter's uncanny phone call and the very last ticket seating me exactly where David couldn't fail to see me, it was clear we were meant to meet. I bought a copy of the latest le Carré hardback, *Single & Single,* from the display and waited in line.

'I know this lady!' David announced to his small army of female minders from Hodder, who were perplexed to see their VIP leave his signing table and advance towards me as I reached the head of the queue. Back at my flat over an hour later, I still had the sensation of being held hard in his big arms, could still feel the urgent press of him against me and the warm damp of the performance sweat that had soaked through the fabric of his suit.

Hello you, he whispered in my ear.

You were wonderful, I whispered back.

He led me back to the table, and as he signed my copy of his book I slipped him my address and phone number, like the tart I may well always have been, and, like the other tart that he always was too, he pocketed it in one deft move.

David's timing was always idiosyncratic, of his own crazy making, though he could never see that it was so, and was no different now. I could only wait for him to get in touch. But *would* he get in touch? Would he call? Would he write? It was the gorilla joke again. This time I had to remember to let him tell it.

I had only a few days to wait. The lecture was on the last Sunday in March. David rang the following Thursday morning. *Of course he did.* Thursday was 1 April, All Fools' Day, and we were two of them.

'My darling girl,' he began. He sounded breathless, as though I'd been the one calling and he'd been running to the phone. He was actually on Hampstead Heath, on his mobile. 'Phew,' he said, exhaling audibly. 'Is it really you? Are we still us?'

I was as dazed as he sounded. The utter strangeness of the situation came from the fact that it didn't feel strange at all. We hadn't spoken in almost fourteen years and yet the words simply flowed between us. The receptors must always have been there, just waiting to be reactivated.

'I'm sixty-seven, my darling,' he said soon into the call. 'Do you realise? In thirteen years, I'll be eighty.'

How funny. He had made exactly the same calculation about how he was going to be sixty-five when he was fifty-two. I didn't make the same remark about coming to see me on his concessionary bus pass. It wasn't funny now that he qualified for one.

'Don't worry about it, David,' I told him. 'You've aged very well. Really.'

'Thanks for saying so. But *you* don't age. I couldn't believe it was you sitting there, so close—'

'I didn't mean to sit so close,' I said quickly, in case he thought I'd planned it. 'I got the last ticket, the only return. I saw how you didn't believe it at first. You did the world's most covert double-take.'

'Well, you *did* give a chap a *turn*.'

He explained how he'd quickly had to hustle his group of guests out of the theatre after the lecture, drawing on all his powers of persuasion to urge them to go on ahead to the restaurant without him, to keep them clear of the signing. I pictured him doing it. Perhaps his performance sweat hadn't just come from the lecture.

'And yet at the same time I believed it utterly,' he went on. 'That you'd simply appeared. It seemed impossible *and* inevitable at a stroke.'

I told him about my dream and what he'd said in it.

'Well, that was very prescient of you. And of me, to appear in it. I think I like us being predestined. Perhaps we always were. Listen, my love, I have to be away for the next couple of weeks or so. They're making final decisions on the new movie, of *The Tailor of Panama*. John Madden thinks he wants to direct. Did you see his *Shakespeare in Love*? No? So I may have to go over to LA. There are other places too. Our timing's only as good as it ever was, I'm afraid. But when I get back, will you let me take you to the world's best ever lunch? Some establishment where I can spend an inordinate amount of money on you?'

That too was as good as it ever was. Going out on our first date those years ago was delicious, delightful and de-lovely, but only a way to delay the inevitable moment when we jumped each other's bones. It was no different now. The same intense vibe I'd felt at the signing transmitted itself over the phone. *All* the receptors were still there.

'I will,' I replied.

'How wonderful,' he said, and paused, letting it sink in. 'Meanwhile, I'll write to you. I haven't yet, but I will. You will be there, won't you? My darling girl.'

An envelope soon fell onto my doormat, the so-familiar blue handwriting delivering my name to me again, but for the first time at this particular address. I didn't open it immediately. At the theatre, I'd first walked around the block before going in – hesitating between the idea and the reality, to see if there was going to be a shadow. But there wasn't. Not then. There would be a shadow – this was David, who always brought his own – but not for a while.

The letter was as enchanting and loving and even chatty as any he had ever written to me. He called me his *most amazing and peerless Our Sue*, telling me again how astonishing it was to see me appear like an apparition in the theatre and how it had not only made his day, but his year so far, as well as all the years in between. He went into further detail about his schedule: first Amsterdam, then Kenya for his new novel, then LA for the movie, which was now going ahead. Ian McKellen had called him at midnight, apparently, and was mad keen to play Pendel, the tailor, though less keen on Madden. He didn't say why Amsterdam, so I guessed it was for an award; those were usually what he made least mention of. He said his plans were ridiculously fluid, but that he looked forward so much to seeing me again and would propose something as soon as he could see the mists clear.

He ended by underlining that I simply wasn't to go away.

His schedule had always been a maze of criss-crossing vapour trails, a many-partnered dance between competing loyalties and obligations, but now it seemed to demonstrate an extra measure of *Hast*. For all that he'd calculated how many years he had left until he was eighty, I imagined there was very likely a nearer number hanging over him. Ronnie died only months before his *seventieth* birthday, and though David had spent his life trying to escape his father that wasn't to say, even a quarter century after his death, he didn't still feel doomed by him. So I didn't expect to hear from him until the mists did clear, supposing with David they ever really could. But then, late one midweek morning towards the end of that month, he called unexpectedly from Hampstead Heath. Over the background chatter of birds and passers-by, his voice sounded unnaturally light, as it always did when something was wrong.

'Hullo, Sue. I just got back from Nairobi.'

He'd been there only a few days, after Amsterdam and LA. I wondered what had brought him back so soon.

'You remember my friend Yvette?' he asked in the same light tone.

I did, of course. His French former lover, whom he'd turned into a family friend, who he'd arranged for me to meet in the hope that she could explain him to me...

Quite suddenly, I knew why he'd called. I absolutely *knew* – not from any leap of guesswork, but from my heart. It was in his voice. He was even going to tell me while he was standing on the Heath perhaps staring out at the distant view of London, just like the first time. Something as singular and dreadful as that had somehow happened all over again, sixteen years later, even in the very same month.

I waited for the old echo, which came as he told me.

'She's dead.'

Boom—

'She went to Albania to help the refugees from Kosovo,' he continued in that same passive tone, 'and died in a car crash with three other people. On Sunday. It was raining heavily and their vehicle went over a ravine.'

Sunday had been the eighteenth. It didn't seem possible, but Yvette hadn't just died sixteen years to the month that Janet had been killed – she had died sixteen years to the very day.

I began to offer my condolences, but David spoke over me.

'Listen,' he said, 'will you have lunch with me tomorrow?'

I said of course I would.

261

'Good,' he said, cutting me off again. 'I'll call you then.'

He rang off.

Next morning he rang first thing to check where best to take me for lunch.

'Would a girl like to go somewhere for some caviar?' he asked.

'Why don't you bring some round?' I suggested.

'I'll be there at twelve.'

I spent all morning getting ready. I showered, then washed my hair again with a different shampoo. I tried on three or four outfits. I changed my lipstick twice. This was ridiculous. Why was I so nervous? It wasn't a new lover who would be arriving at my flat, it was David. *My* David, coming to see *his* Sue. We already knew each other inside out. He wouldn't have cared if I greeted him wearing a burlap sack or, indeed, wearing nothing at all. As I almost finished closing the zip on a fifth and final combo, just a soft blouse and skirt, but with lace-topped hold-up stockings – *and the rest* – underneath, the intercom buzzer sounded. He was there, a quarter of an hour early. Despite his face appearing on the little monochrome screen of the video entry panel, I couldn't believe it. I couldn't believe any of it.

'I'm here,' he said. 'Where do I go to find you?'

'Top floor,' I told him.

I didn't add that it was five flights up; he'd managed seven quite readily at John Wood. The flat was in a grand old Victorian mansion block in North Kensington that had nowhere to install a lift, but the huge roof terrace and the view more than compensated for the hike up the stairs. I gave myself another check in a full-length mirror, slipped on an earlier choice of shoes and retouched my lipstick. By the time I opened the front door he was approaching along the terrace, laden with bags and flowers. He let everything tumble to the ground as I rushed out to wrap myself around him. It was two or three wordless minutes before we let go and went inside.

David promptly took off his suit jacket and hung it on the back of a dining chair, then laid out what he'd brought with him on the kitchen counter, after first putting the flowers – an armful of freesias, which he'd remembered I liked – into the sink, running some water for them and stowing a bottle of vodka in the freezer. Thirty-five seconds inside the flat and it was already as if he lived there. Then he embraced me and kissed me again. I was mildly flustered when his hand went straight to the three inches of still-open zipper below the closed back button on the waistband of my skirt, which for all my double- and treble-checking I'd still managed to overlook.

'You were helping a chap out,' he said sweetly, closing the zip.

Keeping his hand on the small of my back, he showed me what he'd brought. In addition to the Stolichnaya now in the freezer, there was a perfectly chilled bottle of Krug, three types of gourmet cheese, some water biscuits, a baguette, a tin of *paté de foie gras aux truffes*, a tin of caviar and – for a reason known only to himself – a large pork pie.

'I didn't know what a girl likes to eat nowadays,' he explained, opening the champagne as I found a pair of glass flutes.

We sat on the sofa, or rather, he sat and I lay, *maja*-not-yet-*desnuda* style, with my legs across his lap. I held both glasses while David poured and we took in the new-old look of ourselves. He set the bottle aside, but before taking his glass from me he undid his shirt cuff and rolled back his sleeve. He drew back the hem of my skirt and laid the underside of his forearm against my thigh.

'Look,' he said. 'Our skin's still the same. Still the same grain, cut from the same bale.'

He restored my skirt to its former position, primly straightening the hem closer to my knees, as though it were altogether too soon for him to have seen the tops of my stockings. Then he took his glass from me, took a first mouthful of champagne and passed it back to me in a tender, careful kiss.

Plus ça change … Except that when he tried the same move again, we weren't quite co-ordinated and some of his next mouthful of Krug went on my hair.

'My darling—' he said, slipstreaming smoothly into a perfect Noël Coward impersonation. 'Your hair smells of Krug. Strange, since we only drink Dom Pérignon …'

But not everything was quite *la même chose*. David's own hair, which previously had been sandy and only speckled with grey, was fully grey now, pure white in places. His face didn't look too much older overall, but was every year older and then some around his eyes. It was the strain of all that time spent scanning entrances and exits, I seemed to know. The constant vigilance, both inside and outside of his own head, had created a network of permanent creases as his gaze narrowed too many times ever to relax. Whatever the source of that drive in him, the thing that sustained his perpetual surveillance, it was still what made David run.

His mouth had altered a little bit. His top lip seemed to have drawn back, giving the appearance of a slight fixed smile. But it wasn't a smile of contentment, I seemed to know that too, more a rictus of resignation, from having to sip too frequently from the poisoned chalice in a life that still wasn't how he wanted it to be. After all the Round Table references he had put into his earlier books – especially in *Tinker Tailor*, with Merlin, Witchcraft and the Lancelot and Guinevere subplot of Bill and Ann – he was almost Arthurian himself now. The questing knight, still strong, still valiant, but ageing; weary from seeking his elusive, perhaps illusory, personal grail and knowing his time to find it, if he ever could, was running out.

Halfway through the Krug we took our glasses to the bedroom.

'You're a phenomenon,' he told me as we undressed. 'You really *don't* age. There's not a line on you and you still have the breasts of a seventeen-year-old. I can't believe it – you're just a wondrous impossibility. You always were.'

David's admiration sang in my ears. It always did.

'I've become quite fat, as you can see,' he added. 'But I'm determined to lose it now, for a girl.'

He overstated the case, but he'd definitely put on weight. In fact, I thought he'd looked quite Smiley-ish at the lecture, especially when he put on a pair of heavy-rimmed glasses to read from his notes. Or even a little Philby-like, from that old video. Art and Life – Life and Art. With David, there was never a clean sheet of A4 space between the two.

I reassured him that he wasn't fat. 'You've just got a belly on you, that's all.' I ran my hand across it, then down. 'I don't mind a bit, except it rather spoils the view—'

Here was something else that hadn't changed. All my nerves that morning had disappeared the moment I saw David walking towards me and they didn't return now. I *knew* this man and he knew *me*. Our appetite for one another was as insatiable as ever, perhaps even more so now it was unleashed to take its fill after a fourteen-year famine.

Afterwards we lay in bed just looking at each other, David framing my hair around my face with his feather-soft touch. Then tears began to flow from his eyes, though his face remained composed.

'No one will ever love you as I do,' he said solemnly. 'That's my vanity.'

I made no reply, just kissed his tears. He had spoken for both of us.

We made a picnic for ourselves on the living-room rug.

'I remembered you liked big balls,' David remarked with a chuckle as we dug into the golden caviar. The conversation went on happily while we ate and drank and looked at each other some more, but then ebbed strangely. It wasn't awkwardness that was the bar to fluency, it was something else. My new-old renewed-restored lover quickly discerned what it was.

'We need new terms,' he declared.

'Agreed,' I seconded. 'What do you suggest?'

'I think we should just make it easy on ourselves. No more big promises. No more great escapes. Just see ourselves and enjoy the good stuff and get away when we can.'

Again, how funny. That was all I'd ever wanted right from the start, the time-honoured married-man-and-mistress template so exemplified by George and Gigi. It was David who wouldn't take the easy route, who made the ever-escalating promises and needed the ever-greater escapes. Did this mean he'd changed? Had he finally learned to stop overloading and over-complicating everything? I told him it sounded like a good way forward; a little late in the day, I didn't add, but better than never.

'But what about a girl? What are her terms? What does she want out of this?'

Hmm. He had just offered my preferred terms as his own, as though I'd been the one originally wanting something else. It took me a moment to think of an additional clause to the new compact. Then the exact thing came to me. David raised his eyebrows expectantly.

'No more talk about your family.'

Meaning; no more minutely parsed critiques of his marriage, no more stories about his endless sons and how *wonderful* they were and, presumably by now, how wonderful *their* families were too. No more tales at all from the domestic areas of his life, in which I had and wanted no part. Meaning also; no more of the inevitable corollary, the lamentations over how he didn't need all their woes and worries loaded on to him, or even the good things with them very much, and how it all took time away from his writing. I'd never wanted to know any of it and it only ate into our time together to have him tell me about it. But I didn't elaborate, I let my statement stand.

'All right,' he said after a moment. 'Absolutely.'

He nodded affirmatively, rather as though he were committing one further item to memory in an advanced round of 'I-packed-my-bag'.

Now we had terms, we could schmooze properly. The Krug was finished, but David retrieved the Stoly from the freezer and picked up two fresh glasses from a drinks tray on the sideboard by the dining table on his way back. He was my room-mate once again and we settled back on the sofa, resuming our former positions, to talk.

He told me about his new book that was 'just on the go'. It was set in Africa, hence the trip to Nairobi, where he intended to return shortly. He was tackling Big Pharma – the multi-national pharmaceutical companies – and how they were unloading bad drugs on patients there, using them as unwitting guinea-pigs for clinical trials. 'My heroine discovers what's happening,' he explained. 'She's killed because of it at the start of the book and her husband sets out to track down her murderers. It's called *The Mad Gardener*,' he concluded happily.

He didn't talk about Yvette and I had the sense that he wanted to keep his thoughts and feelings about her at bay, at least for the duration of his visit to me. We talked instead about our loves in the intervening years. David didn't seem to have had too many. One that was quite fun and lasted a little bit, with a well-regarded photo-journalist who'd approached him at a publicity event in Washington.

"'Is Mrs Cornwell here for a photograph," she asks enthusiastically, looking all around. "Is Mrs Cornwell here?"' David was smiling as he recalled the scene, acting out her gestures with her camera. 'It was quite a good stunt,' he said admiringly, 'establishing I was on my own. I liked that. We used to talk a lot on the phone—' He drank some vodka from the glass he held cradled to his chest, his other hand resting on my thigh. Then the smile slipped away. 'Jane handles all the household accounts now that she doesn't have Nick to see to anymore. She came to me with a phone bill,' he went on without affect, the way he always spoke about his wife to me. '"I think BT have made a mistake," she said. "We don't know anyone with this number, do we?" It was the photo-journalist's, of course. I looked at her and replied, "I don't think I am accountable to you for the phone calls I make." Well, it was frosty for a few days.'

He took another sip of vodka and his face opened again, while his hand closed more tightly on my thigh.

'But it wasn't a great love, for either of us. The last time we met up, nothing happened – we just agreed to lie in bed together and talk.'

There were some other minor encounters, he added, only a few and all *en passant*.

'But nothing like us,' he concluded. 'No one like Our Sue.'

He paused to drain his glass, then grew quite solemn again.

'I said you were my last love and I meant it. I knew it, you see, even then. I'm deathly sure of it now.'

I believed him without question. The two women who had been his most significant loves before me had now both died, each in the most terrible and sudden of circumstances and one just before we began our relationship *each time*. It wasn't anything even he could write. I could feel David consciously summoning the last of his belief in love to seize this un-looked-for second chance with me.

He set his glass down and took my hand in an oddly chaste gesture.

'Were there any writers amongst yours?' he asked.

No, I told him, and he looked relieved. I didn't say that I'd shared Jeremy's Belgravia mews house for a period only a couple of years back. Cohabiting quite happily and platonically with an ex would have taken far too much explaining for David, who had only ever cohabited platonically with his wives, though never, I think, quite happily. My guess was that he meant *his* kind of writer. He was worried there'd been a successor *of rank*.

I listed my intervening lovers for him by occupation, giving no names: one TV guy (Peter), one Old Etonian City headhunter, and the rest were actors (one of whom, I also omitted to tell him, wrote very good plays for stage and screen). They were all lovely men. (There'd also been one diagnosable psychopath, a mercifully brief rebound relationship I'd had immediately after leaving David, but I didn't want to sully the moment, so didn't mention him at all.)

And there was a mad weekend I'd spent with a reader at the Magic Hotel in Hollywood. David laughed when I told him how 'the Hamlet of his generation' had enacted scenes from his recently failed second marriage, playing all the parts in an impromptu one-man show in his hotel room while completely naked. The actor claimed he'd never told anyone those things before, so I suppose I was briefly his audience of one, too. I mentioned that he'd later published a novel with all the same scenes in it.

'I got a mention in it as "a willowy blonde",' I said, 'though only to say that he never went for that type. I think he meant me, anyway.'

Finally, I gave David one name. A big movie star whose go-to girl in London I'd been for several years. I felt I had to name him since he unquestionably had rank.

'Really?' he said in surprise. 'Well – all I can say is that you have very good taste. And so, of course, does he.'

He considered something for a moment.

'Tell me, my darling, does he know about me?'

Yes, I said; in the same way that he and I were talking now. 'Why? Do you mind?'

'No. Not a bit. But it explains something. I encountered him not so long ago in LA, in the elevator of my hotel. I introduced myself and said how much I admired his work and he gave me this frozen look. He was perfectly courteous, but he got out at the next available floor. I wonder now whether he was afraid I was going to ask him to compare notes!'

I pictured the scene and was sorry for my lovely movie star's discomfort. He was such a le Carré fan too. Perhaps his wife was with him in the lift, which might have accounted for his deer-in-headlights response. But David didn't say and the world's worst investigative reporter didn't ask. I was just exceptionally pleased to learn that something from *my* life had slipped through the impenetrable Cornwell surveillance net into *his*.

'Do you still see Gigi?' he asked next. He hadn't mentioned George's retirement or the fall-out from it. He probably wanted to know if I knew about it from her, which of course I did and which he would assume I did once he established we'd kept in touch. I was familiar with David's interrogation technique this time around.

'Yes, I do,' I replied. 'I'm going down to visit her in her weekend cottage in a couple of weeks.'

'I expect she's still vivacious?'

'She is.'

'I always mistrusted that in her. But if you're friends—'

That was rather sly of him, I thought. Since George and he were no longer on terms, I suppose he felt free to take the shot. (He'd felt free to take a shot at me with them, after all, after I left Tregiffian that first time.) But I didn't let it bother me. I knew how David was, how he could be, and none of it was going to bother me this time around. No doubt Graham would have told me one last time that I had myself snowed.

'I don't think we'll miss the St John's Wood flat, do you?' he asked, casting ahead. He already looked as if he lived here with me now. 'I sold it to Willie Shawcross.'

'Yes,' I said. 'I know.'

'*Do* you? That's very clever of you, then. How did you find out?'

The apprehension on his face indicated he was trying to guess how I'd come by that piece of information prior to his disclosing it. I offered a sphinx-like smile but no explanation. It was more therapeutic to let him sweat through all the paranoid possibilities than reveal the mundane truth, which was that I'd phoned the flat a couple of months after we'd last seen each other there, to see if he was still using it as an escape hatch from his marriage. It was in one of those moments of burning post-break-up curiosity and I'd intended to hang up once I heard him answer. (This was still before caller ID, but did I honestly think he wouldn't have known it was me?) But no one picked up. Instead, the out-going message on an answering machine announced – *This is William Shawcross. Please leave a message.*

'I sold it with all the furniture, by the way,' David said finally, when he saw he wasn't getting the story out of me. 'And with that naked picture of you still hanging over the bed.'

David was still averse to taking showers and so we took a bath together before he left, lest he transfer evidence of *that delicious light scent you still wear* back to Hampstead. I asked him if he ever wore cologne himself; he'd just made me realise I'd never noticed any on him. He told me no, he didn't, and I asked him why not. Wouldn't it have been a useful layer of cover for tell-tale traces of perfume? But he only repeated that he didn't use cologne, confirming that even if I *did* think to ask a follow-up question, I seldom received an answer. But in any case, I'd been coming at the subject the wrong way. He would never have *needed* a scent of his own for *domestic* cover. After his disastrous relationship with Susan Kennaway during his first marriage – possibly as a result of it – David only ever had girlfriends *abroad*. Ours was the only other love affair he ever conducted on home turf – the first since 1965.

'I think we need a trip together sometime soon, don't you?' he said from the tap end as we bathed. 'Switzerland, I think. How does Geneva sound to a girl? That would be fun, wouldn't it?'

Switzerland. Where we had taken our very first clandestine trip together and so many others afterwards. Where David always looked so handsome and relaxed and at one with himself and his surroundings. Where his private company and his head man had been based for so many years and where he still kept a chalet, 'his place', in the mountains. Where he'd first escaped from England to become a fledgling spook. If we were going to have trips to Switzerland again then of course we wouldn't miss the St John's Wood flat. That entire country was David's safe house.

I said Geneva sounded terrific – especially, I thought privately, because he hadn't called it a 'second honeymoon'. I was relieved, too, that he didn't suggest Cornwall. I never wanted to go down to Tregiffian again, though I suspected he wasn't going to ask.

'Excellent!' he said happily. 'I'll make some plans and let you know.'

Before he went, he asked to see my copy of *Single & Single*. He gave the title one of his little twists, calling it *Sniggle & Sniggle*. He opened it at the title page, took a pen from inside his jacket and swiftly added something to his signature and date, which was all he'd managed to produce after our hot clinch at the signing. He snapped the cover shut, set the book down on the table, kissed me as urgently as ever and left.

I opened a front window and leaned out. After a few moments I saw him cross from the building and begin to walk up the street towards the main road for a taxi. I knew he'd look back. That was why he'd crossed the road, so that he could.

When he saw me at the high window, he paused to twinkle up a little wave. I'd dressed again after our bath, and before he turned away, in a sudden recollection of our seeing *Silkwood* together, I opened my blouse and flashed one of my breasts at him in reply. It's what Meryl Streep does to Kurt Russell, before she gets into her vehicle and drives off at the end of the film. With a little more reflection, given what had just happened to Yvette, I wouldn't have risked reminding him of a film in which the crusading heroine meets a vehicular death, though it was perhaps what had put it in my mind. But he only saw the gesture for what it was, a spontaneous invitation to come back soon, and blew a kiss up to me in reply. Then I went to see what he'd written in the book.

David had drawn a line from his signature to the nearest bit of space on the title page to record a personal literary addendum.

John le Carré ——— was born again soon after this predestined encounter, following fourteen years solitary, loyally served.

He surprised me ten minutes later with a phone call from the taxi to tell me how much he loved me – 'The technology's moved on since we originally did this,' he noted – and then again later, to say the same thing from Hampstead Heath.

I didn't hear from David again until he rang late morning the following Wednesday.

'I just got back last night,' he said, and drew a great breath. Back from Yvette's funeral, he meant, held at her farmhouse in southern France. He had taken Jane, he said, and confessed to me how he had simply wept throughout the whole thing. He ended the brief call saying, 'I adore you. Your body is exactly as I remember it. So beautiful. I'll call you tomorrow with some proposals.'

But he didn't call the next day. Instead, a letter arrived the day after that, the last day of April. It had two little faces drawn on the envelope, though only one of them was a smiley. The other looked more like its elderly namesake. I'd forgotten how he used to do that with his envelopes, signalling the tone of their contents with a variety of cartoon expressions on little round faces, though usually only one at a time. Seeing the un-smiley one now, I began to wish I'd added a second condition to my side of our new terms – *No more bloody letters*.

Inside the envelope the smiling face was repeated on what he called letter one, the frown face on letter two. Both parts were written on yellow copy paper instead of his usual white A4.

I was still his darling Sue, it seemed, and what he wrote on all of the first page and most of the second was a memorialisation of our most recent sexual encounter that was so extraordinarily graphic I was almost shocked to read it. But after that he began to cast ahead. We needed a vision that was large enough to allow for our shared life and our separate ones, something that enabled us to feel happy and lucky and free, never caged. This, I already sensed, was his own lifelong fear of a new escape route just leading him to another confinement. He went on to tell me that he loved me and that he had always loved me, but then reminded me how, towards the end of our last relationship, I had thrown some things back at him. He quoted my saying *never do it to anybody else*, meaning, never indulge the worst of himself in another relationship, as he had with me. (I might add that I believe he never did. As his last love, which he always insisted I was, I should have known it was axiomatic that there wouldn't *be* anyone else of consequence for him to do it *to*. From this distance, I can see how the hurt he inflicted was simply concomitant to his letting me so far into his life that he couldn't protect me from the worst of himself. As he told me right from the start in Greece, *It's a rocky path you've chosen, you can't know* …) He went on in the letter to make the nicely ironic point that now 'anybody else' was me. But he acknowledged that we were both possibly wiser and would probably know better.

He claimed to be *very* old, with what he called 'injury time' fast approaching. There were all his commitments – the new book, the movies of old ones, travelling everywhere for everything, including one trip to Panama already made that year with the original director on *The Tailor*, and a second likely to be required now a new director, John Boorman, had been brought in. Of the rapidly diminishing time he felt he had left to him, he feared there would be very little free to spend on us. He wanted to get ahead of the disappointment he saw coming.

He seemed also to be saying, elliptically as ever, that he no longer aimed to get out of what he'd previously called the slammer of his domestic life. From what he wrote, if it had ever been a prison before, it now seemed to be a practical try-out for what would shortly become Guantanamo Bay. He described himself as living in a closely monitored enclave under what seemed to be quasi-carceral conditions, since he appeared to have no friends and neither did Jane, who he claimed never left the house. I had thought our new terms made it clear that I didn't want him to do anything he didn't want to do – 'just make it easy on ourselves', as we'd agreed – but his present frame of mind wouldn't permit that take-it-as-it-comes approach any traction.

He told me again how he'd wept at Yvette's funeral, seeing traces of their old love everywhere in her house and with everyone taking him aside to commiserate with him. But he managed to end the long first section of the letter with something closer to hope: he claimed that love was what would rescue it all and that having gained back in his life what he had lost any hope of recapturing was nothing short of an unimagined blessing. The shorter second section indulged his darkest thoughts and gave further black moments from the funeral, most despairingly when Yvette's closest friends and even her daughter had each told him privately that he was the love of her life.

He ended by saying that he'd be away over the weekend and would ring me once he returned. He didn't explicitly ask me to write back, but said he would call in at Hampstead Post Office before he rang again.

This wasn't unfamiliar territory. After recent events, David appeared to be on the wrong side of his head again. As it happened, I understood better than he knew how he was feeling about Yvette. A former lover and close friend of mine – the big TV exec I'd surrendered to be with David the first time – had died only four months earlier, following eight weeks in intensive care across two hospitals after catastrophic aortic-valve failure. I'd sat next to his bed in the final ICU with my arms around him as he died. He was only sixty-one, the same age as Yvette. There had been a memorial 'do' for him at BAFTA earlier that month, where Barry Took, Bill Cotton and other old friends of his from the Beeb each told me that I'd been – yes – the love of his life. So we'd both recently experienced these terrible too-soon losses and other people's too-well-meaning commiserations. Yet now there was this unexpected second chance for ourselves, this blessing, as he wrote. But so soon after readily seizing both it and me with his two great hands, David was claiming he couldn't see a way to run with the heaven-sent opportunity.

It may seem obvious that it was Yvette's death which had put him into such a tailspin. But I don't believe it was, at least not directly. It may sound brutal, but I'd come to understand that David almost liked to have a quotient of death around him. I don't for a moment mean that he wished it to happen to anyone, least of all to anyone he loved, or that he didn't grieve when it did – only that, should it happen, it was something he could roll with quite comfortably. I think the ultimate loss rendered by death served to validate his belief in the other losses he made himself have in his life – freedom and lasting love, to name only two.

So, as my thesis goes, it wasn't Yvette's death which had so confounded him. It was a different loss altogether, of something he valued above all else, something which, in his whole life, he hadn't believed he would *ever* lose – namely, his *nerve*. It was when he said he'd taken Jane to the funeral that something clicked in my head and made me see it, as though my internal camera had suddenly pulled the focus on the scene David was framing up till then.

I will try and show it here, but the exposition – peeling back the layers – will take a page or two.

David had previously told me that he'd never confessed the affair with Yvette to his wife. The one time I'd asked him what he would do if Jane found out about *us*, he answered flatly, *I'd deny you – I'd deny you utterly*. It was what he'd done when she actually did confront him about Janet Stevens. It was the First Rule of Spy Club: DENY EVERYTHING. All spooks knew it. Until his Fall, Philby was the all-time exemplar. Second Rule of Spy Club was: DENY. EVERYTHING. ALWAYS. Meaning that even two years after Yvette's death, after dedicating *The Constant Gardener* to her and revealing how her tireless aid work had helped inspire the novel, David would still be claiming she was only ever a friend, so thoroughly persuading one interviewer that she wrote how he had only just remarried and started a new family when he met her in '74. As though that confirmed his fidelity! *Sixteen* years after her death, David still barred his biographer from writing about their true relationship. (With the exception of Susan Kennaway, whose story was already in the public sphere, Sisman couldn't write about *any* of his subject's 'other women', including me. More on that later.)

But David had 'turned' Yvette from lover to friend fairly soon into their affair. He had tried to do the same with me, if you recall, though the record shows that a platonic friendship would have been impossible to sustain in our case. Yvette, however, agreed to take the deal. Better to have David in her life somehow, she must have thought, than not at all. Why he pressed for this conversion with each of us goes, I believe, to the notion of imprisonment and escape that had been indelibly imprinted on him, so deeply and from so far back as to be part of the fabric of his soul. His first marriage was an escape from a life of psychological and emotional imprisonment with his father; his second marriage was an escape from the psychological and emotional imprisonment of the first, and then the second marriage – the escape from which he attempted once with me, but never again – finally became Gitmo. David felt constantly that he wasn't free, yet couldn't see it was all his own doing in submitting to his inner demons and letting them run him. He once declared to me that he was *a born architect of slammers*, but even that was an understatement. David carried his own personal slammer around with him, like a snail with its shell on its back. Graham said exactly this in his cut-to-the-chase way on that gloomy day at Wimbledon, after he'd heard all my rationalisations about David's behaviour: *Nah – he's got you snowed. If he's miserable in his marriage it's because he likes it that way – for some miserable reason in himself.* I hadn't liked hearing it at the time, but Graham was right. He so often was. I rather think now that David had himself snowed most of all.

So it was for this reason, I believe, that he so quickly turned Yvette from a lover into a friend – *We'll always have Phnom Penh* – to block his own escape route from leading him to further incarceration. But here's the bigger question: why go the extra step and turn her into a *family* friend?

It was for cover. All his instinct, training and lifelong practice necessitated it. Cover for David, as for any spy, was vital. Without cover there was no deniability. Without deniability he would risk exposure. He could be 'blown'. What better way to dispel any doubts his wife may have harboured about his fidelity, therefore, than to bring the woman he'd betrayed her with into the family fold? To have both women smile and laugh together while he buttled around them – *Fancy a snoot?* – or played *mein Host* so charmingly in restaurants? It was all for cover, of course.

This is the extra quality that made David who he was, that made him *le Carré*. He needed the experience of acting out his fiction for himself so that he could convince other people it was living fact. Because if he could convince others of it, then *it must be true*. I came to understand that this was what all the research trips were really about. Capturing the exact way the sun slipped behind the mountains at a certain location, or the precise flavours of any distant purlieus, was never his primary motivation. Nor was his lead character truly his 'secret sharer', the expression he stole from Conrad and made his own. This commonly held misunderstanding of his creative method has it entirely backwards – as should be clear from the fact that David so often explained it that way himself. *If you're going south, tell them north.* David's secret sharer was always and only *himself*. He needed a lead character for cover, as an adopted persona, a new skin, in order to live through him – through her, once, with Charlie – while he was out in the field. He no longer had the original spook field he was trained for – born for, even – with its high buzz of operational excitement and peril. Philby's personal betrayal – as I believe David always saw his defection, spoiling forever his chance for adventures in the double-double game – had seen to that. So he recreated the tensions, the daring, the deceptions in his fiction and in his personal life.

When David told me he was going out for a walk in Plomari and took a day-old newspaper with him, he transformed his voice and manner to become his character. It was extraordinary to see the whole scene appear in *A Perfect Spy*. But it was a tortuous piece of pretence if you parse it down to its constituent parts. The former real-life spy and current premier spy novelist deceives his secret girlfriend, with whom he is already deceiving his wife, in order to play out a fictional scene wherein his spy hero deceives his wife to meet the secret contact with whom he is deceiving his masters in the Secret Intelligence Service. He did all that just to ginger up the scene. But he *needed* to do it – to create the edge in the experience so that he could recreate it in his writing. I wonder now what would have happened if I'd seen what he was doing and simply asked, *Are you being Pym?* I can't really imagine.

There was a later point too, in our first relationship, when he suggested I join him on research trips to meet people from his father's life with us *both* behaving as though we shared nothing but a work relationship. It was a test of my capacity to take his direction, no doubt a replaying of some erstwhile trick with his Joes, and I declined. Even if I'd wanted to join him in the exercise, there would have been no point in attempting it. His most cloistered maiden aunt wouldn't have been fooled into thinking our relationship was platonic, let alone Ronnie's old lags. But the sheer bravura of David's performance in these deceptions presented a kind of challenge to those who witnessed them. I'd lived through a couple of them myself, after all. It was all about instilling belief, making his fiction, whether lived or written, seem so authentic that it was accepted as the truth – as much in his lies on the phone to his wife while I was in the hotel bed beside him as in his worldwide bestsellers. He had it from Ronnie, who made so many believe in his cons, and from his pulpit-thumping, lay-preaching family on both sides when he was growing up. He was trained to it for years as a spy.

When David channelled all his considerable conjuring powers into *making* people believe him, most were happy to let him pull off the trick, to have him suspend their disbelief. For the longest time, I was one of them. And even if, sometimes, the belief he wanted seemed to strain credulity, who was going to call him out? He was *John le Carré*, for God's sake. Which of us, among the chosen few ever admitted to his world on any level, would want to be the equivalent of the lone kid in the *Peter Pan* audience who refuses to clap to keep Tinkerbell alive? Compelling performance achieved cover and David's instinct for cover overrode all other considerations. Performative control of the narrative in his external life was what took the pressure off his inner dramas, upon which he never succeeded in bringing down the curtain in his head. Had he ever been forced to confess – about something of consequence or of no significance at all – it would have been the end of the entire show.

So Yvette *had* to become a family friend, or else there was no theatre of the real to prove he could still pull off a cover story. Keeping their affair secret from his wife wasn't enough. Keeping it secret while selling her the false narrative of a friendship which had only ever been platonic was what hit the spot. It was a mark of his great regard for Yvette that he included her in his conspiratorial charade. (His estimation of my performance capacity, on the other hand, was entirely misplaced. I would have blown our cover the moment I failed to resist a *double entendre* about 'deep penetration agents' …) And all the while we may imagine that Yvette was silent in her longing to have her lover back – the love of her life – just as Jane would have been silent in what was either her new understanding or the bitter confirmation of an old one, that she didn't possess her husband's heart. The ex-lover was deceiving the wife to please the man she loved, and the wife, if she knew she was being deceived, tolerated the deception for the same reason. And David, who arranged it all that way, had scripted every scene, down to the last unspoken word.

It was a most amazing business, and I think that it would have been better in the eyes of God if they had all attempted to gouge out each other's eyes with carving knives. But they were 'good people'.

No wonder he claimed *The Good Soldier* was the book of his life. I hadn't understood the full degree of parallel until then.

I should add that when Yvette was in London the time I met her, David took to visiting me at my own flat. He'd also asked me for my keys to St John's Wood, saying he was having some work done there. I believed him, of course, though it's quite obvious to me now that he wanted them for Yvette, to put her up at the flat rather than risk her staying at Hampstead. Having his ex-lover maintain the joint fiction of their always-platonic friendship in front of his wife was by then a well-practised show. But expecting her to carry off the same performance after he had just sent her to have a heart-to-heart lunch with his current girlfriend might have called upon levels of dissembling that were beyond David's estimation of Yvette's capacity. That scenario wouldn't have resembled anything from Ford Madox Ford, or even from le Carré – it would have been pure Iris Murdoch.

Again, this must all be understood in light of the fact that maintaining cover was more important to David than anything – *anything in the world*. Maintaining his cover meant maintaining his nerve and he lived constantly in a state of all-points nervous alert lest he ever be *un*covered in any of his deceptions. Eleanor Philby called it *the most tireless watchfulness* in her husband and it was exactly what I saw in David. It never left him, only ever altering as to degree. Even in his sleep, his indistinct mumblings had a fretful, anticipatory edge.

I don't for a moment mean to suggest that he contrived the situation with his wife and Yvette cynically, or did any of it unfeelingly. David felt *everything*, quite as keenly as those poor babies who are born sometimes without a proper top layer of skin. (To pursue the metaphor, Ronnie had flayed David's off him virtually from birth.) I know very well that he was plagued by guilt, not for every hurtful thing he had done in his life by any means and sometimes for that which hurt only himself, but, amortised across the board, there was more than enough to go around. But he could handle guilt. Like death, it was something he could roll with. He was perversely comfortable with both the secret betrayals *and* the secret guilt they engendered in him. One reinforced the need for the other and David needed both. He had never known anything else. Or so my thesis goes. He was simply a perfect spy, always and forever. He had been one long before the British Secret Services harnessed his native capacity for the benefit of Queen and Country and remained one, I dare guess, to the last. An infiltration agent in his own life.

So back now – albeit some few pages later – to his current tail-spin in the letter.

When Yvette died, David took his wife to her funeral. Quite properly; for, despite the initial contrivance, there can be no doubt that Yvette *was* a very sincere friend to both of them for all those years. She had a huge heart inside that tiny little French body and I'm sure she would have made an especially sincere effort with Jane, as reparations for the never-to-be-disclosed original affair. But at the funeral, when David was suddenly confronted with every sad reminder of what Yvette had *truly* once been to him and he to her, he simply couldn't maintain his own fiction any longer. Overwhelmed by the undeniable evidence of their old love, *he lost his nerve.* He 'wept and wept' for her, as he told me, and his tears were his confession of the truth. Even with Jane at his side, for whose continued deception the whole quarter century of dissembling had been undertaken, he couldn't stop himself from revealing that long-held secret of his heart, in a manner that must have been obvious to all, not least to Jane herself. It might have been an extraordinary catharsis for him, as funerals can so often be, if only his wife hadn't been there. But she *had* to be there – to maintain his twenty-five-year fiction that Yvette was only ever a friend. And his wife's presence was the very thing that blew him. Then the other mourners, thinking they were helping to keep his secret for him, only continued to drive the private reckoning home by drawing him aside – *from his wife* – to tell him the very last thing he needed to hear, that he had been the love of his former lover's life. David must have felt the whole house of cards come tumbling down over Yvette's grave.

He returned from France bone-weary from the massive effort that had kept the performance going for so long, drained by the *débâcle* of the final act and shaken to the core by the private mortal shame of losing his nerve – that cardinal failing for any spy – thereby bringing himself to the very brink, if not actually over the edge, of exposure. For all the explaining and justifying in his letter, it was simply to say he felt he had no strength remaining to him to pick up where he had left things with me. No reserves left to maintain his cover for yet another secret love affair, even if it was the continuation of ours.

Long into his retirement, Smiley's tradecraft was as sharp and subtle as ever. It never failed him. Still younger than his aged hero had been at the height of his powers, David had just witnessed the last of his own tradecraft crumble beneath him. He had experienced the sensation of that degree of exposure only once before, when he learned of Philby's defection and believed it had effectively blown his cover as a spy. But he came back from that. The 'fugue state' the experience generated was what drew *The Spy Who Came In from the Cold* out of him and created the nuclear fusion of his past life in espionage with his future life as a world-class writer. Now it had happened again, but this time the exposure was in his personal life, his one remaining area of covert activity. If David couldn't come back from this – if I couldn't bring him back – there was no hope for our relationship to continue.

Schliesse mir die Augen beide
mit den lieben Händen zu!
Geht doch alles, was ich leide,
unter deiner Hand zur Ruh.
Theodor Storm

Once again, I have absolutely no recollection of what I wrote back, *post restante* Hampstead. My only point of true recall is the determination I felt to give it my all. It was a reprise of the situation after my first visit to Tregiffian. David had wanted me to pull him back from the brink of his own apostasy then and he needed me to repeat the manoeuvre now. So, once again, I gave him the sincerest form I could of whatever I thought it was he would eat. Once again, I was relieved to find he ate up every word. It's possible to infer some of what I must have written from his reply, which he sent by special delivery. He even began with the same line he had praised me with before: *That one doesn't go into the shredder, my girl, I can tell you.* (If in fact it didn't, then I suppose there's an outside chance it's still sitting in one of the multiple hundreds of boxes of papers in the le Carré archive at the Bodleian.)

There was another smiley face grinning on the seal of the envelope, this one replete with stick-out ears and stand-up hair. Inside, a much bigger one was positively beaming from the top of the first page above a banner headline that proclaimed all the notes I'd struck were perfect and was signed:– W. A. Mozart

He wrote that my letter was delightful, marvellous, generous and had ended the great battle he realised he had been waging with no one but himself. I had helped persuade him, he said, that it was time to embrace a newer, freer way forward. I must have written in some detail about my former lover, because he asserted that it would be a lucky man who died in my arms and added that he was glad that I too still loved my former lovers. I must have written about Graham as well, because he said he remembered him with a smile. He said again that he would love me always and always had, so much and so constantly that he loved me across rooms where I wasn't present and in restaurants where I wasn't sitting. I believed him too. Only David could have turned such a plangent and paradoxical claim into such a tribute to the power of his love. He declared he couldn't write that morning, but didn't mind, because though nothing moved through his pen, so much was moving in his heart. He quoted the poem by Storm in German. It translates:

> *Close both my eyes*
> *with your beloved hands!*
> *Let all my suffering*
> *gain rest beneath your hand.*

It wasn't possible *not* to love David, you see.

He then explained his immediate itinerary – Ireland first to see Boorman, to discuss the script David had written to replace the one neither of them liked by Andrew Davies, then ten days in the Atlas Mountains on a long-delayed holiday. (He meant with his wife, but knew it would be discordant to say.) But we'd go away together soon, he said finally, and joked that he promised to choose somewhere 'really unpleasant' so that we'd have to spend the whole time in bed. Meanwhile he'd call whenever he could.

He called – and called and called. It was as if there had never been a problem and as if there never would be one again. Right then, he was full of the new movie, which, for his sake, I hoped was going to be an improvement on its predecessors. During the Q&A after the lecture, David was asked to opine about why his films generally failed to set cinema box-office sales on fire. Regarding the failure of the most recent – *The Russia House*, which had Sean Connery in the lead, Michelle Pfeiffer as the love interest, a stellar supporting cast, screenplay by Tom Stoppard, and Fred Schepisi directing – I wondered whether he might be at a loss for an explanation. But I should have had more faith.

'The thing is,' he said sagely to the audience, with a donnish lift of his chin as he prepared to impart a hitherto unremarked detail, 'you can't imperil Bond.'

The quality of voice and the skill in the delivery was still what David's fiction-spinning was all about and the audience bought his entirely specious piece of reasoning with a general murmur of assent. Think about it for a moment. If this were true, then not just Connery but every other action-movie leading man would never have a career beyond his first hit. *We can't cast that guy as the hero again – the audience already knows he's gonna win!* Did I say specious? I meant bonkers. But now the hunt was on for somebody new to imperil. David told me McKellen wasn't in the running for Pendel, which I said was a great shame.

'Do you have any ideas yourself, then, my love?' he asked me. 'Any likely actors? Casting is your field too.'

I said I would let him know if I came up with any candidates.

(At David's urging, Geoffrey Rush would get the part in the end, opposite Pierce Brosnan – not just another peril-proof Bond, in case he hadn't noticed, but actually the current one at the time. And sadly, the film would be another failure-to-launch.)

I went down to see Gigi in her cottage. On my way to the station a charity collector rattled his tin at me.

'Help the Aged?' he asked cheerily.

Lost in thought about my self-described 'very old' lover, I brushed past, telling him emphatically, 'I already gave!'

I hadn't yet told Gigi about this second time around with David. I didn't quite know what was stopping me, except for a mildly shamefaced awareness that she was the friend who had most helped me get over him the first time.

We sat in the riverside garden of her pretty Berkshire cottage, drinking wine in the spring afternoon sunshine and watching the ducks and swans paddle by on the water. She pointed out a clump of bluest blue forget-me-nots from George that were thriving in one corner. She told me I was looking well, then gave me a more sizing glance.

'I know that look!' she exclaimed. 'You've got a new man!'

I didn't confirm or deny her declaration, but I'm sure my face gave me away.

'Come on, Dawson – tell me who he is.'

Can I not, I asked her sheepishly, not just yet? It wasn't that I didn't want to tell her, I said, only that it was all rather new and uncertain at the moment; I was sure she would understand.

'Of course I do, darling. No problem.' She sipped her wine and I thought the subject had passed. But then I saw a sudden thought cross her brow. 'Don't tell me—!' she exclaimed, as her face lit up with a new possibility. 'It's not another impossible famous writer, is it?'

Dearest Gigi. How unconsciously wonderful of her to put it that way. I hadn't wanted to deceive her about what was happening with David and now I wouldn't have to.

'No,' I told her with complete honesty. 'It's not another impossible famous writer.'

I only omitted to say that it was exactly the same one.

On his next visit to my flat, David said he would arrive at ten in the morning but turned up even earlier. I had barely bathed and dressed.

'I haven't put my make-up on yet,' I told him as I let him in.

'No, I thought I wouldn't bother either,' he said sweetly. None of that mattered to him, I'd honestly forgotten.

He was wearing a very spiffy new suit in a fine dark blue cloth. I said it looked very good on him, thinking that even Graham might have approved. He had 'a new suiter', he explained – Douglas Hayward, the man who famously tailored sharp-suited British movie icons such as Terence Stamp and Michael Caine. I'd read that Hayward was the model for Pendel. When I hugged David this time, I could feel a hard shape across the middle of his back under his new suit and for a brief moment I concluded he'd surrendered to the worst of his paranoia – it seemed no more than an inevitability – and was finally packing. But when the jacket came off it wasn't a gun-holster I'd felt, but the leather cross piece on a pair of new braces. He'd already lost enough weight, as he said he would 'for a girl', that he needed them to keep his spiffy new pants from falling down.

He brought an equally snazzy briefcase with him, which must have fitted his cover story, along with the suit, since he intended to spend the whole day with me. There had been a distinct evolution in David's cases since I'd known him, starting with the dull and dated tan briefcase for the *Smiley's People* recording, progressing to a cool black international-traveller-style pilot's case once he acquired the St John's Wood flat, and now there was this ultra-smart flat attaché case, with a very distinctive dark brown covering. I had a suspicion I knew what it was.

'Two-hundred-year-old Russian reindeer hide,' David announced as he saw me admire it. 'They brought up bales of the stuff with an old shipwreck off the Cornish coast and the Duchy awarded licences to local artisans. They've made it into everything possible.'

'Yes,' I said, pleased to have my guess confirmed. 'I know someone who re-upholstered an old Lagonda with it.'

'You know people in Cornwall?' He looked a little startled.

'Yes,' I said again. 'All sorts. I spent six months down there a couple of years ago.'

'You didn't tell me.'

'You didn't ask.'

'Well, that's true.'

'I rented a cottage from some friends,' I told him, not offering the explanation I knew he wanted to dispel his immediate suspicion that I'd had a lover in his own county besides himself. I could see him picturing me riding shotgun in the Lagonda, or something more graphic over the hood. Not that anything close had been the case. I'd simply wanted to be away from my London flat when the outside of the building was being renovated and the offer of the cottage happened to come up. Once again, I didn't want to interfere with the potential therapeutic benefits of leaving him guessing.

'But it was in the habitable part, where trees grow and birds sing and they don't bury cows with their hooves sticking up out of the ground,' I explained, relenting a little, but wishing to make the point about Tregiffian, which I hadn't before. 'So not near your end.'

'Ah.'

I don't think this entirely dispelled his fear of there having been another tall man from Cornwall in my past, but he seemed relieved that he still retained exclusive territorial rights at the *Straw Dogs* end of the county. He was less relieved when I told him I'd picked up some gossip about him while I was there.

'What was that?' he asked gingerly.

I named a local painter, a man with a modest national profile, someone I knew he would have encountered. The mother of the friend I'd rented the cottage from was a painter herself and Cornwall, in terms of social circles, particularly artistic ones, was a very small place. It was she who'd told me the rumour.

'It was believed,' I said, 'that you'd had an affair with his wife.'

'God,' David said quietly. His shoulders rose defensively and he offered a small involuntary gagging sound from the back of his throat.

'So you're saying it was just a groundless rumour, then,' I asked. 'You didn't have a fling with her?'

'Under *no* circumstances.' He looked genuinely appalled.

I believed him, but couldn't resist the tease.

'You were kind to call him a painter, though,' he said to conclude the matter. 'I shouldn't put him above a dauber.'

I hadn't given credence to the story, though it was strenuously urged upon me as being true. I knew David wouldn't so much as flirt with anyone so close to home, particularly in such a socially incestuous place as that county. But it made me wonder, as I hadn't at the time, how he might have responded if I'd contacted him myself while I was down there.

The attaché case contained a copy of his script for *The Tailor*, which he wanted me to have. I noticed a large, leather-bound desk diary in there too, though it wasn't clear why he would want to carry one around. It was a gift from his publisher, apparently, with a literary quotation for each day.

'And not one from me,' David said pointedly.

Though ostensibly bound by our new terms, wherein he'd agreed not to talk about his family, David nevertheless appeared to feel free to talk at length about his wife. Things that didn't start off being about her often devolved into sidelong complaints. He told me he'd started a charity, to return a portion of his own good financial fortune to those less well off.

'It's called the David and Jane Cornwell Charitable Trust. It's a way of paying back, you see. Tithing.'

I asked what sort of aid the charity was set up to offer.

'Small things for now, mostly local. But where it's needed most. Helping a young mother with the train fare to take the kids to see their dad in jail. That sort of thing.'

I imagined David felt for that kind of need very keenly, given Ronnie's incarceration during his own childhood.

'Jane's quite involved with it,' he continued. 'I started it in part to give her something to do. She can patronise them all there to her heart's content.'

I recalled how she had tried her hand with me when she rang about the *Drummer Girl* abridgement.

'I've given her the house in Hampstead,' he went on, warming to his theme. 'And I've made her a millionaire in her own right. But she doesn't *do* anything with it. She came to me recently to ask whether I thought it permissible for her to arrange to have something funded. From the uncertain way she was approaching the possibility, I thought she meant by the Trust. Then I realised she meant the money *I'd* given her.' David raised his eyebrows, to reflect his astonishment at her diffidence. '"My dear woman," I told her, "it's *your* money to do with *as you wish.*"'

I suppose he couldn't see it. George had, when he remarked to Gigi how Jane seemed 'hoovered up' since her marriage. I'd heard it for myself, on that call, when she said 'we' so often and never once said 'I'. But David couldn't see it at all. He'd made his wife's every thought and deed subservient to his own for nearly three decades and yet still felt free to be critical of her when she demonstrated uncertainty over acting on her own initiative. Not that he said absolutely nothing in Jane's favour. Before, he'd said that she was a devoted mother. Now, with their son grown and living away, David insisted that she was 'a very fine editor'. But that was about it. As before, I don't believe it was out of any consideration for my sensibilities that he held back on her praise. In a wry aside at the lecture, he'd said that he deliberately put a new generation of heroes into his novels nowadays, because he wanted to 'write about younger men who had sex lives'. This drew a titillated laugh from the audience, as well as a knowing smile from me. But now he told me quite frankly that his marriage had been sexless since *before* we met the *first* time. Well. I only wish he'd told me then, when it would torture me to think of him still having what he'd made a point of calling 'rotten little duty fucks' in those intervals when I couldn't see him.

'We should have just moved in together, you and I,' he said, smiling distantly, 'and fuck the lot of them.'

There was no point in asking him who had stopped us from doing just that – supposing I'd wanted to in the first place.

'You were my best shot at it, Our Sue – getting out of the slammer. But I can't leave a sixty-two-year-old woman now.'

Again – was that anything I'd ever yet asked him to do?

We had a happy early lunch at a local Lebanese restaurant, where David either forbore or forgot to correct me about raising food to my mouth with my left hand. But he made another observation in its place. Reaching out to hold my hand, he looked at my wrist and asked, 'What's the story with your watch?'

There wasn't one. I'd simply liked the look of it in Bloomingdale's on a recent trip to New York. Then I realised what he was really asking. It was a man's watch – probably unisex – and he suspected it had come from the wrist of a lover.

'It's just a watch,' I said. 'No story.'

He tilted his head a little as he continued to look at my wrist. The story for David was that it wasn't the gold watch he'd given me.

'Perhaps you'll let me buy you jewellery again,' he said unassumingly. 'This time, some pieces that you'll actually like to wear.'

It must have hurt him, that I hadn't kept his original pieces. He didn't need to ask if I still had them. He would know I'd have worn them for him if I did. I had kept them for a while, but then it had begun to hurt *me* to see them. I should have said something to this effect by way of gentle explanation at the time – it needn't have been anything more than I've written here – but for some reason I didn't. It's these little moments, not the bigger scenarios, that I so wish I could replay differently now.

We returned to the flat and went straight to bed, taking a pair of tumblers and the Stoly I now always kept in the freezer. Prompted by our conversation, I noticed that when David removed his own watch it wasn't the lovely flat white gold Rolex he had always worn before. I asked him what the story was there and he told me how he had given it to a jeweller to clean, to be told that it subsequently 'disappeared' from the premises.

'Did you sue?' I asked. I imagined him getting Special Branch on the case.

'No,' David replied, with that *Weltschmerz* sigh I hadn't heard in a long while. 'They gave me this one in its place.'

It was funny, mystifying in fact, how he let some slights slide and took other ones to task. Even if we'd ever taken that mythical extra step of moving in together, I should still never have been able to guess which way he would land on things.

He declared our trip to Geneva was on at the end of the month and I asked if the spook travel agents were arranging it.

'No,' he said. 'I've no spooks left anywhere. I'm completely out of tradecraft, my darling. It's all gone. Everything's got to be strictly cash-cash now.'

It was how he'd described Pym's under-the-counter payments for the room at Miss Dubber's, his autobiographical hero's final safe house. Art/Life was with us again, though time had moved inexorably on. Rainer was dead, George was retired and the spook travel agent in the City, like the Cold War and the Berlin Wall, was no more. David took a thick envelope from his attaché case. It contained far more than enough Swiss francs for my plane ticket and instructions as to which flight to book myself on. But it surprised me that he hadn't kept even one covert line open in the whole vast economic enterprise that was John le Carré. He must have believed he'd never need one again.

He'd already be in Switzerland and would meet me at the airport. He would try and call me before then, but it was only two weeks away. It was going to be wonderful, he said, kissing me before he went. Really wonderful. I waved to him again from the bedroom window and he blew up another kiss to my naked breast.

My diary entry for the day has David arriving at my flat at 9.45 am and leaving at 4 pm. It ends with his telling me as he left, *We're married, you and I. So that's it.*

Late afternoon a couple of days later, the face of a uniformed policeman appeared in the little video-entry panel at the flat and asked for me over the intercom. I had a minute or so while he climbed the stairs to wonder what I'd done to put myself on the Met's radar, but I came up clean. Apart from revisiting the married-man's-mistress thing, hardly illegal, I was a model citizen. When I opened the front door and saw that there were actually two uniforms approaching along the terrace, one of them a woman, I began to suspect something else. The policewoman was already giving me *that look* as they asked to come inside.

They'd come to tell me that my mother had died and that my father had collapsed and been taken to the nearest hospital. They were unable to tell me his condition, or indeed anything more. They said how sorry they were to have to bring me this news and, once they were satisfied that I wasn't going to collapse myself, they left.

I rang the hospital immediately, to learn my mother had probably died of a heart attack and there would need to be a post-mortem. My father had been sedated and was resting as comfortably as could be expected. It was only an hour's journey to get there by train (I still didn't drive), just over two hours door to door, but it was still too late to visit him that evening. I said I'd be there the following morning and left my phone number in case anything happened overnight.

I was left to contemplate the sudden news and the complete turn-around it brought with it. It had been the unquestioned assumption throughout my parents' marriage and for my entire life that my father, who was fourteen years older than my mother, would die first. He had been showing mild but increasing signs of dementia for the past few years. He was still lovely, still good humoured and kind, still very much himself, but was growing increasingly forgetful and very unsteady on his feet. My mother needed to watch him like a hawk in case he injured himself if he fell over, or endangered them both if he left an electrical appliance to overheat or put something on the stove and forgot about it. The constant worry of it all – which she insisted on carrying by herself, refusing almost all offers of help from me and from friends who lived nearby – seemed finally to have put too much strain on her heart.

I began to make a list of everything I would need to do. Take an early train down next morning; see my father in hospital; find out what condition he was in; hope I could console him just a little bit. Find out when my mother's post-mortem would happen. Find out how to register her death. Find a funeral home and arrange her cremation. Find a nursing home for my father. Obtain power of attorney for my father's affairs. Sort out their finances. Sort out their papers. Sort out their stuff. Call their friends, most of whom lived nearby, and remaining family members, all of whom did not. I was sure there was more than that to do, but my mind was a blur. I'd never wished for siblings before, but now wished for half a dozen, all married to obliging spouses, with some helpful young adult offspring between them, so that I wouldn't have to do it all by myself. I had no head space left to register that I had just lost my mum.

When my father saw me at the hospital he held out his arms in a dreadful gesture of helplessness mixed with abject relief. I sat on his bed and held him while he wept and wept. My mother and father were in love with each other from the moment their eyes met across a crowded dance floor back in the fifties and they stayed in love throughout the whole of their long marriage. Now my father was still in love, but suddenly bereft and overwhelmed by his loss. The hospital doctor said he hadn't been injured when he collapsed, but they would keep him on the ward for observation till the end of the week, just to be sure. That seemed more than reasonable. Whatever else they might be able to do for him, they couldn't mend his broken heart.

In the ensuing days I managed to get through everything on my list, plus further additional tasks that cropped up in the process. I was operating in a kind of automated blur, a strangely efficient state of mind that lasted right into the day of the funeral, because there were so many people to greet and my father to look after and the flowers and messages to acknowledge. It lasted right up until the moment I saw my darling dad silently raise his hand to wave goodbye to my mother's casket as it rolled behind the curtains at the crematorium. Then I was lost.

There was no alternative to a nursing home for my father and with the invaluable help of my mother's best friend I found a wonderful place for him. They advised me to admit him directly after the funeral and then leave him in their care. I said I'd come back and spend time with him over the next few days, but was told it was better if I didn't. The manager, a kind and capable women whom I would get to know well – whose name happened to be Jane – explained that this was the kindest thing to do. Residents settled in much faster if they were left to adjust to their new surroundings by themselves for a while, not unlike children starting at boarding school. I saw my father into his new accommodation, where I'd already sent some of his belongings so that he'd have familiar things around him, made certain he understood I'd be back to see him in a few days and told him that I was sure everyone would look after him. Then I sat with him until he fell asleep in his new bed and left. It was a strange new reality for us both.

I was back in London the next morning with two days to go before leaving for Geneva. David had left a reel of messages on the answering machine (I hadn't yet acquired my first mobile), wondering with increasing urgency where I'd gone. It was strange – and two weeks ago I wouldn't have believed it possible – but I hadn't thought of him once since the police arrived at my door. He was a huge figure in my life, but he didn't have a presence in this part of my world.

I was there next time he called. He sounded relieved to hear my voice. I was out of town for a few days, I told him, but for some reason didn't tell him why. I knew I would tell him, at some point, just not yet. A problem shared with David wasn't necessarily a problem halved; not this one, anyway. He would be kind, I was sure, but I wasn't ready to handle even the most delicate response from him. When I'd come closer to understanding how I felt myself, I'd feel more prepared to let him that far in.

A Canadian girlfriend was passing through London just then and came to stay for those last two nights. I was running on ghost energy and wasn't sure I could cope with seeing anybody else, let alone having a house guest, but Kate was just the restorative I needed. Over a meal and wine at the Lebanese restaurant and more wine back at the flat, we exchanged all our news, mine being the lion's share. Kate was sorry to hear about my mother's passing, but it was when I told her the story of how David and I had met again after all those years that the tears began to well in her eyes. Well, it *was* one of *those* stories. We talked till the small hours and next morning hit the stores in the West End.

I'd told her how David said he hoped I'd let him buy me jewellery again.

'He's rich, right?' she said, before she pulled me into Cartier in Bond Street, where we looked at some 'Tank' pieces; the watches, but the rings too, a variety of which I tried on. 'Let him know you've been here and checked your ring size,' she told me on our way out.

In another store I bought a simple dark blue linen shift to fly out in, and some ultra-sheer hold-ups and a lace teddy to complete the package when I arrived.

Lausanne

I had dropped several pounds dealing with the events of the last fortnight and hadn't been overweight to begin with, so right then I was essentially all leg. David was waiting for me at Geneva airport and the expression on his face when he saw me was entirely composed of wonderment. He was looking his handsome best Swiss self and every lovely thing he had ever said to me was locked into his expression. I don't know whether other travellers stared at us as we stood wrapped around ourselves for what seemed timeless minutes, but it didn't matter. It was just so perfect to be there in his arms.

'Hello, my darling,' he said into my ear. 'You're here. We made it.'

He'd already raided the airport concessions for provisions. Wedged between his suitcase and another black leather bag on his trolley was a paper carrier with caviar and champagne.

'So we can go straight to bed when we get to our hotel,' he explained. 'Just enough to tide us over until we go out to supper later. Come on, we've got a train to catch.'

He put my bag on the trolley and led the way, announcing that we were going to Lausanne; the train we wanted ran directly from the airport. I'd assumed a weekend in Geneva, but David still liked to move on from first places, that old but still very active instinct to present a moving target.

'Come on, this way,' he urged, not understanding my hesitation as he awkwardly forced the trolley down a short escalator ramp clearly marked UP ONLY. 'This way to the train, quick, quick.'

As the train slipped smoothly along, I realised again how much I liked being in Switzerland. It was true that I had only known the country with David, under the easy affluence and familiarity he always provided, with everything always seeming to be of the most effortless quality. But then it was also true that the effortlessly perfect mountains and lakes and sky were all entirely free.

David ordered champagne and we talked happily – about how good the train was, clean, comfortable and stylish – about how good the champagne was, too, available by the glass and perfectly chilled – how everything was, well, Swiss.

About two-thirds of the way through the first glass, just enough to soften the edge of things, David asked me how I was. He knew I'd been away but he also knew something had happened. I knew he knew because it wasn't his habit to ask me how I was. Over the phone, yes, but not in person. It was axiomatic we'd be naked together at some point on every occasion we met, which would tell him how I was more intimately and exactly than any answer I might give. He clearly had his suspicions that there'd been something since he saw me last.

I was fine, I told him. Wonderful.

And it *was* wonderful, just sitting there across the little table from him, with the champagne gently flowing and the scenery whisking by. It would have been wonderful under any circumstances, but especially so after recent events, about which I was determined still to say nothing.

'Well, you *look* wonderful, too, my love,' he said. 'But there's a particular gloss to you. You've been through something and it's left its mark.'

'I've been busy,' I answered. 'I'm just a bit tired, that's all.'

It was lame, of course, but there was no point in attempting a more elaborate cover story. I was with the Master! I began to wonder whether he thought I'd been with another man.

We talked some more, about nothing in particular, but if it had been one exercise not to say anything on the phone at my flat, it was another altogether to withstand David's interrogation face to face, even though I knew the trick of it perfectly well. *Talk to your subject as though you already know everything, thereby rendering any resistance pointless.* And he wasn't even asking questions, just looking at me as though his private guess was quite good enough.

'You'll tell me,' he said gently, just when I was hopeful we'd moved the conversation along. 'I'll get it out of you, I know I shall.'

I continued to resist right through most of another glass of champagne. But then I folded – I didn't want to wait for the thumbscrews – and told him without elaboration that my mother had died.

'Wow,' he said quietly. 'That's big stuff, Our Sue. Crikey. When exactly did this happen?'

I told him when the police had called at the flat.

'Wow,' he said again, looking at me steadily. 'That's nearly two weeks ago.' He took a large mouthful of champagne, as though he needed it after the impact of my answer. 'Well, all I can say is, I admire you for that. I admire you *so* for that, my love – more than you can ever know.'

I was happy to hear him say this – I could always soak up David's compliments like a sponge – but couldn't quite see what it was he found so admirable. Other than the fact I'd handled everything myself and was still standing, which spoke to a certain capacity for endurance, I'd only done what I'd had to.

David stared silently out of the window for another long minute, holding his glass but not drinking. Then he looked back at me again. It was clear I'd impressed him quite substantially and in a way that he was taking his time to formulate. But I might never have guessed how if he hadn't just then explained.

'I think you're astonishing for not telling me. Simply marvellous. *I* shouldn't have been able to do it. I should've *had* to tell you, straight away. But if I hadn't pressed a girl, I don't think you would have told me at all. You're an amazing woman, Sue – I always knew it – but now you've earned my admiration for life.'

So that was it. My perfect spy admired me most for not telling him my own secret. I suppose I should have known.

*   *   *

Our hotel was a red-roofed neo-gothic lakeside château and our room was at the very top of the building in its own separate turret, with a private elevator to take us there. With Swiss efficiency and dispatch, our bags were sent up ahead of us as David signed us in. As we stepped into our own lift together, I noticed how David held his breath when the door slid to.

'I don't care for lifts,' he said with a dry swallow.

After seventeen years of occasionally wondering, I finally had the answer to why he'd taken the stairs up to the studios that first day. It wasn't to make a silent entrance. He was claustrophobic.

Our room was decorated in the luscious but slightly faded fin-de-siècle style that David had seemed to favour in the past. It was a lot like our first hotel in Vitznau, except that it was Lake Lucerne then and Lake Geneva now, but with the view still stretching for miles and the placid water still sparkling gently in the late afternoon sun. When I opened the window and leaned out, the air carried the sound of the mast ropes on all the little sail boats moored below us clacking like busy waterfowl in the breeze.

The bed took us almost immediately as we shut ourselves into our private tower and then once again, after we'd assailed the caviar and champagne that David had thoughtfully stowed in the ice bucket. Then he made me a present of the black leather bag I'd seen on the trolley; a Tumi weekend bag that he'd bought with our comestibles at the airport. I'd brought presents for him too, obtained on my West End excursion with Kate. The first was a silk tie from Hardy Amies; it had an abstract pattern that contained all the colours in his eyes.

'I love it,' he told me. 'I really do. How clever of you to choose it.'

'You can say you bought it at the airport,' I said, thinking of when he took it home. 'They have a concession, I checked.'

'Listen. So I bought a tie – so what? The less attention you bring to anything the less anyone else notices. I shall wear it whenever I choose, whenever the colours work. It looks like they always will.'

The second present was a black pinseal notepad with gold corners, from Asprey.

'Oh, how perfect,' he said sweetly. And whether or not he had a drawer full of them at home, he made me feel as if it actually was.

After that we bathed and dressed, David wearing a fresh shirt with his new tie and his notepad slipped inside his jacket, myself in a different shift, this one with pale stripes and slightly translucent, and ventured outside again, into one of those sweet-scented, mauve-tinted evenings to which Switzerland seemed to own the eternal copyright. We sat out at a lakeside restaurant and both marvelled how anybody, including either of us, could freely choose ever to be anywhere else in the world.

My heart had gone back to David completely. His, apparently, had never left me. Just being there with him on that balmy silvered evening absorbed all my senses, all my understanding. He had cast his magic spell again and this time what he conjured seemed more real than ever. But for all the loveliness we had so suddenly regained – all the love that must always have been there – some small watchful part of me was trying so hard not to be fearful that at some point it would have to hurt. David didn't know any other way.

Back in our turret-room that night we made love again, this time with an accompaniment to the proceedings that David had never suggested before. It took him a few moments to figure out the remote control for the television, but eventually he found the channel he wanted and we continued with blue movies playing silently on the screen.

Next morning we had an early al fresco breakfast at the end of the hotel's jetty. The people at the next table clocked David as soon as we sat down, I could tell from the startled expressions of recognition they quickly wiped from their faces. But they didn't approach. This was Switzerland, where even bank accounts had the right to remain anonymous.

Then we set out for an explore. The sun was more intense than I'd anticipated and to save me from burning in what I was wearing – a mid-length unbleached linen skirt and a favourite khaki T-shirt – David offered me one of his shirts to wear as well. It was pale tan and, with the cuffs turned back and unbuttoned, made a nice combo, so he decided I should also wear the cream-coloured Augustus John-looking hat he'd brought with him. David said he didn't have a head for hats, but once I put it on at a rakish angle declared that I did. The hatband matched the colour of my T-shirt, so quite by chance it all looked deliberately styled; Banana Republic meets Calvin Klein meets Herbert Johnson. David told me I looked like Karen Blixen as we set out.

We took the ferry across to Évian-les-Bains on the French side of the lake and had a glass of champagne at each of three separate places along the front. Then we took a taxi inland to David's restaurant of choice for our lunch, Le Relais de la Chevrette, where we ate outside at a rustic table. Afterwards we went for a stroll through the nearby countryside. David had a lovely calm about him that day. It was the effect this part of the world always had on him – the mountains, the altitude, the air. My effect – *our* effect – on him too. I never went with him to his chalet, but would guess that he was a lot like this whenever he went skiing in Wengen, where the exhilarating exercise would help to further tone him down. Though I think I have to say, because it strikes me as being as true as anything else about him, that he'd also had the benefit of exhilarating exercise here. We'd already had five bouts of extraordinarily intense sex, including once in the middle of the night and once again before breakfast that morning, and had only arrived at the hotel late yesterday afternoon.

We found an old tree in a lovely meadow and sat down by it. I kept in its shade with my back against the trunk and David sat in the sun with his arms around his knees. The grass was lush and deep and dotted with yellow and purple flowers. White flowers growing on taller stems above them seemed to catch the sunlight in a haze. High on the horizon, the snow-capped mountains were like clouds and the clouds above them were like more snow-capped mountains and the gentian-blue sky sat atop it all. It was so perfectly Alpine that I wouldn't have raised an eyebrow if Heidi and the Grandfather had appeared on the spot. Or perhaps that was us.

As we sat in comfortable silence in the meadow I began to think how much my mother would have enjoyed this place, on this timelessly lovely day. But now, suddenly, there were no more sunny days for her. I had simply assumed, as I think the adult children of elderly parents too often do, that there were always going to be other summers ahead for her to enjoy.

David must have been operating his uncanny mind-radar again, because without leading up to the subject he asked me, 'What are your thoughts on the Big Moo, my darling? I've never asked you before.'

'The big what?'

'Moo. God. It was Kennaway's expression. Do you think there's anything out there?'

He was right that we'd never ventured onto the topic before. I hadn't ventured onto it for a while with anyone. My parents had always been 'no sale' about religion and I was enormously grateful for it. But David had been raised in the pulpit-thumping West Country and as a child he'd frequently been left by Ronnie in the care of relatives who took it all very seriously indeed. They may even have bashed their Bibles with particular vigour on those occasions, to atone for the fact that they were enabling his godless narcissistic psychopath father to run his ruthless scams by providing childcare.

'Not in the way that any of the religions would have us believe,' I said, after I'd thought about my answer for a moment. 'So, no.'

'Well, I agree with you there, my love,' he replied. 'Religion is one of the institutions I've failed to penetrate in my life, though not for the want of trying at one time.'

I recalled he'd once had a very brief flirtation with joining Miller and Michael in their 'lay brotherhood' in Cornwall. Not that I could ever recall that episode without going for the obvious gag. David had been taking himself way too seriously to see the idiocy of it at the time. It had been another abortive attempt to get out of the 'slammer' at Hampstead and I made no reference to it now.

'But about God Himself,' he persisted gently. 'Or Herself? No?'

I shook my head. 'No. Not the imaginary one we were required to sing praises to every morning in school assembly, nor any of the imaginary others that we weren't.'

'So you don't believe we go on in any way?'

'Actually, I do. I just don't think there's any invoking or worshipping or obeying required for it to happen.'

David cocked his head. 'How so, then?' he asked.

'I think we recycle,' I said. 'Everything else does – matter, light, energy, so I don't see why one's soul or spirit shouldn't recycle somehow too. Just as a basic principle of the way things go.'

I didn't consider this to be a terribly advanced theory – more akin to dinosaurs being thin at one end, fat in the middle and thin at the other – but David listened with great attention.

After a thoughtful pause he said, 'That's a very elegant belief, my darling.'

'But it's *not* a belief,' I corrected him. 'That's the point. It doesn't require any faith. In fact, it's pretty much inductive reasoning. You know – Smiley stuff.'

That drew a wry smile.

'How about you?' I asked in return.

Now it was David's turn to shake his head.

'No,' he said flatly.

'So nothing? Nothing beyond at all?'

'I think we die and that's it. I don't think I know what spirit is. Beyond life, anyway.'

I wasn't particularly surprised to hear him say this. David was very cerebral; the cessation of brain activity and consciousness must have seemed particularly absolute to him. Having been raised in such a harsh religious environment and consciously rejecting all traces of it, he had then failed to find any more sympathetic substitute. I'd already seen how seriously he took his age, how little time he felt he had left. Nearer my God to Thee must have seemed a very bleak proposition to him, with no Thou out there.

'So are your books going to be your immortality?' I asked. 'Is that how you see things?'

'Some of them, yes,' he replied, nodding as he looked out at the mountains. 'I think some will last. But who knows? This new one feels wonderful, full of all sorts of life.'

He would be going back to Africa soon, he said, to continue his interrupted research. The story was shaping up; he was beginning to see how his hero, Justin Quayle, would set about his journey to track down his wife's killers.

'Another chap on his personal odyssey,' I suggested.

'Yes, that's exactly it. Now, tell me, Sue – because you'll know – why was it that Odysseus went on his odyssey in the first place? What was he doing all that travelling for?'

I hesitated before answering. I was waiting for a knowing grin, to show me he was aware of asking the exact same question, in almost those exact words, on our Greek beach all those years before. But David was quite serious in his enquiry. He'd already told me how 'great swathes, whole chapters' of his life were closed to him and, though he may have believed it, I didn't quite believe they were. Some were selectively dormant, perhaps; others lying doggo, waiting for their master's whistle; but none were permanently closed. David remembered everything. Now, quite suddenly, I understood that this was how he kept going, by processing the same things over and over again – the same desires, the same fears, the same concerns, even the same loves – generating ever more layers of complication for himself and everyone around him, while obscuring anything that might lead him to reach resolution. He *was* Odysseus, in a way, as he'd claimed once before. Travelling and travelling, each adventure taking him on to another, but in his case every time ending up back on the same shore where he'd started, yet never really knowing it for the first time. Perhaps, I thought a little sadly in the end, he wasn't really Tigger after all, as he'd liked me to say, bounding enthusiastically from one thing to the next until he found what he liked best. Perhaps he was really poor old Pooh Bear, walking round and round the tree in the snow, getting more and more alarmed as he saw more and more footprints appearing ahead of him, fearing they were made by unknown beasts in the forest, not realising that he had made them all himself.

'Odysseus didn't mean to go anywhere,' I said at last, hearing my own words echo in my ears. 'He was only trying to get home.'

We took a taxi back to Évian. Before taking the return ferry we stopped to have more champagne and a double sugar cone each at an ice-cream parlour by the lake. After our conversation about the Hereafter, I now had something of an existential epiphany myself, which was that if anything came close to manifesting the concept of Eternal Bliss for me, it was a lakeside ice-cream parlour – with an Alpine view – that also served champagne. As we were only a few yards onto French soil, I credited my private revelation to the Swiss, thinking it was no wonder they stayed neutral in wars. They didn't need to fight anyone for anything. They already had the best of everything life could offer right where they were.

My new family situation returned with a bump once I was back in London after our four days *en Suisse*. Thereafter, I was constantly dividing my time between my parents' place, to look after the house and sort their stuff and see my dad, and London, for work and David, and meantime living on the trains that took me to and fro. It was like existing inside a split-screen film with two complex storylines running concurrently and no easy way to completely follow either. Now it appeared to be my turn to keep all the plates spinning on top of all the poles. To keep sane, I purchased my first mobile phone the moment I was back. It and my new Tumi bag were my constant companions as I shuttled between my two lives.

I'd always kept some of my past belongings at my parents' house, but as I went through everything I soon discovered that my mother had kept so much more. My scholar's gown from Oxford; my school uniform blazer; my christening gown she made from the satin of her wedding dress; the miniature cardigan she knitted for my favourite doll to match one she'd made for me. She had kept the first Mother's Day card I'd made for her, aged six, and all my earliest school exercise books with the clumsy printing in pencil and the eager pictures in crayon. She'd kept postcards from me from everywhere. And, in a little blue Tiffany's box that originally contained some earrings I'd bought her on a trip to New York, she'd kept a lock of my baby hair, transferred from its first home in an old blue envelope. It was strawberry blonde and still tightly curled. It broke me to see it and, finally, I wept for my mother from the bottom of my heart.

I always knew what a lovely man my father was, but every time I visited him in his nursing home I learned it anew. He was born just before the First World War and because his own father was serving in France throughout his infancy I always imagined him as a version of the little boy in the A.A. Milne poem who took very great care of his mother though he was only three. Once he met my mother, his one ambition was to take very great care of her and then, when I came along, of us both. Which he did – and always with a smile, good humour and simply endless love. I took him flowers and chocolates and books whenever I visited and sat with him in the quiet sitting room that overlooked the garden, or sometimes in the garden when the weather was fine. He'd been a keen gardener and still liked to name all the flowers – aubretia, chionodoxa, alstroemeria and all the different roses. It was strange but not entirely discouraging to see what remained in his memory and what had slipped away. While he would tell me tale after tale from his childhood, his unmarried youth and the war, all of which remained with him in living detail, losing my mother already seemed to have become a distant event. The sadness hadn't left him, but the immediacy of his grief had gone, as if he'd already been widowed for many years when it wasn't even many weeks. It made me think that his form of dementia, the gently increasing time and memory slippage of old age, was actually rather a merciful condition, something provided by Nature to cushion the emotional blow. The manager at the home told me he might forget my mother altogether one day, but I knew that would never happen – though I could imagine a time when he might altogether forget that she was gone.

When we couldn't see ourselves, David continued to call and call and call, to my new mobile, to the number at my parents' house and to the landline at the flat, leaving long messages when he didn't get through and talking for what seemed like hours when he did. If I didn't manage to pick up before the answering machine clicked on in London, some of the calls were recorded. I kept notebooks through this period, and one of them has verbatim transcripts of his messages and the taped calls. In my diary there's a note that suggests I intended to have the recordings copied by an audio engineer friend, but it didn't happen. I suppose I couldn't find the time. But the transcripts survive. This one is dated three days after we returned from Geneva. David is speaking first.

9.36 am, Thursday 3/6/99

– Hello, my darling. How are you?
– I'm still wonderful. How are you?
– OK. OK. I'm all right.
– Oh. How was it going back? Was it awful?
– Mmm. Pretty awful. Just very sad.
– How was Jane?
– Mmm. She was in a bad way. Thought I'd gone off for less than a good reason. You know.
– What did you say to that?
– Oh, nothing. Never excuse, never explain, of course. But I think she just got it through instinct. So. We just had to go through it. Accusing glances from across the room. You know ... So we'll just have to be careful. Talk and write and see ourselves pragmatically ... We'll just have to be a bit nimble about it.
– When weren't we?
– Quite so. When weren't we? How is it with your people, your dad?
– Oh, I went down yesterday, planning to stay till Sunday. I got to the station and phoned a local cab driver I'd used for years to pick me up. When he pulled up outside the house I realised I hadn't brought my keys.
– Oh, no!
– Yes. So I said 'fuck' about seventeen times in the back of the cab and cast around for alternatives – getting a locksmith, breaking a window. The nice cab driver was very helpful. 'Can I help you break in?' he said to me.
– I'll bet. Can I help you break in? Can I look after you—?
– I decided the easiest thing to do was just to come back. So I took the taxi to see my dad and came back here afterwards. I'm going back there later this morning, *avec mes clefs*.
– Poor love.

– My head just isn't in the right place at the right time always.

– No. Of course. And how is your dad?

– Oh, doing well, I suppose. They all think the world of him at the home. They tell me he's trying to get on with everyone, trying to laugh and smile and talk a bit, trying to appreciate everything they do for him.

– And they're all making a tremendous fuss of him.

– Yes. They love him. I don't know which is worse really, which is saddest – that he's trying to adjust or if he weren't. Anyway – I'll be there till the weekend. Sunday probably. How was Boorman?

– Oh, really very good. I like him a lot, I think. I really do.

– I've got an actor for you, by the way. But go on—

– Have you? Well, he likes the script. Likes it very much. The book was written to end with—

– With the handover of the Canal in the year 2000, yes—

– Which will be a historic event by the time this film is made. So we've decided to start with the handover ceremony and take the story back from there. So Boorman wants me to write twenty minutes to start the film, using documentary footage they'll have from the handover. Then he'll take my script as written and work on it himself. He likes to write his own stuff, but he'll have a hotline to me and the chance to make further use of my services. It's a good deal and it means I can be free to get on with the new book.

– Wonderful. Do you want to hear my actor?

– Yes.

– OK. Don't react straight away, because it's going to sound like a crazy idea, but I know he'd be perfect.

– All right.

– Michael Caine …

– Ha-ha-ha-*ha*. That's very good and very funny. So Boorman says to me, 'I've got the perfect actor in mind. You'll think it's a crazy suggestion at first, but I know he's right and he's even

Jewish.' So I said, 'Michael Caine,' and he said, 'Absolutely. Michael Caine.' So you're bang on the money, Our Sue. How clever.

– He'd be brilliant.

– Ever since *Little Voice* – he was supposed to be so good in it. Have you seen it?

– No. Just the trailers. But I think he was probably extraordinary in it.

– I'm chipping away at that idea. I'm saying Geoffrey Rush or Tom Wilkinson.

– Hmm. Istanbul Productions. [i.e. a turkey]

– You think so? [laughs]

– Go with Caine.

– You may be right, Our Sue. [I was. He should have.]

– I love you.

– And I love you, enormously. I'll call you tomorrow night, my darling. When I'm back from Scotland seeing my man.
[ex-MI6, someone who had worked in Africa]

– Fine. I love you. Travel safely.

– I will. I love you, my darling.

– I love you.

– Bye.

I next saw David later the following week. He called me at about nine thirty in the morning.

'I've just put Jane on the train. Can I come round?'

He arrived at ten forty-five and was hardly inside the flat before he fell on me, fired with a pent-up urgency that was off even his own intense scale, saying my name over and over and over.

'I had to have you,' he told me afterwards.

We stayed in bed, helping ourselves to the goodies he'd brought with him. (I found a yellowed receipt from Selfridges Food Hall inside one of the notebooks, time-stamped 10.17 am and listing exactly what he'd bought: vodka, caviar and a carton of white and green asparagus spears from the deli counter. He was definitely in a hurry to see me!) Two vodkas down, David began to talk of what it would be like to be together all the time.

'The floodgates would open,' he said. 'I'd write all the time. We'd fuck all the time too. I'd write in my room and you'd write in yours and I'd come and take you and fuck you and then go back to work.'

(What was it that Judy Garland is supposed to have said to the Munchkin actor on *The Wizard of Oz*, who claimed he could show her a really good time? 'Well, if you do and I find out about it …')

Whole-cloth fantasy though the vision seemed to be, I believe for David, in that moment, it was very, *very* real. And he was very nearly making *me* think it could be real, too. In another life we'd have to try it, like Daisy Gamble and Dr Marc. Perhaps, on a clear day on a distant time-line, we already had.

Then, out of nowhere, David asked me if I wanted a child.

The straight answer to that question was *no*. But a flat no to anything, particularly something you resolutely wish to avoid, tends to send a challenge out into the ether to deliver the exact thing back to you, to test your resolve. After recently coming off the pill I was a little twitchy about the contraception I was using, so, not wanting to challenge the Universe on that subject, I gave my all-purpose non-denial denial.

'Well – never say never.'

'How marvellous!' he exclaimed.

Funny. He seemed to have heard me say yes anyway.

'I think you'd make a marvellous mother,' he went on. 'Especially if you had a boy. And if it had something wrong with it, you'd be superb. It would be simply marvellous.'

'What would you do if I *were* pregnant?' I asked after a few moments.

314

'Leave,' he answered without hesitation. I assumed at first he meant leave me, but he went on. 'Get out. Of Hampstead. Join you to look after the nipper.'

To this day, I don't know if he was actually making the offer. It certainly seemed as though he might have been floating the possibility. Perhaps it was some sort of unconscious projection of the child – the damaged one, at that – he saw in himself. Perhaps for some reason – even that one – he needed to have the women with whom he had serious relationships either become or already be mothers. Not to start on the Oedipal thing, since David had been so motherless himself, but Susan Kennaway had a small brood at the time of their affair, Yvette had a natural daughter and an adopted son and went around the globe saving children (the title of her biography was *Femme aux mille enfants*), and Janet Stevens was pregnant when she was killed, possibly with his own child. Then there were his four sons by his two wives.

Perhaps, though, it was something with even more of a David spin to it. Because now there was Dawson – again – to whom no man in his right mind would have attributed the desire for motherhood. But David's right mind was only ever the one that he was in at any given period and served – indeed created – his quotidian reality. I'd seen how hard he was endeavouring to maintain his belief in our renewed us-ness this time around, to make his belief stick. So – *was* it an offer? Did he see it as his last chance to leave the 'slammer' in Hampstead? The one undeniable reason and the unshakable cover it would give him for finally 'getting out'?

Lady Ann Smiley was childless and expressed no desire to be otherwise. It wasn't a question in any of the books. The monkish Smiley kept that slate clean and there was never a whisper that any of her 'First Eleven' succeeded where he failed. When she left him – which occurred in the very first paragraph of the very first book – her name remained behind, turning her into the besetting indefinite article of Smiley's life. *I think Smiley's Ann may be you,*

David had said to me all those years before. It was an extraordinary statement, one he didn't make lightly and which he never rescinded. I wonder now whether he was trying to get me to defect from it myself, so that he could fuse together the two warring elements of escape and imprisonment and finally bring the fantasy home.

Well, the wonderings over David, I've found, can go on forever. Whatever the impulse that made him say this, it clearly suited his vision of me then and that was always what reality was for him, his inner persuasion at any one time. It wasn't always momentary, not all of it was fleeting. That he loved me as truly as he did for as long as he did – over decades, in fact, and, as he wrote, across rooms where I wasn't even present – spoke to the constancy he could bring to his inner reality where it ran deep. But when his own extraordinary power of conjuring made the inner reality start to take hold in the external world, it was usually his cue to defect. The only thing he would never have defected from was another child. It was what Miller had told me right at the very start. David always had to have a reason for leaving …

He stayed until late afternoon, then said he would go home, pack his things and pick me up again for an early supper before he went to the airport to go back to Nairobi.

That evening we went to The Brasserie in South Ken and sat at a table outside for an early supper. While we were deciding what to order, David asked me if I liked Schnitzler.

For a half-second, I swear I looked for it on the menu: *Wiener Schnitzler*, my brain had told me, which wasn't so off the mark, since that writer was actually from Vienna. Then the name clicked in connection with something I'd read about the next and probably last film starring Tom Cruise and Nicole Kidman.

'*Eyes Wide Shut*, you mean?'

'Mmm. *Traumnovelle*. Have you read it?'

Of course not.

'No.'

'Kubrick asked me to write the screenplay.'

I'd read that Kubrick had asked just about everybody to write it at one time or another. But I hadn't come across David's name in the throng.

'Why didn't you? Frederic Raphael did in the end, so I read.'

'I went down to his place in Hertfordshire for the day. I don't think we see this movie the same way, Stanley, I told him in the end. He was really quite mad, I decided. He had all these videos sent in by film students. Hundreds, if not thousands. He never looked at them, just kept them and had them wiped, then sold the tapes off second hand.'

David's mood began to slip before we finished the meal. I'd forgotten that it was never a good idea to see him so close to when his head had either been somewhere else – as on that first trip to Cornwall – or, as now, was about to be somewhere else. He always seemed to need a pause between courses when I was on the menu. I should have just let him leave the flat and wend his way to the airport by himself.

The moody letter I anticipated arrived a couple of days later. He must have delayed his departure, or else given me a fictive date for it in the first place, because I wrote back to the Hampstead dead letterbox, with more of my usual soft-soap reassurances that seemed always to work on him (I don't write that cynically, but he was sometimes so much like a little boy wanting someone to check under the bed for monsters), and he wrote straight back again, sending me a parcel of books, non-fiction titles, *The Surgeon of Crowthorne* and *Nathaniel's Nutmeg* among them. He enclosed a note saying that these were the kinds of books he imagined me writing. I'd told him I was happy ghost-writing at the present time, but he didn't seem to like the idea of it. Beginning with the Ronnie biog, he'd always wanted me to write non-fiction. He also enclosed a picture postcard of a couple on the deck of the *Titanic*. He'd drawn arrows to each of them with captions. The woman's was TOO GOOD FOR HIM and the man's was DOESN'T KNOW HIS LUCK. On the back of the card he'd written simply *Then yes*. He let the subtext of the photograph speak for itself.

Total Eclipse

Once David was back from Kenya in early July – after 'a pretty heavy mugging' in Nairobi, a city he detested – it was as if he couldn't tell me enough about absolutely everything else in his life. For the next few weeks, whenever I saw him or we spoke on the phone, he seemed to want to cram in everything he hadn't yet told me, as though he somehow had to shore himself up with me, before his time to tell me all of it ran out.

The mugging, he said, was a natural consequence of his 'white colonial guilt'. Some guy had approached pleasantly, asked David to go with him on some ruse and he'd fallen for it. Then his accomplice appeared with a knife. They'd only taken what cash he had on him, not even his credit cards, and hadn't used the knife, but he'd clearly been shaken by the experience. Then he spoke about talking to the Médecins Sans Frontières doctors who treated the boy soldiers from the various militias, out in the farther reaches of the country.

'They told me that the most disheartening thing was you knew you were only patching the kids up so they could go out and fight again and maybe get permanently maimed or killed the next time.'

The movie was progressing with Boorman and David hoped he wouldn't have to go back to LA for a while.

'Charlotte's out there,' he said. 'She's got a new man. She told me his name, so I decided to get my friend John Calley to check him out.'

Calley was a big-time studio exec.

'He rang me back after he'd asked around. *One word*, he said to me. *Hustler.*'

He told me of his rebarbative falling-out with Hollywood producer Sydney Pollack. Pollack had bought the rights to *The Night Manager* for an exorbitant sum, but then messed him around over how and when to make the film, which ultimately didn't happen. David said he'd felt himself to be just the latest blue-eyed blond boy Pollack had taken up, referencing Robert Redford.

'I simply couldn't stand for it any more. There were never any straight answers. *I think, Sydney,* I told him on our last call, *that you and I should never speak again.*'

David said he'd also had to dispense with the services of his long-time representative in New York, Georges Borchardt, and told me why.

'He used to bring his *wife* to our meetings.'

He didn't see fit to mention – I only discovered it later – that Borchardt's wife was also his partner in his business. He didn't say anything at all, good or bad, about his present UK agent, Bruce Hunter, whom he'd gone to after leaving Farquharson's, or say why he'd left his former agency, though George had already told me that after he retired, Farquharson's had substituted a woman in his place. David asked me how I got along with Ed Victor. I'd been telling him how Graham C. Greene had got me into ghost-writing when I hadn't known what to write after my Galsworthy sequel, how I found I enjoyed it, though I knew David didn't really approve. Graham was someone I liked tremendously, a man of impeccable courtesy and twinkly good humour. David inferred from this that I didn't harbour the same sentiments towards Ed. I answered by relaying something Ed had said to me one time, not long after Graham signed me on.

'*When I get to know you better, Sue*, he said, *Carol and I will have you over to the house*. I was tempted to reply that when I got to know *him* better, I might not want to accept. I think he didn't hear himself.'

'No,' David said, agreeing. 'Ed's a joke. He came to me years ago, when he was still working for George at Farquharson's. He took me to lunch and made his pitch. *Let's you and I go it alone, David,* he said to me. *We'll make millions.* Well, it wasn't pretty.'

'What did you say?'

'I told him I was George's man and that was it. But he didn't seem to think he'd done anything wrong.'

David asked me what I'd thought of the BBC's production of *A Perfect Spy.* Sadly, I said, not a lot.

'Nor I,' David concurred. 'It was astonishing to me how they'd taken this Swiss roll I'd made of my story and managed to flatten out every bit of it. What did you make of Egan?'

'Literally nothing,' I said.

'Nor I,' David said again, and we agreed that the part of Pym had somehow become a cipher in the production. I told him I'd worked with the actor in the studio.

'What was he reading for you?'

I found I couldn't recall – rather underscoring the point – but remembered that the client had been very pleased with the finished recording. (A few years later, I saw Egan in the West End in *Art,* playing opposite my great chum Anthony Valentine, and he was really good. Casting is everything.)

David had got to know Peter Cook in his final years.

'I used to go round to his place and drink vodka with him. He had porn videos playing silently on multiple TV screens around the room while we talked.'

That explained the episode at the Château d'Ouchy. Cook was another inveterate rulebreaker and iconoclast, much like Kennaway, who might well have done the same had he lived into the age of VCRs. David still liked the type, evidently, and still liked to try out some of their native ways for himself. The idea of porn movies playing silently in the background would recur in *The Tailor of Panama* film, in a scene with Geoffrey Rush and Pierce Brosnan.

And when we were lying together in bed he read me pages from the new book, just as he had before. His voice still had the same magical power to transport, to conjure up the characters as if they were with us in the room. But I couldn't help thinking that Gooders had been right when he remarked on David's esses all those years ago. There were moments when Justin Quayle sounded completely 'Brideshead' and very prissy indeed.

I was beginning to see some of the characteristic tropes appear in the new novel. First, the almost Dickensian naming of his characters. After giving us the un-smiling Smiley, the recursive Turner, all-dough Aldo, Magnus Pym's minuscule mother, Dot, and so many others, David was now giving us Quayle, the timid desk-bound husband who nevertheless finds the courage to seek out his wife's killers, only to be hunted down and killed like a game bird himself. And there was the fact that Tessa Quayle was dead at the start of the book, her throat slashed for knowing too much about what the bad guys were doing, for not knowing her place in the male system. Stella Rode meets with a similar fate for similar reasons at the start of *A Murder of Quality*; Elsa Fennan has her neck broken in *Call for the Dead*. The women die by injury to their throats, the female organ of reproach. I can't say how much of this he recognised in his writing. I rather think it hovered just below the surface of his conscious use, the way a great chef reaches for and uses a certain knife without really looking, his thoughts already several stages ahead in the feast he's preparing. He'd previously told me that, until it was pointed out to him, he hadn't realised how often he included 'the watching child' in his books – Roach, the new-bug with another Dickensian name in *Tinker Tailor*, being the best-known example.

'"Her cat-like grace",' David repeated from a passage about Tessa Quayle, stroking my thigh. 'Who's that, then, do you think?' he asked me.

He had Justin growing cacti at the start of the book, a detail he decided to modify when I told him I'd read that in feng shui they were supposed to be bad *chi*.

And just in passing, he mentioned he'd turned down another K that year. Still no Sir David, then, though it might have quite suited the Arthurian touches I'd noticed in him now, which he seemed not to see in himself.

There was going to be a total solar eclipse on 11 August, and the press and media were all over it throughout the summer. David was planning a big gathering of the Cornwell clan at Tregiffian for the occasion, but seemed to be dreading it. He had to go down there at the beginning of August and planned to stay the whole month. He made me promise to write, saying he'd be desperate to hear from me in all the madness of the massing throng. He made it sound as though Land's End would resemble the Gaza Strip.

I checked that I was still to send my letters to Sancreed.

'No,' he said, a little quizzically, as if his own answer puzzled him. 'No, my love. Miller's no good now.'

I gathered from this that they'd had a falling-out of some sort, but he didn't choose to elaborate. He gave me a different address for a new friend, Dave Humphries, another writer who lived down there. His recent credit was the LWT fire-station drama series, *London's Burning*.

Hearing what sounded like his estrangement from Miller made me think of Tangye, who had died in '96. I'd seen David's obituary piece on him. My mother had cut it out of the newspaper and sent it to me. It was something she'd always done since I first left home for college and was one of the thousand things I would miss about her. (It was such a shame that she didn't live to enjoy the full internet age, when she could and surely would have sent me links to everything going.)

'Yes,' David said, his voice growing sombre at the recollection of a man he had sincerely considered a friend. 'He lived for ten years without Jeannie. At first, when she died, if he saw a bird at the window he'd say, *That's Jeannie! There she is – her spirit's come back!* By the end he was pissing and shitting in containers and keeping it all round the house. Jane used to go over to help clean him out.'

For all those years I'd been certain there couldn't be a more revolting image of the man than the one I already had, but David had just proved me wrong. My mother never read his books again after I'd told her about the lunch. She'd believed what she read about their Cornish idyll at Minack and afterwards thought them both frauds. I wondered what she'd have made of Tangye's final chapter. But then, she died before I'd told her about my own latest chapter with David.

The last time I saw him before he had to go down to Cornwall, for what by then had become 'the bloody eclipse', he sounded truly pained at the thought of the big family event.

'But at least they'll make use of the place for once. I've spent half a million there and it really looks like it's had the money spent on it, too. It's just amazing. But it's like *Elective Affinities* or *The Forsyte Saga* – they should never have finished the fucking house and garden …'

His voice tapered off with one of his desolate smiles.

'I thought it was always full of family and friends?' I queried.

'No, not at all. Just the two of us. We don't even have the dogs now. It's deadly.'

Before he left that time, he made a point of saying how easy it was to talk to me, how much he appreciated being able to talk to me as he had.

'We live complete lives when we're together, Our Sue.'

The letters he sent me were all really good, the envelopes sporting beaming smiley faces again. They were so uniformly good, in fact, that I teased him in one of mine that the Nairobi mugging must have involved a substantial blow to the head. He wrote of the sex, very extensively, and of what he considered my elegance, and of our love. He said how I'd made him recall the interconnectedness of fucking and writing. He said he'd make every excuse possible to get away as soon as the eclipse was over and come and see me again.

He was in the papers quite a bit at this time and sent me cuttings. He was in a dispute with the farmer who had sold him the land and cottages thirty years ago. The farmer had applied for planning permission for outbuildings and David had lodged an objection with the local authorities. He had his reasons – suspecting that it was the first step towards a separate more substantial dwelling – but was inevitably tagged with nimbyism in the press. He gave me an account of a local meeting he'd had to attend. His mobile had rung before it convened and David had explained it was an important call from LA that he had to take and excused himself. Twenty minutes later, having concluded the call, he rejoined the locals.

'Ere, David told me that one of them asked him, *'owever much did that cost you then?* To which he replied stony-faced, *The other end pays …*

Peckinpah had evidently been onto something.

It sounded like a tiresome battle and possibly one that David thought he might not win. Next time he called he said he'd come up with a devilish plan.

'I'm giving my whole fucking mile of cliff to the National Trust! They can fight the farmer now. Stuff him!'

He wrote a piece in the *Observer* to mark Al Alvarez's seventieth birthday. He was the one member of the inner circle I never met. I never found out why, but put it down to some more delicate sensibility on the part of the academic, poet and poker player than had been the case with the others. (I learned subsequently from Sisman that David had once asked Alvarez if he would receive letters for him, as Miller originally did, but Alvarez refused.) He wrote in the article that Alvarez was one of only two people who were permitted to disturb him while he was working. I hadn't heard this rather precious diktat from David himself and concluded the other of the two was his wife, meaning that even his sons weren't allowed that level of access. I had a vision of Jane (only it was Terry Jones in drag) warning one of his sons (played by Eric Idle), *Don't disturb your father – you know what he's like after a few novels ...*

Mobile telephones weren't such an asset in Cornwall at that time. David's next call was from a tor. He said he'd had to walk miles to get to a high point for a signal and even then he sounded as if he were speaking under six feet of water. But he just had to hear my voice.

'I've rewritten the bit about feng shui and bad *chi* from cactus,' he told me, 'and now it really works.'

He called me very early on the morning of the eclipse. He'd walked to a different place and found better reception.

'I'm just going to say quickly that I love you and I'm *surrounded* by people and it's *pissing* with rain. I've got your lovely letters, though, my darling, and cor, you can't half write a letter.'

He rang again the day after the eclipse, another very brief call. It sounded as if this time he was calling from the house.

'It really *was* like a rebirth, just as it was supposed to be,' he said, sounding invigorated by the experience, a renewed energy in his voice. 'Your whole life really does march before you – and who was leading the procession? You, my darling. You.'

He rang again later, when I was expecting a call from my friend Emily, who was just over from the States.

'Hi!' I said.

'*Hi*,' David said back deliberately. 'I'm not even going to ask who *that* was for.'

326

He asked if I'd got his latest package of non-fiction books, more titles of the sort he was gently suggesting I might write. Because of this persistent suggestion, gentle though it was, I said I wondered whether he'd perhaps found my first attempt at fiction a little hard going.

'Now, listen,' he responded sternly. 'The only fiction we must cease here is about your somehow sucking on the hind teat of literary talent. I have read your book, Our Sue, and it *simply* isn't *true*. And in that I am your staunchest supporter.'

I had to re-run the convolutions of this for a second or two before deciding it was a fairly major compliment from the Great Man.

He'd arranged our trip, he said excitedly, when he rang again the next day. We were on for the start of September, Bern and then Elba.

Bern, I thought when he rang off. Not just Switzerland this time, but *Bern*. For David, there was no place where he could take me further 'in'.

He called again later with explicit travel details. It was Elba first now, Bern after.

'I want you to travel out on Wednesday 1st on Air Engiadina from London City Airport. I'll spell it for you—' He did. I'd never heard of the airline and never flown from the new City Airport. 'I just can't manage any time for us before then, but we'll have a lot of time together once we're away.'

'That's all right,' I said. He sounded worried whether I'd make it there. 'I love you, David. It's all fine.'

'And I love you too. Very much. I'll call you later tonight. And I'm sending you a little letter. Maybe a long letter. And the money for your ticket.'

He was always so concerned that I shouldn't spend a penny of my own money on anything to do with him. But without the Authors Workshop as a cut-out and with his wife now handling the household accounts directly, he couldn't write a cheque. This time the cash came inside a French paperback novel. Its spine wasn't cracked, so he hadn't read it before packing the money inside. There was a lovely letter with it and a back copy of Granta where an essay of his, *The Unbearable Peace*, had appeared. It all arrived in a padded envelope he'd addressed to a P. Drax Esq., at my flat, so it must have gone with his wife to the post office in Cornwall.

The next time he called I was out with Emily and hadn't taken my mobile with me. When I told her about being back with David, how it had happened, Emily – like my friend Kate before her – had tears in her eyes. Well, it just *was* one of those stories. I came back to a message on my answering machine.

'I'm just calling again to tell you I love you and I dream of you and I am *surrounded* by people, but I had to call you. I've sent you a fat letter. And I adore you. I wanted to tell you, but you aren't there.'

I kept my mobile with me at all times after that and the next time he caught me while I was trying on a Jaeger dress in Kensington.

'Guess where I am,' I said.

'The sauna! The bath! Anywhere naked!'

It was another of his uncanny guesses, since I very nearly was.

'I'm trying on something to wear for you,' I told him, naming the store, 'but I think it's the wrong colour. Or I am.'

'So are you standing there bollock-naked, Our Sue? That's really what I was asking.'

'Pretty much,' I said. 'Only without the bollocks.'

'Cor,' he purred. 'But me on my knees with my head between your legs, all right?!'

I looked at myself in the long mirror in the changing cubicle and saw that David had just made me blush.

So how did it end, and why, when everything was going so well?

As always with David, the answer was in the question. Just as there ought to have been a word, solely for him, to mean a man who was so especially and so magically attentive to his mistress, there ought to have been another adjective with his name on it offering some brain-spinning hybrid of axiomatically paradoxical and paradoxically axiomatic. (It wouldn't surprise me if there is such a word in German.) It had to go wrong because it *was* going so right.

I was still visiting my father as often as possible and, much as he never gave anyone a moment's unnecessary trouble in his life (unlike some, as Graham might have observed), there were still all the attendant issues for me to deal with. And seeing him meant that I was still living part-time on the train, my Tumi bag slung permanently over my shoulder as I shuttled between my two realities. I don't think I fully realised the strain I was under, but I was beginning to realise that while I'd heard all of David's problems, he really didn't try to elicit mine. He occasionally asked me how my father was, but didn't ever prompt me to say more, about how the situation was affecting me. But it was. And though I was looking forward to going away with him again – it had been more than a couple of months since Lausanne – something was bugging me about this trip. When I worked out what it was, it seemed so obvious. It was one thing to once again be a married rich guy's secret girlfriend – I trust I've shown I was always fine with that – and to be whisked away on fabulous trips. I liked the whisking; it compensated for the other restrictions in the relationship and was especially welcome now, given what I'd had on my plate all that summer and would continue to have for as long as my father was alive. But somehow, being sent a bundle of cash and told to make my own arrangements wasn't whisking. I realised I wasn't OK with it. I was quite capable of making travel arrangements for myself, of course, but the point was, these were not my arrangements. They were David's. And much as I was happy to accompany him and very much wanted to be with him on his travels, there was something that didn't sit right with me about having to go about things this way. It seemed demeaning somehow, to us both. More so because he was a multimillionaire ex-spy who couldn't find a more elegant way to manage the issue and didn't seem to be looking for one either. It was too close to leaving money on the dresser.

I decided I would find a way to put this to David when we were in Elba. A gentle – *careful* – suggestion that he might think of making a separate arrangement somewhere, as he had before with Rainer; just one credit card that his wife didn't see, to facilitate things for us. I hoped he'd see the nuance in what I felt. But David rang me before I'd had the chance to properly formulate what I would say, how I'd put it to him. He asked if I'd got my ticket to Elba and I told him that I hadn't yet. And then I made the cardinal mistake of just asking him straight. Not unpleasantly, certainly not whiningly – just straight. As if that had *ever* been the way with him.

'Do you think, David, that you could maybe arrange just one credit card your wife doesn't know about to use on these trips?'

I knew the second the words were out of my mouth that I shouldn't have said them. I felt a bristling silence at the other end of the line. It was axiomatic – *of course* – that if he *could* have done that, he *would* have. If Hampstead was practice for Guantanamo Bay then Tregiffian was a revival of Alcatraz, and I'd just reminded him that he was only ever out on licence from either one.

'I think that's a bit stiff—' he said at last.

I tried to explain, I even began to back-pedal – not a thing I was good at because it wasn't a thing I ever did – but I knew it was no use. David half-mumbled some excuses and quickly rang off. I called him back, but got no answer. I didn't stop calling him back for several days. I wrote too – to our latest dead letterbox in Cornwall and to the first one, *poste restante* Hampstead – but nothing elicited a response. I couldn't bring him back from the edge this time. That dated, pink-gin expression – *a bit stiff* – was the last thing he ever said to me. And when he said it, it was as if a light had gone out in his voice.

David wrote to me eventually, but only to underline what I already knew. He claimed I'd 'bawled him out', which I hadn't at all. Not even the tiniest bit. I'd only thought to suggest that it really wasn't too much to ask my ex-spook secret lover to facilitate our secret trips with just one secret account. After I'd spent the previous three months dealing with everything to do with my parents' lives and mother's death; after I'd travelled so frequently on the same train line, back and forth between London and their place, that the train company should have named a carriage after me; after I'd run out of resilience to the slightest challenge myself; after I'd got David back as my lover and all *that* entailed – I hadn't thought it was so much to ask. But after he'd put almost thirty years of his life into what he'd already called a sexless empty marriage, I suppose it was. Though the flesh had still been extraordinarily willing to continue with 'us', his spirit was weak – just about beaten down, I reckon – and so that tiny bit of oh-so-gentle reproach from me had been enough. And far, far too much. My tentative request had confirmed that John le Carré had finally run out of tradecraft.

But then he went on to say that he was grateful I'd done it, because now he knew he had to settle for the life he had, which he described only as 'not the worst'. It was the saddest phrase. If I understood one new thing about David then, it was that the only close relationships he had that didn't end miserably were the ones that continued so.

It was over. *Fin d'histoire*, as Graham always used to say.

But really, this time.

Le Fin De L'histoire

I seem to see poor Edward, naked and reclining amid darkness, upon cold rocks, like one of the ancient Greek damned …

Ford Madox Ford, *The Good Soldier*

I immediately went back to Elizabeth, expecting to cry uncontrollably in her consulting room. But as I told her how David and I had met again, had fallen in love again and now it was over – again – the tears were in her eyes, not mine. Well, it just *was* one of *those* stories. And as Elizabeth helped me realise, the story finally had its right and proper ending.

After a long session with her, I returned home and wrote David one last letter, not even covering a full page, just saying I love you and thank you and goodbye. We didn't see each other or speak or write to each other ever again.

Over the years, David had seen off many would-be biographers, scaring them with lawyers or seeming to offer openings that he later blocked, even agreeing to a posthumous publication; anything to stop his life becoming anyone's material save his own. But as he neared the rise to eighty he gave up trying to be King Cnut holding back the tide of his own life story and finally let another writer 'that far in'.

Adam Sisman's biography was published in 2015. But while his extraordinarily comprehensive six-hundred-page book gives the tangled relationship with Susan Kennaway and her husband in some detail, it barely touches on the rest of David's extra-marital life. The whole topic is covered in just a few lines, describing 'impulsive, driven, short-lived affairs', words David supplied himself, Adam told me. For the sake of concluding the project smoothly, they had come to an agreement not to include any specific mention of his sexual relationships, with Yvette, with Janet or with me, or with any of his hitherto nameless second XI, several of whom Sisman had also tracked down. Having at first said publicly that he had no time for 'authorised biographies', David evidently decided he still didn't want the whole truth to come out. The biographer's free hand seemed to be rather more like Bosinney's in the matter of finishing Soames Forsyte's house; 'a free hand in the terms of the correspondence'. Perhaps David had originally assumed he wouldn't be quite so thorough in finding all the women, including me.

I always intended to write my own memoir of my time with David and had even completed an early first draft. But the combination of UK libel laws, EU privacy laws and, for a period, a legal gagging device called a super-injunction – which errant celebrities were readily using to keep their sexual indiscretions hidden – would have all weighed disproportionately on David's side of the scales of justice, had he ever chosen to avail himself of them against me or any publisher who took the manuscript on. It had made me see that any publication of mine would probably have to wait until he was dead. Since it looked as if our mutual subject was going to live to be a hundred and ten in the shade, I agreed to tell the biographer the key elements of my story, only to have it come to nothing when David insisted that part of his life still shouldn't be told.

'I told him I'd spoken to you, though,' Adam said to me after he'd published.

'What did he say?' I asked, all ears to know what the response had been.

Adam replied simply, 'He said – *Oh, God.*'

I confess I found the Great Man's reaction strangely gratifying.

And oddly enough, for all his intention to mask the topic, David had composed an almost entirely truthful description of his love encounters for the biography. They really weren't much more than brief affairs – the longest of them, with Susan Kennaway and Janet Stevens, not lasting more than a few months in each case and with Yvette even more swiftly converted to a family friend. The one exception was the relationship he had with me. If you were to calculate the combined time David spent with all his 'other women' it still wouldn't amount to as long as we had together. Not even close.

My phone rang around 10 pm on 13 December 2020. It was my friend Peter's ringtone. Over the years that we've known each other, it's become his way often to dispense with any greeting and go straight to the subject he's calling about. This time he was more direct than ever.

'He's dead.'

I thought at first he meant Biden. The election result had only recently been called and the gathering alt-right storm in the States made it seem a horrible possibility.

But it was David. He had died from pneumonia after a fall. It was only a few weeks after his eighty-ninth birthday. *Flights of angels* was the phrase that ran through my mind when Peter said his name.

At the start of the new year, raiding old files for earlier drafts and notes, rounding up the letters and my diaries, I began to write. And I rather think I fell in love with David for the third time as I did. Never more so than when I re-read his letters, and saw again how very much he had opened his heart and his life to me.

So this is it – the story of my time with le Carré the writer and with David the man. I hope I've made him seem as lovely as he was and as loving. I hope I've shown the magic. I trust I've helped elucidate the rest. Did I crack the code? Did I discover what made David run? Perhaps a little. But life – any life – isn't about finding the answers so much as it's about uncovering the clues.

His wife, who died only a short while later, is supposed to have said of him, *No one can have all of David.* I tend to think she had his affairs in mind when she said this and I find myself wanting to say in reply – Well, who can? Even supposing such a thing were possible, who would want the *all* of anyone? But it seems to me now that the exact opposite is what was true of David; that, in fact, there was no 'all' to be had. I think he was entirely fractal. Every piece of him felt like the whole, because he always presented it as if it were, and to him, in each moment, it was the truth. What all the pieces added up to, I rather think that he himself was the very last to know. He once wrote to me that there were at least ten thousand versions of himself, so perhaps, in the end, there are only clues to be had. Lovely, fascinating, baffling, infuriating clues about the essential enigma of him, the puzzle that I think he always wanted me to try and solve. It's what I've tried to do here. He once told me that I was part of the best thing he had so far written. He is the entirety of mine.

The first dream I ever had about David – when his face suddenly appeared, telling me so sweetly that he thought 'we should see ourselves again' – was what led this story to have its final ending. But I had a second dream about him in the course of writing the story down.

I arrived alone at a supper party for ten or a dozen people and was surprised to find myself seated opposite him. I was further surprised when he called me *my darling*, just as he ever had, as I sat down at the table.

'*Am* I still your darling?' I asked him.

'Yes,' he replied, as paradoxical as ever. 'Always.'

Glossary

The Circus – the 'in-house' name for le Carré's fictional Intelligence Service, his MI6, taken from the location of its London headquarters in Cambridge Circus.

dead letterbox – secure temporary hiding place for the exchange of written information; a drop-box.

fallback – agreed alternative arrangements to a plan, in case of emergency.

Joes – agents operating in the field, working to an agent-runner.

lamplighters – surveillance agents, also responsible for clearing drop-boxes and mail intercepts.

legend – cover story involving false biographical details.

Martha – a female recruit to the Intelligence Service.

mole – deep-penetration agent; a long-term 'double'.

Moscow Rules – strictest levels of secrecy and security for operating safely in enemy territory.

mothers – female ancillary staff working for the senior men in the Circus.

Reptile Fund – untraceable money available to fund covert operations.

safe houses – secure premises for clandestine meetings.

Sarratt – le Carré's fictional training school for spooks.

soft-route – the least traceable or accountable way into a country or region.

Acknowledgements

My sincere thanks go to my agent, Jane Graham Maw, to my publisher, Joel Simons, and to all the team at Mudlark/HarperCollins, without whose individual and combined experience, care and commitment my story could not have become this book.